6th Workshop on Cognitive Aspects of the Lexicon 2020 (CogALex VI)

Held online due to COVID-19

Barcelona, Spain
12 December 2020

ISBN: 978-1-7138-2823-5

CogALex VI - 2020

The Workshop on the Cognitive Aspects of the Lexicon

Proceedings of the Workshop

December 12, 2020
Barcelona, Spain (Online)

Introduction

Supporting us in many tasks (thinking, searching, memorizing, categorizing, communicating) words are a key aspect of natural language and human cognition. Yet they are large in number, and complex in form, hence the question, how are they learned, accessed and used? These are typical questions addressed in this kind of workshop that looks at words from a cognitive perspective.

More specifically we are interested in the creation, use and enhancements of lexical resources (representation, organization of the data, etc.). What are their limitations, and how can they be overcome? What are the users' and the engineers' needs (computational aspects)?

Given these goals, the CogALex workshop series, which this year has reached the sixth edition, has become a venue to discuss these issues from multiple viewpoints: linguistics (lexicography, computational- or corpus linguistics), neuro- or psycholinguistics (tip-of-the-tongue problem, word associations), network-related sciences (vector-based approaches, graph theory, small-world problem).

Also, just like in previous workshops (CogALex IV and V) we proposed a 'shared task'. This year the goal was to provide a common benchmark for testing lexical representations for the automatic identification of lexical semantic relations (synonymy, antonymy, hypernymy) in various languages (English, Chinese, etc.). Discovering whether words are semantically related or not – and, if so which kind of relation holds between them – is an important task both in language (writing, production of coherent discourse) and cognition (thinking, categorization). Semantic relations also play a central role in the organization of words in the lexicon and their subsequent retrieval (word access, navigation).

We received 25 submissions of which we accepted 7 for oral presentation, 6 as posters, and 3 as shared task papers (which means, we had overall an acceptance rate of about 65%, and 32% for oral presentations). We were pleasantly surprised to see that a growing number of authors combine work done in linguistics and psychology. Actually, the most highly rated paper came from two teams favorably complementing each other in this respect, which shows that it is possible to work together, and to produce excellent results which may benefit not only the respective teams but also the rest of the community. We hope that such results encourage other researchers or research teams to build on the strengths of other disciplines.

Obviously, none of the results here presented would be possible without the dedication of the authors and the efforts of the reviewers, who have considerably contributed to helping the authors to improve their work. We would like to thank both of them.

The CogALex Organizing Committee
Michael Zock
Emmanuele Chersoni
Alessandro Lenci
Enrico Santus

Organizers:

Zock, M. (CNRS, LIS-AMU, Marseille, France)
Chersoni, E. (The Hong Kong Polytechnic University, China)
Lenci, A. (University of Pisa, Italy)
Santus, E. (Bayer Pharmaceuticals, U.S.A)

Program Committee:

Arenas, A. (Universidad Rovira i Virgili, Tarragona, Spain)
Barbu Mititelu V. (RACAI, Bucharest, Romania)
Biemann, C. (Language Technology group, Universität Hamburg, Germany)
Brysbaert, M. (Experimental Psychology, Ghent University, Belgium)
Camacho-Collados, J. (Cardiff University, Cardiff, UK)
Carl, M. (Kent State University, Cleveland, Ohio, U.S.A.)
Chersoni, E. (The Hong Kong Polytechnic University, China)
Chiarcos, C. (Goethe-Universität Frankfurt am Main, Germany)
Cristea, D. (Al. I. Cuza University, Iasi, Romania)
de Melo, G. (Hasso Plattner Institute, University of Potsdam, Germany)
deDeyne, S. (School of Psychological Sciences, University of Melbourne, Australia)
Delmonte, R. (Department of Computer Science, Università Ca' Foscari, Italy)
Erk, K. (University of Texas, U.S.A.)
Espinosa-Anke, L. (COMSC, Cardiff University, UK)
Evert, S. (University of Erlangen, Germany)
Fairon, C. (Catholic University of Louvain, Belgium)
Ferret, O. (CEA LIST, France)
François, T. (Catholic University of Louvain, Belgium)
Fellbaum, C. (Princeton University, U.S.A.)
Gala, N. (Laboratoire Parole et Langage, Aix Marseille University)
Grefenstette, G. (Institute for Human and Machine Cognition, Florida, U.S.A.)
Hirst, G. (University of Toronto, Canada)
Hovy, E. (CMU, Pittsburgh, U.S.A.)
Hsieh, S.K. (National Taiwan University, Taipei, Taiwan)
Iacobacci, I. (Huawei Noah's Ark Lab, London, UK)
Kenett, Y. (University of Pennsylvania, Philadelphia, PA, U.S.A.)
Langlais, F. (DIRO, University of Montreal, Canada)
L'Homme M.C. (University of Montreal, Canada)
Lafourcade, Matthieu (LIRMM, University of Montpellier, France)
Lenci, A. (University of Pisa, Italy)
McCrae, J. (Data Science Institute, NUI Galway, Ireland)
Padó, S. (University of Stuttgart, Germany)
Pihlevar, T. (Iran University of Science and Technology, Teheran, Iran)
Pirrelli, V (ILC, Pisa, Italy)
Polguère, A. (ATILF, CNRS and University of Lorraine, Nancy, France)
Purver, M. (King's College, London, UK)
Raganato, A. (University of Helsinki, Helsinki, Finland)
Saggion, H. (Universitat Pompeu Fabra, Spain)
Sahlgren, M. (SICS, Smart AI, Sweden)

Santus, E. (Bayer Pharmaceuticals, U.S.A.)
Schulte im Walde, S. (University of Stuttgart, Germany)
Schwab, D. (LIG, Grenoble, France)
Stella, M. (Complex Science Consulting, Lecce, Italy)
Tiberius, C. (Institute for Dutch Lexicology, Leiden, The Netherlands)
Tufis, D. (RACAI, Bucharest, Romania)
Zock, M. (CNRS, LIS-AMU, Marseille, France)

Shared Task Organizers:

Chersoni, E. (The Hong Kong Polytechnic University, China)
Iacoponi, L. (Amazon)
Santus, E. (Bayer Pharmaceuticals, U.S.A.)
Xiang, R. (The Hong Kong Polytechnic University, China)

Best Paper Award:

Markus J. Hofmann, Lara Müller, Andre Rölke, Ralph Radach and Chris Biemann.
Individual corpora predict fast memory retrieval during reading

Keynote Talk

Vito Pirrelli (ILC, Pisa, Italy)
Emerging words in a vanishing lexicon: prospects of interdisciplinary convergence

In the wake of the 'cognitive revolution' (Miller 2003), scholars believed in a parsimonious form of direct correspondence between grammar rules, their organization and processing principles on one hand, and psychological and even neurological processes on the other. Grammatical rules and syntactic structures were claimed to have psycholinguistic reality, i.e. to be mentally represented, and speakers were believed to use the representations offered by linguists (e.g., Clahsen 2006, Jackendoff 1997, Levelt et al. 1999, Marslen-Wilson and Tyler 1998, Miller and Chomsky 1963). This straightforward assumption has been shared and popularized by Steven Pinker (Pinker 1999, Prasada and Pinker, 1993).

According to the Declarative/Procedural model (Pinker and Ullman 2002), the distinction drawn by linguists between regular and irregular morphology is not just a matter of classificatory convenience, but is motivated by the way linguistic information is processed in the human brain. Different cortical and subcortical areas are recruited to process and retrieve word forms like walked and sang. The former is decomposed into its sublexical constituents (walk and –ed), while the latter is stored as a whole. Likewise, the classical organization of the language architecture into two sharply compartmentalized modules, namely a word-based lexicon and a rule-based grammar, was viewed as reflecting the neuro-functional divide between a long-term store of static units (or knowledge of "what") and a procedural system (or knowledge of "how") (Ullman 2002). Accordingly, the irreducible building blocks of language competence are stored in and accessed from a redundancy-free mental lexicon. Rules, in turn, are responsible for the assembly and disassembly of these blocks when complex structures (e.g. morphologically complex words, phrases or sentences) are processed in production or recognition. Despite this seemingly clear division of labour, researchers disagreed considerably on matters of detail. Some of them assume that full words are the minimal building blocks in the mental lexicon (Butterworth 1983, Manelis and Tharp 1977), others claim that only sublexical units are stored (Taft 1979, 2004, Taft and Forster 1975), yet others propose a combination of the two (Baayen 1992, Frauenfelder and Schreuder 1992, Caramazza, Laudanna and Romani 1988, Laudanna and Burani 1985). Nonetheless, the largely dominant view was that storage and computation are distinct processes, subserved by different brain areas, in line with what Harald Baayen (2007) humorously dubbed the 'pocket calculator metaphor'.

This general picture was challenged by the 'connectionist revolution' (Medler 1998, Pirrelli et al. 2020). Multi-layered perceptrons proved to be able to process both regularly and irregularly inflected words with a unique underlying mechanism (Rumelhart and McClelland 1986). Accordingly, morphological structure was not modelled as an all-or-nothing issue. Rather, it was an emergent property of the dynamic self-organization of subsymbolic, distributed representations, contingent on the processing history of input forms. In fact, artificial neural networks appear to mark an even more radical departure from traditional language processing architectures. First, in neural networks, lexical representations are not given but learned. Thus, aspects of how they are acquired and eventually represented are not taken for granted, but lie at the core of connectionist modelling. Secondly, and most importantly, lexical representations and processing routines are not assigned to different components, but they both rest on the same level of weighted connections.

On the one hand, storage implies processing. Network nodes that have been repeatedly activated in processing an input word are the same units representing this word in long-term memory. On the other hand, processing implies storage. The online processing of an input word consists in the short-term re-activation of processing routines that were successfully triggered by the same word in the past. Ultimately, processing and storage only designate two different points in time (i.e. immediate response to stimulus, and response consolidation) of the same underlying learning dynamics.

McClelland and Rumelhart (1986) published their pioneering book on Parallel Distributed Processing 35 years ago. Strange as it may seem, the theoretical consequences of this radical shift of paradigm have not been fully appreciated. In my talk, I will try to reappraise their contribution by showing how it can deal with issues like word representation and processing. In doing so, I will consider evidence from several interrelated lines of research. The first one revolves around evidence from human word processing and lexical acquisition, suggesting that a lot of lexical information is inextricably related to processing. The second line of research focuses on recent advances in the neurobiology of human memory and its tight connection with language processing. Last but not least, I will consider neurobiologically inspired computer models of the language architecture.

Drawing on an analogy with recent developments in discriminative learning and morphological theory (Baayen et al. 2011, Blevins 2016, Ramscar and Gitcho 2007, Ramscar and Yarlett 2007), I will suggest that speakers' knowledge about words is the resulting state of a dynamic, self-organizing process. According to this view, words are abstractions emerging from interrelated patterns of sensory experience, communicative and social interaction and psychological and neurobiological mechanisms (Elman 2009). The information associated with them is hardly ever stable, time-independent or context-independent. Their content is continuously updated and reshaped as a function of the moment (when), the reason (why) and the frequency (how often) of its access and processing. Such flowing activation state is reminiscent of the wave/particle duality in quantum physics (Libben 2016) or the inherently adaptive, self-organising behaviour of biological dynamic systems (Beckner et al. 2009). Hence, if we look for particles (i.e. individual word representations) we may not be able to find them. It all depends on the task or the context.

This discussion leads to an apparently paradoxical state of affairs. We know that the linguists' view of the lexicon as a redundancy-free container of word representations fails to capture our current understanding of how words are accessed, used and processed. Can then we talk about the reality of words in any non-metaphorical or non-epiphenomenal sense? I believe that we can. After all, speakers have lexical knowledge. However, the mental reality of words resides in the collective behaviour of nodes and connections in a lexical network engaged in a particular word processing task. It cannot be deduced from any individual and stable representation. As the context or task changes, also the pattern of these connections will change, and so our perception of individual representations.

Language sciences address different Marr's (1982) levels of understanding of a complex cognitive system. Theoretical linguistics addresses Marr's level one (i.e. what speakers do when they use language), while psycholinguistics is mostly concerned with level two (i.e. how speakers use language), and neurolinguistics with level three (i.e. where in the brain language processes take place). Due to the dominant focus of theoretical linguistics on the basic units of language and the principles of their combination, linguists have laid nearly exclusive emphasis on representation issues. Conversely, psycholinguists and neurolinguists have mainly been concerned with behavioural and physiological evidence of the human processor. As suggested by Anderson (1972), inter-level mapping rarely implies the extrapolation to level Y of properties holding at level X. It is thus not surprising that moving from Marr's level one to another level is often a matter of discovering new laws and concepts, and requires a creative shift from quantitative to qualitative differentiation. Decade-long developments in recurrent neural networks have proved instrumental in shedding light on the psychological nature of classical linguistic categories and basic units (Elman 2009, Marzi and Pirrelli 2015). Ultimately, they appear to lend support to Poggio's (2010) claim that (language) learning is key to the appropriate methodological unification of Marr's epistemological levels: units in language crucially depend on the way they are acquired, organized and used by the speakers. From this perspective, any attempt to put all these units directly into the speaker's mind is dubious, if not futile.

References

Anderson, P. W. 1972. More Is Different. Science 4047 (177). 393–396.

Baayen, R.H. (1992). Quantitative Aspects of Morphological Productivity. Yearbook of morphology 1991. Dordrecht: Springer Netherlands, 109-150.

Baayen, H. (2007). Storage and computation in the mental lexicon. In G. Jarema and G. Libben (eds.) The Mental Lexicon: core perspectives, 81-104.

Baayen, R. H., Milin, P., Filipović Đurđević, D., Hendrix, P. and Marelli, M. (2011). An amorphous model for morphological processing in visual comprehension based on naive discriminative learning. Psychological Review 118 (3). 438–481.

Beckner, C., et al. (2009). Language is a complex adaptive system: Position paper. Language learning, 59(s1): 1-26.

Blevins, J. P. (2016). Word and Paradigm Morphology. Oxford, UK: Oxford University Press.

Butterworth, B. (1983) Lexical representation. In B. Butterworth (Ed.) Language Production, 2, 257-294. San Diego, CA: Academic Press.

Caramazza, A., Laudanna, A. and Romani, C. (1988). Lexical access and inflectional morphology. Cognition, 28(3), 297-332.

Clahsen, H. (2006). Linguistic perspectives on morphological processing. In Wunderlich, D. (ed.) Advances in the Theory of the Lexicon, 355–388. Berlin: Mouton de Gruyter.

Elman, J. L. (2009). On the meaning of words and dinosaur bones: Lexical knowledge without a lexicon. Cognitive science, 33 (4): 547–582.

Frauenfelder, U.H. and Schreuder, R. (1992). Constraining psycholinguistic models of morphological processing and representation: The role of productivity. Yearbook of morphology 1991. Dordrecht: Springer Netherlands, 165-185.

Garrett, M. (1988). Processes in language production. in F.J. Newmeyer (Ed.) Linguistics: The Cambridge Survey III. Language: Psychological and Biological Aspects. Cambridge: Cambridge University Press. 69-96.

Jackendoff, R. (1997). The Architecture of the Language Faculty. Cambridge, MA: MIT Press.

Laudanna, A. and Burani, C. (1985). Address mechanisms to decomposed lexical entries. Linguistics, 23, 775-792.

Levelt, W., Roelofs, A. and Meyer, A. (1999). A theory of lexical access in speech production. Behavioral and Brain Sciences, 22, 1-75.

Libben, Gary. 2016. The quantum metaphor and the organization of words in the mind. Journal of Cultural Cognitive Science 1: 49–55.

Manelis, L. and Tharp, D. (1977). The processing of affixed words. Memory and Cognition, 5, 690-695.

Marr, D. (1982). Vision. San Francisco: W.H. Freeman.

Marslen-Wilson, W. D. and Tyler. L.K. (1998). Rules, representations, and the English past tense. Trends in Cognitive Sciences, 2: 428-435.

Marzi, C. and V. Pirrelli. 2015. A neuro-computational approach to understanding the Mental Lexicon. Journal of Cognitive Science, 16 (4): 493-534.

McClelland, J.L. and Rumelhart, D.E. and the PDP Research Group (eds.). (1986). Parallel Distributed Processing, Cambridge, MA: MIT Press.

Medler, A. D. (1998) A Brief History of Connectionism. Neural Computing Surveys, 1: 61-101.

Miller, G. A. (2003). The cognitive revolution: a historical perspective. Trends in cognitive sciences, 7 (3): 141-144.

Miller, G. A. and Chomsky, N. (1963). Finitary models of language users. In Luce, R. D., Bush, R. R., and Galanter, E. (eds.) Handbook of Mathematical Psychology, 2: 419–491. New York: John Wiley.

Pinker, S. (1999). Words and rules: the ingredients of language. New York: Perennial.

Pinker, S. and Ullman, M.T. (2002). The past and future of the past tense. Trends in cognitive sciences, 6(11), 456-463.

Pirrelli, V., Marzi, C., Ferro, M., Cardillo, F.A., Baayen, H.R. and Milin, P. (2020). Psychocomputational modelling of the mental lexicon. A discriminative learning perspective. In Pirrelli, V., Plag, I. and Dressler, W.U. (eds.) Word Knowledge and Word Usage: a Crossdisciplinary Guide to the Mental Lexicon, 21-80. De Gruyter.

Prasada, S. and Pinker, S. (1993). Generalisation of regular and irregular morphological patterns. Language and cognitive processes, 8(1): 1-56.

Poggio, T. (2010). Afterword. Marr's Vision and Computational Neuroscience. In D. Marr, Vision, 362–367. MIT Press.

Ramscar, M. and Nicole Gitcho, N. (2007). Developmental change and the nature of learning in childhood. Trends in cognitive sciences, 11 (7): 274–279.

Ramscar, M. and Yarlett, D. (2007). Linguistic Self-Correction in the Absence of Feedback: A New Approach to the Logical Problem of Language Acquisition. Cognitive Science 31 (6). 927–960.

Rumelhart, D. E. and McClelland, J. L. (1986). On learning the past tenses of English verbs. In J. L. McClelland, D. E. Rumelhart and the PDP Research Group (eds.), Parallel Distributed Processing, 2: 216-271, Cambridge, MA: MIT Press.

Taft, M. (1979). Recognition of affixed words and the word frequency effect. Memory and Cognition, 7: 263-272.

Taft, M. (2004). Morphological decomposition and the reverse base frequency effect. The Quarterly Journal of Experimental Psychology, 57A(4): 745-765.

Taft, M. and Frost, K.I. (1975) Lexical storage and retrieval of prefixed words. Journal of Verbal Learning and Verbal Behavior, 14(6): 638-647.

Ullman, M.T. (2001) A neurocognitive perspective on language: the declarative/procedural model. Nature Reviews Neuroscience, 2; 717–726

Table of Contents

Conference Program

No Day Set (continued)

17:50–18:00   **Break**

18:00–18:45   **Session 2: Oral Presentations**

Characterizing Dynamic Word Meaning Representations in the Brain
Nora Aguirre-Celis and Risto Miikkulainen

Contextualized Word Embeddings Encode Aspects of Human-Like Word Sense Knowledge
Sathvik Nair, Mahesh Srinivasan and Stephan Meylan

Automatic Word Association Norms (AWAN)
Jorge Reyes-Magaña, Gerardo Sierra Martínez, Gemma Bel-Enguix and Helena Gomez-Adorno

18:45–19:00   **Closing Remarks**

Individual corpora predict fast memory retrieval during reading

Markus J. Hofmann, Lara Müller, Andre Rölke, Ralph Radach
Bergische Universität Wuppertal, Max-Horkheimer-Str. 20, 42119 Wuppertal
{mhofmann,lara.mueller,roelke,radach}@uni-wuppertal.de

Chris Biemann
Universität Hamburg, Vogt-Kölln-Straße 30, 22527 Hamburg
biemann@informatik.uni-hamburg.de

Abstract

The corpus, from which a predictive language model is trained, can be considered the experience of a semantic system. We recorded everyday reading of two participants for two months on a tablet, generating individual corpus samples of 300/500K tokens. Then we trained word2vec models from individual corpora and a 70 million-sentence newspaper corpus to obtain individual and norm-based long-term memory structure. To test whether individual corpora can make better predictions for a cognitive task of long-term memory retrieval, we generated stimulus materials consisting of 134 sentences with uncorrelated individual and norm-based word probabilities. For the subsequent eye tracking study 1-2 months later, our regression analyses revealed that individual, but not norm-corpus-based word probabilities can account for first-fixation duration and first-pass gaze duration. Word length additionally affected gaze duration and total viewing duration. The results suggest that corpora representative for an individual's long-term memory structure can better explain reading performance than a norm corpus, and that recently acquired information is lexically accessed rapidly.

1 Introduction

There are three basic *stages* of memory (e.g. Paller and Wagner, 2002). All memories start with *experience*, which is reflected by text corpora (e.g. Hofmann et al., 2018). The training of a language model then reflects the process of memory *consolidation*. The final stage is memory *retrieval*, which can be examined in psycholinguistic experiments. In this paper, we measure the correlation of computational language modelling and cognitive performance.

We collected individual corpora from two participants reading on a tablet for two months and compared them to an extensive corpus mainly consisting of online newspapers (Goldhahn et al., 2012). To consolidate differential knowledge structures in long-term memory, word2vec models were trained from these corpora. For stimulus selection, we relied on these three language models to compute word probabilities and sentence perplexity scores for 45K sentences of a Wikipedia dump. Perplexity rank differences were used to select sentences with uncorrelated word probabilities for the three language models, allowing to estimate the independent contribution of the word probabilities in multiple regression analyses. The resulting 134 stimulus sentences were read by the participants in an eye tracking experiment. In the multiple regression analyses, we used these predictors to account for the durations of the first fixation on the words. We also predicted gaze durations, in which the duration of further fixations during first-pass reading are added. When the eye revisits a word after first-pass reading has been finished, the durations of further fixations are added into the total viewing duration (see Figure 1 for an overview of the present study). The underlying hypotheses of our research are that semantic expectancy has a top-down effect on word saliency at the visual level (Hofmann et al., 2011; Reilly & Radach, 2006), and words appearing in more salient contexts, are processed quicker by human subjects. Therefore, language models on individual reading corpora, realized e.g. by word2vec, should predict the processing speed.

Proceedings of the Workshop on Cognitive Aspects of the Lexicon, pages 1–11
Barcelona, Spain (Online), December 12, 2020

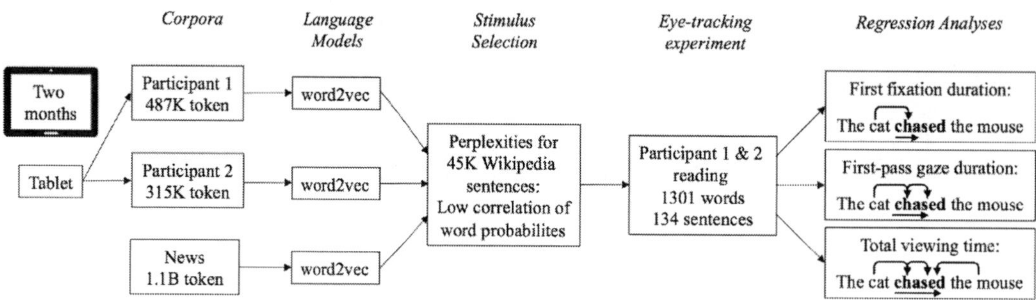

Figure 1. Overview of the present study

2 Learning history and memory consolidation

2.1 Norm corpora as a representative sample of human experience?

When selecting a corpus as a sample of the learning experience of human participants or language models, the question arises which corpus is most representative for which person. For instance, the knowledge of young adults is better characterized by corpora consisting of books written for younger adults, while older adults are more experienced – when therefore searching for corpora that account for their performance best, more diverse fictional and literature books are chosen (Johns, Jones, & Mewhort, 2018). Rapp (2014) proposed that corpus representativeness should be measured by the Pearson correlation of corpus-derived computational measures and an external measure of human performance. The knowledge of an average reader may be well represented by balanced corpora containing all sorts of content, such as Wikipedia. However, a previous study revealed that a newspaper corpus often provides higher correlations than Wikipedia when accounting for human cloze completion probabilities, as well as eye tracking or brain-electric data (Goldhahn et al., 2012; Hofmann et al., 2017). This result pattern could on the one hand be explained by the fact that typical German readers very frequently visit online newspapers. On the other hand, the encyclopedic nature of Wikipedia with one article per topic does not reflect the frequencies of exposure. Therefore, a newspaper corpus may be more representative. In his seminal work, Rapp (2014) avoided the possibility to observe the average language input of test persons, noting that it would be effortful and unpractical to collect corpora from the language of participants. In the present work, we directly address this problem by collecting individual corpora from two test participants, which is made possible by technological advances and cheaper hardware, i.e. tablets with cameras for eye-tracking.

When choosing a corpus, a key issue is its size. In general, a larger corpus may provide better word frequency estimates that allow for better human performance predictions than a small corpus (Rapp, 2014). For high frequency words, however, a corpus of 1 million words already allows for predictions comparable to larger corpora (Brysbaert & New, 2009). For low frequency words, performance predictions improve for corpora up to 16 million words, while there is hardly any gain for corpora greater 30 million words. Rather, extremely large corpora of more than a billion words may even decrease performance predictions. "For these sizes, it becomes more important to know where the words of the corpus came from" (Brysbaert & New, 2009). Movie subtitles represent spoken language, which humans typically encounter much more often than written language. In this case, the corpus is probably more representative, because it incorporates the more frequently produced and received language mode. Therefore, it appears that the representativeness for the language input can outperform sheer size.

Whether such smaller corpora are also sufficient to characterize contextual word probabilities has also been examined by Mandera et al. (2017). They showed that size does not always trump representativeness in predicting semantic priming, i.e. the facilitation of word recognition as a consequence of processing a preceding prime word. In general, the everyday social information represented in subtitles corpora may be more accessible for human subjects. Therefore, they tend to elicit effects in early eye-movement measures, particularly when combined with a language model that can generalize, such as neural network models, for instance (Hofmann et al., 2017, 2020).

Though personalized language signals are obviously used to optimize search engine performance, tempting us to purchase products by means of individualized advertisements, we are not aware of any scientific approach towards assessing corpus representativeness at the level of real individual participants. Jacobs (2019), however, showed that language models can well characterize fictional characters. He used SentiArt to analyze Harry Potter books and found that theory-guided contextual properties of the characters can provide a face valid approach to personality. Voldemort occurred in language contexts indicating emotional instability, thus he scored high in the pseudo-big-five personality trait of neuroticism. Harry Potter's personality, in contrast, can be most well characterized by the personality dimension of conscientiousness. Both, Harry and Hermione score high on the personality trait of openness to experience and intellect. With such a face valid characterization of the personality of fictional characters, we think that it is an ethical necessity to stimulate a scientific discussion about the potential of individual corpora, because they may tell us a lot about real persons.

2.2 Language models reflecting memory consolidation

Psycholinguistic reading and comprehension studies were dominated for a long time by latent semantic analysis (Deerwester et al., 1990). Pynte et al. (2008) showed that such a document-level approach to long-range semantics can better predict gaze duration than an earlier eye movement measure. In this case, however, the Dundee corpus was examined, in which discourse rather than single sentence reading was examined. Griffiths et al. (2007) showed that topics models may outperform LSA in psycholinguistic experiments, for instance by predicting gaze durations for ambiguous words (Blei et al., 2003). McDonald and Shillcock (2003), on the other hand, suggested that a word 2-gram model may reflect low-level contextual properties, given that they can most reliably account for first fixation duration rather than later eye-movement measures. Smith and Levy (2013) showed that a Kneser-Ney smoothed 3-gram model can also predict a later eye-movement measure, i.e. gaze duration, probably because a larger contextual window is used for the predictions of discourse comprehension using the Dundee eye-movement data set (cf. Pynte et al., 2008). Frank (2009) showed that a simple recurrent neural network is better suitable to address gaze duration data than a probabilistic context-free grammar (Demberg and Keller, 2008). The capability of neural networks to well capture syntax was also demonstrated by Frank and Bod (2011), who showed that an echo-state network better predicts gaze duration data than unlexicalized surprisal of particular phrase structures. For predicting first fixation durations of words that have been fixated only once during single sentence reading (Hofmann et al., 2017), a Kneser-Ney-smoothed 5-gram model provided good predictions, but a slightly better prediction was obtained by a recurrent neural network model (Mikolov, 2012). In the same work, Hofmann et al. (2017) showed that an LDA-based topic model (Blei et al., 2003) provided relatively poor predictions, probably because sentence- rather than document-level training more closely reflects the semantic short-range knowledge.

Since Bhatia (2017) and Mandera et al. (2017), word2vec models can be considered a standard tool for psycholinguistic studies. It is well known for eye-tracking research, that not only the predictability of the present, but also of the last and next word can influence fixation durations (e.g. Kliegl et al., 2006). Viewing durations of the present word can even be influenced to some extent by the word after the next word (Radach et al., 2013). As the present pilot study will be based on a limited number of observations, we used word2vec-based word embeddings trained to predict the probability of the present word by the default contextual window of the last and next two words (Mikolov et al., 2013). With such a contextual window of two during training, we intended to subsume the effects of the last and next words on the fixation duration of the present word during retrieval. Therefore, we decided to use this simple standard approach to natural language processing.

3 Memory retrieval in eye-tracking analyses

As has been summarized in Figure 1 and already introduced above, there are a number of different eye-movement parameters that can be used to address early and later memory retrieval processes during sentence reading (e.g. Inhoff and Radach, 1998; Rayner, 1998). When the eyes land on a word within a sentence during left-to-right reading, they remain relatively still for a particular amount of time, generally referred to by the term fixation duration. The first fixation on a word duration (FFD) is generally assumed to reflect early orthographic and lexical processing (Radach and Kennedy, 2004), but has also been shown to be sensitive for readily available predictive semantic (top-down) information for a given word (e.g. Roelke et al., 2020). The sum of all fixation durations before the eye leaves the word to the right is referred to by (first-pass) gaze duration (GD), which reflects later stages of word processing including lexical access. After leaving the word to the right, the eye may come back to the respective word and remain there for some time, which is further added into the total viewing duration (TVD). Such late eye movement measures reflect the time needed to provide full semantic integration of a word into the current language context (Radach and Kennedy, 2013).

Word length, frequency and word predictability from sentence context are generally accepted by the eye-tracking community to represent the most influential psycholinguistic variables on eye-movements (e.g. Engbert et al., 2005; Reichle et al., 2003). Word length is particularly affecting medium to late cognitive processes, while word frequency seems to affect all eye-movement measures (e.g. Kennedy et al., 2013). In psychology, word predictability from sentence context is typically estimated by cloze completion probabilities (Ehrlich and Rayner, 1981), which can be well approximated by language models (Shaoul et al., 2014). There are numerous studies examining the influence of predictability on eye movement measures, which found that predictability affects both early and late eye movement parameters: Therefore, Staub's (2015) review suggested that cloze-completion-probability-based predictability is an all-in variable confounding all sorts of predictive processes. We believe that language models provide the opportunity to understand different types of "predictability", therefore allowing for a deeper understanding of how experience shapes memory and how memory acts on retrieval than current models of eye-movement control (Reichle et al., 2003).

While Rapp (2014) proposed to use single-predictor regressions to approach corpus representativeness, a typical analytic approach to eye movements are multiple regression analyses. In this case, the fixation durations are approximated by a function:

$$f(x) = \Sigma \ \beta_n{}^*x_n + \beta + error \ (1)$$

In Formula 1, x_n is the respective predictor variable such as length, frequency or predictability, and the free parameters are denoted by β. β_n reflects the slope explained by the predictor variable n, while β is the intercept of the regression equation. Error is minimized by ordinary least squares. In single-predictor analyses, correlation coefficients inform about the relative influence of a single variable. To see how much variance is explained by a single predictor, the correlation coefficient is often squared to give the amount of variance explained. Though the typical variance explained by a single predictor can vary as a function of the variables included in the regression model, an $r^2 = 0.0095$ ($r = 0.097$) for the frequency effect in GD is a good benchmark at this fixation-based level of analysis (e.g. Kliegl et al., 2006, Table 4).

A critical factor influencing multiple regression analyses is the correlation of the predictor variables itself. If they surpass an $r > 0.3$, multicollinearity starts to become problematic and the variance inflation factor reaches a first critical level of 1.09 (e.g. O'Brien, 2007). Therefore, we here relied on a sentence-perplexity- and word-probability-based stimulus selection procedure, to allow for an independent prediction of the major variables of interest, i.e. our word2vec-based word probabilities (WP) of the individual and the norm-based training corpora.

4 Methodology

4.1 Participants and corpora

For data protection purposes, we do not provide the exact age of the two German native participants, but they were 40-70 years old and male. Verbal IQ scores due to the IST-2000R were 106/115 for participant 1/2, respectively (Liepmann et al., 2007). Active vocabulary was estimated in the percentile ranks of 100/81 and passive vocabulary by 31/81 (Ibrahimović and Bulheller, 2005). The percentile ranks of reading fluency was 97/48 and comprehension percentiles of the participants were 52/31 (Schneider et al., 2007). Further assessment revealed a clearly differentiable interest profile peaking in medicine and nature as well as agriculture for Participant 1, vs. education and music for Participant 2 (Brickenkamp, 1990).

Individual reading behavior of both participants was recorded on a Microsoft surface tablet. During corpus collection, we also recorded eye movements by an eye tracker mounted on the tablet (60 Hz, EyeTribe Inc.). Therefore, future studies may constrain the individual corpora to only those text regions that have actually been looked at. Participants were instructed to spend a maximum of personal reading time on this tablet. They were instructed to examine content matching their personal interests over a period of two months. A java script collected screenshots, when the display changed. The screenshots were converted into greyscale images and rescaled by a multiplicator of 5. In addition, a median filter was used to remove noise, while contrast intensity was further enhanced. Finally, these pre-processed images were converted to ASCII by optical character recognition (Tesseract Software OCR; Smith, 2007). Next, we reviewed samples from the output data and the word-level confidence scores. At a confidence score of 80, a large majority of words (> 95%) were correctly identified by the OCR script, which we used as threshold for the inclusion into the corpora. In a final step, the data were cleaned from special characters and punctuations. The resulting corpus of participant 1 contained 486,721 tokens, and the corpus of participant 2 included 314,943 tokens. For computing individual word frequency (WF), we stemmed all words of the resulting token sample. To obtain comparable measures to norm-based WF, individual WF was calculated in per-million words and log10-transformed. The norm corpus was the German corpus of the Leipzig Wortschatz Project consisting of 1.1 billion tokens (Goldhahn et al., 2012).

4.2 Language models and stimulus selection

To generate stimulus materials containing words that are either predictable by the training corpora of one of the two participants or under the norm corpus, we trained word2vec models from the three different corpora, using genism 3.0.0 (Rehurek and Sojka, 2010)[1]. We trained skip-gram models with 100 hidden units in 10 iterations with a minimum frequency of 3 for the individual corpora and 5 for the norm-based corpus.

Stimulus selection started by computing WPs of 44,932 sentences of a German Wikipedia dump for the word2vec models under the three training corpora. For sentence selection, sentence perplexity (PP) scores were computed from the WP_i for the n words of a sentence:

$$PP = 2^{-\frac{1}{n}\sum_{x_i}^{n} log_2 p(WP_i)} \quad (2)$$

PPs were rank-ordered for the three training corpora. To select sentences that are either predictable by one of the participants or by the norm corpus, we computed rank differences of these perplexity scores. Then we selected approximately one third of the sentences that provide a relatively low perplexity under one corpus, but a higher perplexity under the other two training corpora. Finally, we searched for words providing a WP = 0 under the individually trained language models and replaced them by highly probable words if this led to a meaningful and syntactically legal sentence. The 134 selected sentences contained 5-15 words ($M = 9.78$, $SD = 1.92$) and the 1,301 words ranged in length from 2 to 17 letters ($M = 5.49$, $SD = 2.67$). In the final stimulus set, there was a low correlation/multicollinearity of the individual and the norm-based WP (see Table 1 below), which allows to estimate the contribution of individual and the norm-based WP to word viewing durations independent from each other.

4.3 Eye tracking study

The eye tracking study was conducted approximately 1-2 months after the end of the individual corpus collection period. Eye tracking data were measured with a sampling frequency of 2000 Hz by an Eye-Link 2k (SR Research Ltd.). The participant's head was positioned on a chin-rest and stimuli were presented in black color on a light-grey background (Courier New, size 16) on a 24-inch monitor (1680x1050 pixel). With a distance from eye to monitor of 67 cm, the size of a letter corresponded to 0.3° of visual angle. A three-point eye-position calibration was performed at the beginning of the experiment and after each comprehension question (see below). After an instruction screen, the 134 sentences were presented in randomized order in two blocks of 67 sentences, intermitted by a 5-minute break. For each sentence presentation, a fixation point appeared on the screen. Then, a sentence was presented in one line, with the first word located 0.5° of visual angle to the right. 2° to the right of the end of the sentence, the string "xxXxx" was presented. Participants were instructed to look at this string to indicate that sentence reading has been finished, which automatically initiated the continuation of the experiment. To make sure that participants read for comprehension, 17 yes/no and 13 open questions were presented after randomly selected sentences. All questions were answered correctly from both participants.

Right-eye fixation durations were analyzed by multiple regression analyses ($N = 1673$). Fixation durations lower than 70 ms were excluded from analysis, as well as outliers longer than 800 ms for FFD, 1000 ms for GD, and 1500 ms for TVD. The first and last words of a sentence, as well as words with WPs or WFs of zero were excluded, leading to $N = 1291$ fixation events remaining for all analyses. The

---

[1] https://radimrehurek.com/gensim/

predictor variables in the multiple regressions were word length, norm-based and individual WF, as well as norm-based and individual WP. The word probabilities due to the two individual corpora, together with a stimulus and viewing time example is presented in Figure 2.

Participant 1:
WP = 1.5e-5   Auch der junge Baron **befand** sich im Liebeswahn.

FFD = 229 ms

Participant 2:
WP = 9.4e-4   Auch der junge Baron **befand** sich im Liebeswahn.

FFD = 176 ms

[Even the young baron **dwelled** in the madness of love.]

Figure 2. Individual word probabilities of an example word and the resulting viewing time: The language model trained by the corpus of Participant 1 provided a lower word probability (WP) than the corpus of Participant 2 in the example sentence. The higher word probability for Participant 2 predicts a faster first fixation duration (FFD).

5   Results

5.1   Correlation analysis and single-predictor regressions

The examination of the correlation between individual and norm-based WPs in Table 1 revealed that there was no significant correlation between these predictor variables. Therefore, our perplexity-based stimulus selection procedure will allow to examine whether these two predictors account for eye-movement variance independent from each other in the multiple regression analysis below. There were, however, typically large correlations between frequency and length and between the two frequency measures (e.g. Kliegl et al., 2006). Therefore, the question of whether length or frequency effects occur, cannot be answered unequivocally and e.g. frequency effects may be estimated by the predictor of word length in the multiple regression. All other correlation coefficients were smaller than 0.3, thus providing an uncritical level of multicollinearity.

	1.	2.	3.	4.	5.	6.	7.	8.
1. Word length		-0.68	-0.71	0.02	-0.10	0.00	**0.14**	**0.19**
2. Norm-based WF	<.0001		0.80	0.09	0.13	-0.05	**-0.13**	**-0.16**
3. Individual WF	<.0001	<.0001		0.06	0.07	-0.01	**-0.10**	**-0.15**
4. Norm-based WP	0.4774	0.0013	0.0222		**0.03**	-0.02	-0.04	-0.04
5. Individual WP	0.0005	<.0001	0.0174	**0.3427**		*-0.12*	*-0.08*	*-0.06*
6. FFD	0.9447	0.0864	0.6284	0.4048	*<.0001*		0.74	0.37
7. GD	**<.0001**	**<.0001**	**0.0003**	0.1277	*0.0029*	<.0001		0.53
8. TVD	**<.0001**	**<.0001**	**<.0001**	0.1610	*0.0380*	<.0001	<.0001	

Table 1: Correlation of the predictor variables and the three word viewing time measures. Correlation coefficients are given above diagonal and correlation probability below.

When considering this correlation table as a single-predictor regression on the eye tracking data, there were effects of length, norm-based and individual word frequency in the GD and TVD data. While larger word length increased fixation durations, a larger norm-based and individual word frequency decreased the viewing times. No such effects were obtained in FFD data. Norm-corpus based WPs did not reveal any effects, while there were significant effects of individual WPs for FFD, GD, and TVD data, showing the largest correlation for FFD (r = -0.12), followed by GD (r = -0.08) and TVD (r = -0.06). Higher word probabilities decreased fixation durations.

5.2 Multiple regressions

The FFD analysis including all predictor variables provided a highly significant multiple regression model, $F(5,1285)$ = 4.629, p = 0.0003 (Table 2). In all, it accounted for 1.77% of the variance. We obtained a significant effect of individual WP: Negative t-values indicated that high individual WP decreased FFD. Word frequency marginally failed to reach significance, with high frequency tending to diminish reading times.

	β	$SE\ \beta$	t	p
(Constant)	268.793017	16.4469826	16.34	<.0001
Word length	-1.7378111	1.61136469	-1.08	0.2810
Norm-based WF	-5.2127476	2.83947993	-1.84	0.0666
Individual WF	2.54936544	3.79117063	0.67	0.5014
Norm-based WP	-73835.943	152204.436	-0.49	0.6277
Individual WP	-26123.236	6394.71736	-4.09	<.0001

Table 2: Results of the multiple regression analysis for FFD.

The multiple regression on GD data revealed a highly significant regression model, $F(5,1285)$ = 0.756, p < .0001 (see Table 3), which in total accounted for 2.89% of the variance. We found a significant effect of word length, with longer words increasing GDs, as well as a significant effect of individual WP, with highly probable words reducing GDs.

	β	$SE\ \beta$	t	p
(Constant)	245.517945	20.9540141	11.72	<.0001
Word length	6.44767908	2.05293331	3.14	0.0017
Norm-based WF	-4.988601	3.61759382	-1.38	0.1681
Individual WF	4.76546508	4.83008007	0.99	0.3240
Norm-based WP	-282605.29	193913.618	-1.46	0.1453
Individual WP	-18673.72	8147.08699	-2.29	0.0221

Table 3: Results of the multiple regression analysis for GD.

For the TVD analysis, we obtained a highly significant multiple regression model, $F(5,1672)$ = 10.56, p < .0001 (see Table 4). Overall, the predictors accounted for 3.95% of variance. Only word length provided a significant effect. Longer words lead to an increase of the TVD.

	β	$SE\ \beta$	t	p
(Constant)	312.913912	36.015215	8.69	<.0001
Word length	13.5909502	3.52852843	3.85	0.0001
Norm-based WF	-6.498011	6.21782625	-1.05	0.2962
Individual WF	1.23816155	8.30181612	0.15	0.8815
Norm-based WP	-448879.23	333293.688	-1.35	0.1783
Individual WP	-17982.923	14003.0014	-1.28	0.1993

Table 4: Results of the multiple regression analysis for TVD.

6 Discussion

To examine the representativeness of different training corpora for the learning experience, we here collected corpora for two individuals. These individual corpora were compared against a norm-based corpus (Goldhahn et al., 2012). We computed individual and norm-based semantic long-term memory structure based on word2vec models (Mikolov et al., 2013). Then we computed WPs for a sample of 45K sentences from Wikipedia and selected 134 sentences providing no significant correlation between the norm-based and the individual WPs to avoid multicollinearity in our multiple regression analyses on eye movement data.

Single-predictor and multiple regression analyses revealed that there are no significant effects of norm-based WP with any eye movement measure. One possible reason for these zero findings could be that we replaced words with a WP = 0 by words that are highly expectable under the individual, but not under the norm-based corpus. This might have increased the sensitivity for successful predictions of individual corpora. The stimulus selection procedure optimized the eye-tracking experiment for the representativeness for our participants' individual knowledge structure. This may compromise the representativeness for other types of knowledge.

The individual WP, in contrast, revealed reliable single-predictor effects. These effects were largest in FFD data and decreased for later GD and TVD data. When comparing the 1.44% of explained variance of individual WP in the FFD data to the total variance of 1.77% explained in the multiple regression, this result pattern suggests that most of the variance was explained by individual WP. The slight increase in explained variance primarily results from norm-based WF, which marginally failed to reach significance in the multiple regression analysis on FFD data. In general, the amount of explained variance in these analyses are comparable to other multiple regression studies predicting each fixation duration, without aggregating across eye-movement data (e.g. Kliegl et al., 2006).

Single and multiple regression analyses revealed that the effect of individual WP tends to become smaller, but apparent in GD data. This suggests that individual corpora are most suitable to predict early to mid-latency eye movement measures (cf. Figure 1). In the multiple regression analysis of GD data, an additional effect of word length was observed, confirming the finding that length has a larger effect on such later eye movement parameters (e.g. Kennedy et al., 2013), because multiple fixations are more likely in longer words. In TVD data, we observed no effect of individual WP, but a large effect of word length in the multiple regression analyses.

The largest limitation of the present study is the low statistical power of eye tracking data from two participants only. As Rapp (2014) already noted, the collection of individual corpora is effortful, but we think that this effort was worthwhile, even when the present study relied on a limited amount of statistical power. We were positively surprised by the reliable effect of individual WP in early and mid-range eye movement parameters. Nevertheless, the present work should be seen as a pilot study that will hopefully encourage further examinations of individual corpora. But there is also a second power issue that makes these results convincing. Our norm-based training corpus was at least 140 times larger than the individual training corpora. Therefore, we think that this is sound evidence that representativeness of a corpus for individual long-term memory structure can outperform size in predicting individual reading performance (e.g. Banko and Brill, 2001, inter alia).

One reason for our conclusion that individual corpora may better predict eye movements lies in the time period, in which the text corpus reflecting human experience was acquired. The individual corpora were collected in a two-month time period that preceded the eye tracking study by about 1-2 months. Therefore, the individual corpora may primarily reflect more recently acquired knowledge. Ericsson and Kintsch (1995) proposed multiple buffer stores in their theory of long-term working memory (cf. Kintsch and Mangalath, 2011). Recently acquired knowledge is held in these buffers before it is integrated into long-term memory. Therefore, participants can stop reading a text, and when carrying on reading later, only the first sentences are read slower as compared to continuous reading of these texts (Ericsson and Kintsch, 1995). Our early eye-movement effects may be explained by the proposal that the recently acquired knowledge still resides in Ericsson and Kintsch's (1995) long-term buffer stores. While they argue that football knowledge can well predict comprehension of football-related texts, for instance, it is hard to answer the question of which knowledge has been acquired in which time period. First, individual corpora may help to free such studies from the investigation of one particular type of knowledge, because each individual corpus reflects the knowledge of this individual. Second, individual corpora collected at different time periods may provide a novel approach to the question of how long information may persist in these knowledge buffers. Our results suggest that information still residing in long-term memory buffers elicits faster and more efficient memory retrieval.

There are several studies, in which participants are required to write diaries, which can be considered as extremely small individual corpora (e.g. Campbell & Pennebaker, 2003). Another example is the task to write emails to predict individual traits: For instance, Oberlander and Gill (2006) found that participants with high extraversion tend to use "will not" for expressing negation, while participants with low extraversion tend to use "not really" (see Johannßen and Biemann, 2018, for a recent overview). While such studies focused on the language output, the present study provided two input variables. First, individual corpora allow to estimate individual experience. Second, we selected the materials based on a language model to specifically capture the individual experience of the participants in the eye-tracking experiment. The language models can be considered an algorithmic approach to the neurocognitive system between the inputs and the output.

Much as differences of the cognitive architecture of the participants, there are "interindividual" differences between language models. For instance, n-gram models may reflect the capability of participants to remember particular words in context of specific other words, while neural network models more closely reflect the human capability to generalize from experiences (e.g. Hofmann et al., 2020; McClelland & Rogers, 2003). Thus, comparing such models with respect to the question of which model predicts which participant may provide information about the cognitive architecture of the respective participant. With respect to human intelligence testing, individual corpora should be a suitable approach to face Catell's (1943, p. 157) challenge of "freeing adult tests from assumptions of uniform knowledge".

For future work, we would like to proceed in three directions. First, we would like to improve the collection procedure: the corpora collected via screenshots and OCR contain a high number of artifacts stemming from non-textual material, as well as non-contiguous texts as a result from complex webpage layouts. Second, we like to increase the number of participants in future studies. Third, it would be interesting to compare our word2vec results with more recent contextual embeddings such as BERT (Devlin et al., 2019), which have been shown to achieve better performance across a wide range of natural language processing tasks than language models with static word embeddings. While it is non-trivial to use BERT's bi-directional architecture and its masking mechanism for language modelling tasks, Salazar et al., (2020) have recently shown how to obtain prediction values for BERT and other architectures trained with masking loss. Subword representations as used in BERT may also help to compensate OCR-based errors, when only a few letters have been falsely recognized. On the downside, it is questionable whether the present corpus sizes of 300/500K token are large enough to obtain reliable estimates for the large number of BERT's parameters. A potential solution is to rely on a BERT model pre-trained by a large corpus, and to use the individual corpora to fine-tune the language model. Though such fine tuning may enhance the predictions over the pre-trained model only, such an approach would mix norm-based and individual corpus information. The aim of the present study, in contrast, was to focus on the comparison of norm-based vs. strictly individual corpora, so we leave this extension for future work[2].

References

Banko, M., & Brill, E. (2001). Scaling to very very large corpora for natural language disambiguation. In *Proceedings of the 39th annual meeting on association for computational linguistics* (pp. 26–33).

Bhatia, S. (2017). Associative judgment and vector space semantics. *Psychological Review, 124*(1), 1–20.

Blei, D. M., Ng, A. Y., & Jordan, M. I. (2003). Latent dirichlet allocation. *Journal of Machine Learning Research, 3*, 993–1022.

Brickenkamp, R. (1990). *Generelle Interessenskala*. Göttingen: Hogrefe.

Brysbaert, M., & New, B. (2009). Moving beyond Kučera and Francis: A critical evaluation of current word frequency norms and the introduction of a new and improved word frequency measure for American English. *Behavior Research Methods, 41*(4), 977–990.

Campbell, R. S., & Pennebaker, J. W. (2003). The secret life of pronouns: Flexibility in writing style and physical health. *Psychological Science, 14*(1), 60–65.

Catell, R. B. (1943). The measurement of adult intelligence. *Psychological Bulletin, 40*(3), 153–193.

Deerwester, S., Dumais, S. T., Furnas, G. W., Landauer, T. K., & Harshman, R. (1990). Indexing by latent semantic analysis. *Journal of the American Society for Information Science, 41*(6), 391–407.

[2] This research was partially supported by a grant of the Deutsche Forschungsgemeinschaft to MJH (DFG-Gz. 5139/2-2). We like to thank Saskia Pasche, Steffen Remus, Dirk Johanßen, and Christian Vorstius for help during data collection and analyses.

Demberg, V., & Keller, F. (2008). Data from eye-tracking corpora as evidence for theories of syntactic processing complexity. *Cognition, 109*(2), 193–210.

Devlin, J., Chang, M.-W., Lee, K., Toutanova, K. (2019): BERT: Pre-training of deep bidirectional transformers for language understanding. Proceedings of the 2019 Conference of the North American Chapter of the Association for Computational Linguistics: Human Language Technologies, Volume 1 (Long and Short Papers) (pp. 4171–4186).

Ehrlich, S. F., & Rayner, K. (1981). Contextual effects on word perception and eye movements during reading. *Journal of Verbal Learning and Verbal Behavior, 20*(6), 641–655.

Engbert, R., Nuthmann, A., Richter, E. M., & Kliegl, R. (2005). SWIFT: a dynamical model of saccade generation during reading. *Psychological Review, 112*(4), 777–813.

Ericsson, K. A., & Kintsch, W. (1995). Long-term working memory. *Psychological Review, 102*(2), 211–245.

Frank, S. (2009). Surprisal-based comparison between a symbolic and a connectionist model of sentence processing. In *Proceedings of the annual meeting of the Cognitive Science Society* (pp. 1139–1144).

Frank, S. L., & Bod, R. (2011). Insensitivity of the human sentence-processing system to hierarchical structure. *Psychological Science, 22*(6), 829–834.

Goldhahn, D., Eckart, T., & Quasthoff, U. (2012). Building large monolingual dictionaries at the leipzig corpora collection: From 100 to 200 languages. In *Proceedings of the 8th International Conference on Language Resources and Evaluation* (pp. 759–765).

Griffiths, T. L., Steyvers, M., & Tenenbaum, J. B. (2007). Topics in semantic representation. *Psychological Review, 114*(2), 211–244.

Hofmann, M. J., Biemann, C., & Remus, S. (2017). Benchmarking n-grams, topic models and recurrent neural networks by cloze completions, EEGs and eye movements. In B. Sharp, F. Sedes, & W. Lubaszewsk (Eds.), *Cognitive Approach to Natural Language Processing* (pp. 197–215). London, UK: ISTE Press Ltd, Elsevier.

Hofmann, M. J., Biemann, C., Westbury, C. F., Murusidze, M., Conrad, M., & Jacobs, A. M. (2018). Simple co-occurrence statistics reproducibly predict association ratings. *Cognitive Science, 42*, 2287–2312.

Hofmann, M. J., Kuchinke, L., Biemann, C., Tamm, S., & Jacobs, A. M. (2011). Remembering words in context as predicted by an associative read-out model. *Frontiers in Psychology, 2*(252), 1–11.

Hofmann, M. J., Remus, S., Biemann, C., & Radach, R. (2020). Language models explain word reading times better than empirical predictability. Retrieved from https://psyarxiv.com/u43p7/download?format=pdf

Ibrahimovic, N., & Bulheller, S. (2005). *Wortschatztest – aktiv und passiv*. Frankfurt am Main: Harcourt.

Inhoff, A. W., & Radach, R. (1998). Definition and computation of oculomotor measures in the study of cognitive processes. In G. Underwood (Ed.), *Eye Guidance in Reading and Scene Perception* (pp. 29–53). Oxford, England: Elsevier Science.

Johannßen, D., & Biemann, C. (2018). Between the lines: Machine learning for prediction of psychological traits- A survey. In *International Cross-Domain Conference for Machine Learning and Knowledge Extraction* (pp. 192-211). Springer, Cham.

Johns, B. T., Jones, M. N., & Mewhort, D. J. K. (2019). Using experiential optimization to build lexical representations. *Psychonomic Bulletin & Review, 26*(1), 103-126.

Jacobs, A. M. (2019). Sentiment analysis for words and fiction characters from the perspective of computational (neuro-)poetics. *Frontiers in Robotics and AI, 6*(53), 1–13.

Kennedy, A., Pynte, J., Murray, W. S., & Paul, S. A. (2013). Frequency and predictability effects in the Dundee Corpus: An eye movement analysis. *Quarterly Journal of Experimental Psychology, 66*(3), 601–618.

Kintsch, W., & Mangalath, P. (2011). The construction of meaning. *Topics in Cognitive Science, 3*(2), 346–370.

Kliegl, R., Nuthmann, A., & Engbert, R. (2006). Tracking the mind during reading: the influence of past, present, and future words on fixation durations. *Journal of Experimental Psychology. General, 135*(1), 12–35.

Liepmann, D., Beauducel, A., Brocke, B., & Amthauer, R. (2007). *Intelligenz-Struktur-Test 2000 R (I-S-T 2000 R)*. Göttingen: Hogrefe.

Mandera, P., Keuleers, E., & Brysbaert, M. (2017). Explaining human performance in psycholinguistic tasks with models of semantic similarity based on prediction and counting: A review and empirical validation. *Journal of Memory and Language, 92*, 57–78.

McClelland, J. L., & Rogers, T. T. (2003). The parallel distributed processing approach to semantic cognition. *Nature Reviews Neuroscience, 4*(4), 310–322.

McDonald, S. A., & Shillcock, R. C. (2003). Eye movements reveal the on-line computation of lexical probabilities during reading. *Psychological Science, 14*(6), 648–652.

Mikolov T. (2014). *Statistical language models based on neural networks* (PhD Thesis). Brno University of Technology, Brno.

Mikolov, T., Chen, K., Corrado, G., & Dean, J. (2013). Efficient estimation of word representations in vector space. In *Proceedings of Workshop at ICLR* (pp. 1–12).

Oberlander, J., & Gill, A. J. (2006). Language with character: A stratified corpus comparison of individual differences in e-mail communication. *Discourse Processes, 42*(3), 239–270.

O'Brien, R. M. (2007). A caution regarding rules of thumb for variance inflation factors. *Quality and Quantity, 41*(5), 673–690.

Paller, K. A., & Wagner, A. D. (2002). Observing the transformation of experience into memory. *Trends in Cognitive Sciences, 6*(2), 93–102.

Pynte, J., New, B., & Kennedy, A. (2008). On-line contextual influences during reading normal text: A multiple-regression analysis. *Vision Research, 48*(21), 2172–2183.

Radach, R., Inhoff, A. W., Glover, L., & Vorstius, C. (2013). Contextual constraint and N + 2 preview effects in reading. *Quarterly Journal of Experimental Psychology, 66*, 619–633.

Radach, R., & Kennedy, A. (2004). Theoretical perspectives on eye movements in reading: Past controversies, current issues, and an agenda for future research. *European Journal of Cognitive Psychology, 16*(1–2), 3–26.

Radach, R., & Kennedy, A. (2013). Eye movements in reading: Some theoretical context. *Quarterly Journal of Experimental Psychology, 66*(3), 429–452.

Rapp, R. (2014). Using collections of human language intuitions to measure corpus representativeness. *COLING 2014 - 25th International Conference on Computational Linguistics, Proceedings of COLING 2014: Technical Papers*, 2117–2128.

Rayner, K. (1998). Eye movements in reading and information processing: 20 years of research. *Psychological Bulletin*, 124(3), 372–422.

Rehurek, R., & Sojka, P. (2010). Software framework for topic modelling with large corpora. In R. Witte, H. Cunningham, J. Patrick, E. Beisswanger, E. Buyko, U. Hahn, K. Verspoor, & A. R. Coden (Eds.), *Proceedings of the LREC 2010 Workshop on New Challenges for NLP Frameworks* (pp. 45–50). Valletta, Malta: ELRA.

Reichle, E. D., Rayner, K., & Pollatsek, A. (2003). The E-Z reader model of eye-movement control in reading: comparisons to other models. *The Behavioral and Brain Sciences, 26*(4), 445–476.

Reilly, R. G., & Radach, R. (2006). Some empirical tests of an interactive activation model of eye movement control in reading. *Cognitive Systems Research, 7*(1), 34–55.

Roelke, A., Vorstius, C., Radach, R., & Hofmann, M. J. (2020). Fixation-related NIRS indexes retinotopic occipital processing of parafoveal preview during natural reading. *NeuroImage, 215*, 116823.

Salazar, J., Liang, D., Nguyen, T. Q., & Kirchhoff, K. (2019). Masked Language Model Scoring. Retrieved from https://arxiv.org/pdf/1910.14659.pdf

Shaoul, C., Baayen, R. H., & Westbury, C. F. (2015). N-gram probability effects in a cloze task. *The Mental Lexicon, 9*(3), 437–472.

Schneider, W., Schlagmüller, M., & Ennemoser, M. (2007). LGVT 6-12: Lesegeschwindigkeits- und -verständnistest für die Klassen 6-12 (p. 6). Göttingen: Hogrefe.

Smith, R. (2007). An overview of the Tesseract OCR Engine. In *Proceedings of the Ninth International Conference on Document Analysis and Recognition (ICDAR 2007)*, Vol. 2. IEEE Computer Society, Washington, DC, USA, 629–633.

Smith, N. J., & Levy, R. (2013). The effect of word predictability on reading time is logarithmic. *Cognition, 128*(3), 302–319.

Staub, A. (2015). The effect of lexical predictability on eye movements in reading: Critical review and theoretical interpretation. *Language and Linguistics Compass, 9*(8), 311–327.

Investigating Rich Feature Sources for Conceptual Representation Encoding

Lu Cao♣, Yulong Chen♠♡, Dandan Huang♡ , Yue Zhang♡◇ *

♣ Singapore University of Technology and Design, Singapore
♠ Zhejiang University, China
♡School of Engineering, Westlake University, China
◇Institute of Advanced Technology, Westlake Institute for Advanced Study, China

Abstract

Functional Magnetic Resonance Imaging (fMRI) provides a means to investigate human conceptual representation in cognitive and neuroscience studies, where researchers predict the fMRI activations with elicited stimuli inputs. Previous work mainly uses a single source of features, particularly linguistic features, to predict fMRI activations. However, relatively little work has been done on investigating rich-source features for conceptual representation. In this paper, we systematically compare the linguistic, visual as well as auditory input features in conceptual representation, and further introduce associative conceptual features, which are obtained from Small World of Words game, to predict fMRI activations. Our experimental results show that those rich-source features can enhance performance in predicting the fMRI activations. Our analysis indicates that information from rich sources is present in the conceptual representation of human brains. In particular, the visual feature weights the most on conceptual representation, which is consistent with the recent cognitive science study.

1   Introduction

How a simple concept is represented and organized by human brain has been of long research interest in cognitive science and natural language processing (NLP) (Ishai et al., 1999; Martin, 2007; Fernandino et al., 2016). The rise of brain imaging methods such as fMRI technology has now made it feasible to investigate conceptual representation within human brain. In particular, fMRI is a technique that allows for the visualization of neuron activity in brain regions, which has become an essential tool for analyzing the neural correlates of brain activity in recent decades (Mitchell et al., 2004; Mitchell et al., 2008; Pereira et al., 2009; Pereira et al., 2011; Just et al., 2010).

Neuroscientists have shown that distinct patterns of neural activation are associated with both encoding and decoding the concepts of different semantic categories in brains. Mitchell et al. (2008) first introduced the task of predicting fMRI activation and proposed a featured-based model which takes a semantic representation of a single noun to predict the fMRI activation elicited by that noun. Subsequent studies (Pereira et al., 2018) introduced distributed based methods to build correlations between distributed semantic representations and patterns of neural activation. However, previous work mostly focuses on a single source of input features, e.g. count-based word vectors (Devereux et al., 2010; Murphy et al., 2012; Pereira et al., 2013; Pereira et al., 2018) to explore the in brain encoding process, which builds correlation between neural signals and distributed representation, and thus can be useful for better understanding both the brain and the word representation. But there has been little work systematically investigating the effect of different modalities on predicting fMRI activations.

We address this limitation by empirically investigating two forms of rich source features: multimodal features and associative conceptual feature. First, we systematically compare input features that come from linguistic, visual and auditory sources into fMRI activation encoding. To investigate the influence of each source of information in the brain conceptual representation, we build and evaluate a multimodal

---

*Corresponding author.

This work is licensed under a Creative Commons Attribution 4.0 International License. License details: http: //creativecommons.org/licenses/by/4.0/.

Reference	Stimuli	Presentation mode	Subj.
Mitchell et al. (2008)	60 concrete nouns	Word, Image	9
Pereira et al. (2018)	180 words	Word cloud, Sentence, Image	16

Table 1: fMRI datasets for language-brain encoding.

Categories	Words
animal	bear, cat, dog, horse, cow
vegetable	lettuce, carrot, corn, tomato, celery
body part	eye, arm, foot, leg, hand
man-made	telephone, key, bell, watch, refrigerator
building	igloo, barn, house, apartment, church
kitchen	spoon, bottle, cup, knife, glass
vehicle	truck, car, train, bicycle, airplane
clothing	dress, skirt, coat, pants, shirt
furniture	chair, dresser, desk, bed, table
build part	door, chimney, closet, arch, window
insect	fly, bee, butterfly, ant, beetle
tool	hammer, chisel, screwdriver, saw, pliers

Table 2: 60 nouns, organized by categories (Mitchell et al., 2008).

conceptual representation model with different modal input features and their combinations. Second, we investigate associative thinking of related concepts. We assume that associative thinking for concepts has individual difference, and it is insufficient to reflect such differences via distributed semantics representation. To verify this assumption, we propose an associative conceptual embedding that predicts brain activity by using associative conceptual words other than the concept presented to the subjects when collecting the brain activity data.

Experiments of multi-sense representation show that not only linguistic features, but also visual and auditory features, can be used to predict fMRI activations. It demonstrates that multimodal information is present in the conceptual representation in human brains, and we also observe that the weights of various modalities in brain conceptual representation are unequal. In particular, we find that performances of visual feature grounded multimodal models are overall improved compared with unimodal models, while the performances of auditory feature grounded models are not consistently improved. This observation leads to a conclusion that the visual information weights the most in brain conceptual representations. In addition, experiments of associative conceptual representation show that the associative conceptual words, which though are distinct in distributed semantic vector space, are related in conceptual representation in human brains.

2   Related Work

Previous studies on conceptual representation mainly focus on correlation between words and corresponding fMRI activations, including feature based methods and distributed representation based methods. Seminal work of Mitchell et al. (2008) pioneered the use of corpus-derived word representations to predict brain activation data associated with the meaning of nouns. This feature based method selected 25 verbs (*i.e.,* 'see', 'say', 'taste'.), and calculated the co-occurrence frequency of the noun with each of 25 verbs. In this regard, a noun word is encoded into 25 sensor-motor features. Subsequent work including Jelodar et al. (2010) used WordNet (Miller, 1995) to compute the values of the features. Obviously, such feature based methods are constrained by corpora, and only focus on linguistic unimodal.

Pereira et al. (2013) proposed a distributed semantics based method using features learnt form Wikipeida to predict neural activations for unseen concepts. Since then, various studies have shown

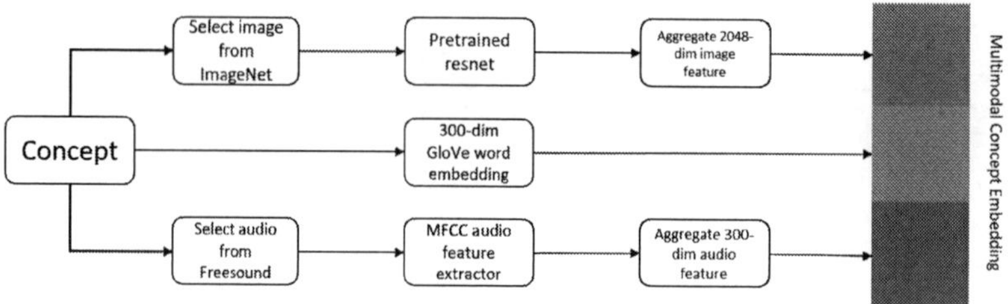

Figure 1: Compute multimodal embeddings.

that distributed semantic representations have correlations with brain concept representation (Devereux et al., 2010; Murphy et al., 2012; Pereira et al., 2013; Pereira et al., 2018; Bulat et al., 2017). However, though these methods outperform the feature based methods, they still ignore the fact that the information in the real world comes as different modalities. In contrast to their work, we investigate the human conceptual representation mechanism via evaluating the effects of multimodal features rather than only unimodal linguistic feature.

More closely related to our work, Bulat et al. (2017) presented a systematic evaluation and comparison of unimodal and multimodal semantic models in their ability to predict patterns of conceptual representation in the human brain. However, they only focused on the model level, contrasting unimodal representations and multimodal representations that involve linguistic and visual signals, but not the effect of each modality. While little previous work studied the influence of each source of information in the brain conceptual representation, our study is more extensive by evaluating multiple modalities data and their combinations. To our knowledge, we are the first to report auditory data in exploring human conceptual representations. More vitally, we explore their importance in concrete noun representations. Different from all work above, we are also the first to introduce associative conceptual words as input features to human conceptual representation.

3   Task: Predicting the fMRI Activation

The task is to predict the corresponding fMRI activations with elicited stimuli. The encoder operates by predicting fMRI activation given feature vectors. Each dimension (voxel) of fMRI activation is predicted by using a separate ridge regression estimator. More formally, given the matrix X and the matrix Z, we learn regression coefficients b and b_0 that minimize

$$\|Xb + b_0 - z\|^2 + \alpha\|b\|^2 \tag{1}$$

for each column of z of Z matrix. X is the semantic matrix, the dimension is the number of words (training set) by the dimension of semantic vector (300 for GloVe); and Z is the corresponding fMRI activation matrix, the dimension is the number of fMRI activation by the imaging dimension (amount of selected voxel, 500 for Mitchell et al. (2008) dataset and 5000 for Pereira et al. (2018) dataset).

We investigate three types of multi-sense inputs, namely, linguistic, visual and auditory sources. And further we use associative conceptual input, namely, the associative conceptual words which is obtained from Small World of Word game. In the next two sections, we will introduce how to obtain multi-sense representations and associative conceptual representations.

4   Multi-Sense Representations

Following Bruni et al. (2014) and Kiela and Bottou (2014), we construct multimodal semantic representation vector, V_m, by concatenating the linguistic, visual and auditory representations as shown in Figure 1:

$$V_m = V_{linguistic}\|V_{visual}\|V_{auditory}, \tag{2}$$

where $\|$ is the concatenation operator.

4.1 Linguistic Representations

The linguistic representation can be a dense vector that represents a word associated with a concept. Distributed word representations have been applied to statistical language modeling with considerable success (Bengio et al., 2003). This idea has enabled a substantial amount of progress in a wide range of NLP task, and was also shown useful for brain conceptual representation (Devereux et al., 2010; Murphy et al., 2012). The approach is based on the distributional hypothesis (Firth, 1957; Harris, 1954) which assumes that words with similar contexts tend to have similar semantic meaning. The intuition underlying the model is ratios of word-word co-occurrence probabilities have the potential for encoding some form of meaning. GloVe (Pennington et al., 2014) provides multiple versions of pre-trained word embeddings. In this paper, we use a 300-dimensional version of GloVe, which trained on a corpus consisting of Wikipedia 2014 and Gigaword 5.

4.2 Visual Representations

Visual representation is used to represent an image associated with a concept in a dense vector. Our approach to constructing the visual representations component is to utilize a collection of images associated with words representing a particular concept. For example, given a stimulus *'carrot'*, the associated images are a collection of *'carrot'* images that we retrieve from the dataset. In our implementation, we use Deep Residual Network (ResNet) (He et al., 2016) to produce the image feature map.

ResNet is widely used in image recognition as it is a deep neural network with many convolution layers stack together and can extract rich image features. The network is pre-trained on ImageNet (Deng et al., 2009), one of the largest image databases. Then, we chop the last layer of the network and use the remaining part as the feature extractor to compute the 2048-dimensional feature vector for each image. To represent a particular concept, we extract the image features of all images belong to that concept. Then, we directly compute the average of all image features as the visual representation.

4.3 Auditory Representations

Auditory representation is a dense vector used to present the acoustic properties of a concept. For example, given the concept *'key'*, correlated sounds are keys hitting or rubbing together; and for *'hand'*, correlated sounds can be applause. For the auditory representations, we retrieve 3 to 100 audios from Freesound (Font et al., 2013) for each concept. To generate the auditory representation for each noun, we first obtain Mel-scale Frequency Cepstral Coefficients (MFCCs) (O'Shaughnessy, 1987) features of each audio and then quantize the features into a bag of audio words (BoAW) (Foote, 1997) representations. MFCCs are commonly used as features in speech recognition, information retrieval, and music analysis. After obtaining a BoAW set, we take the mean of each BoAW as the auditory representation. In this paper, we use MMFeat (Kiela, 2016) to generate 300-dimensional auditory representations. The code is available at `https://github.com/douwekiela/mmfeat`.

5 Associative Conceptual Representation

Associative conceptual representation is a dense vector obtained from the associative conceptual words that are produced by humans in a game scene, and it is used to presented human's associative thinking related a concept. To investigate that whether associative thinking can be reflected in the fMRI activation, we fuse the word vectors linearly and use it as our associative conceptual representations. The linear fusion is represented as:

$$V_m = V_{stimuli} \| V_{associate}, \tag{3}$$

where $\|$ is the concatenation operator.

6 Experiments

We apply three sources of features to predict fMRI activations with unimodal model and multimodal models, and compare their performances. Further, we compare the performances of models with irrelevant words and associative conceptual words as inputs respectively.

	Linguistic		Visual		Auditory		L+V[1]		L+A[2]		V+A[3]		L+V+A[4]	
	W/I	B/W	W/I	B/W	W/I	B/W	W/I	B/W	W/I	B/W	W/I	B/W	W/I	B/W
P1	0.49	0.91	0.61	0.95	0.68	0.76	0.58	0.95	0.62	0.87	0.63	0.92	0.64	0.92
P2	0.47	0.75	0.60	0.81	0.55	0.67	0.52	0.80	0.54	0.70	0.54	0.77	0.52	0.78
P3	0.68	0.85	0.57	0.83	0.57	0.66	0.61	0.85	0.59	0.78	0.62	0.83	0.63	0.84
P4	0.55	0.89	0.57	0.92	0.51	0.71	0.57	0.92	0.51	0.85	0.58	0.91	0.55	0.92
P5	0.58	0.79	0.58	0.80	0.53	0.64	0.61	0.81	0.48	0.75	0.54	0.79	0.58	0.80
P6	0.55	0.77	0.59	0.80	0.53	0.65	0.55	0.80	0.57	0.77	0.62	0.79	0.60	0.78
P7	0.57	0.75	0.54	0.81	0.68	0.73	0.53	0.81	0.68	0.80	0.64	0.83	0.61	0.83
P8	0.61	0.76	0.52	0.67	0.54	0.63	0.56	0.69	0.62	0.70	0.55	0.68	0.61	0.70
P9	0.57	0.83	0.57	0.83	0.59	0.69	0.60	0.84	0.53	0.79	0.57	0.84	0.57	0.85
Mean	0.56	0.81	0.57	0.82	0.58	0.68	0.57	0.83	0.57	0.78	0.59	0.82	0.59	0.82

[1] LINGUISTIC+VISUAL [2] LINGUISTIC+AUDITORY [3] VISUAL+AUDITORY [4] LINGUISTIC+VISUAL+AUDITORY
W/I WITHIN CATEGORY B/W BETWEEN CATEGORY

Table 3: Accuracies of within and between-category examples for all participants (Pi). Within-category refers to stimuli coming from the same category (e.g. bear and cat come from the category of the animal) whereas between-category refers to stimuli coming from different categories.

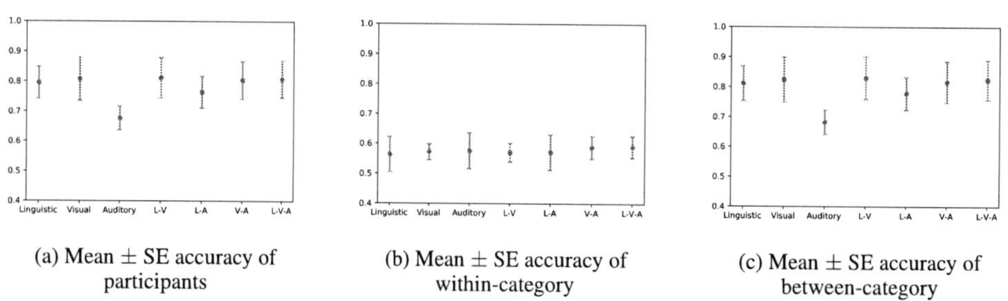

(a) Mean $\pm$ SE accuracy of participants

(b) Mean $\pm$ SE accuracy of within-category

(c) Mean $\pm$ SE accuracy of between-category

Figure 2: Mean $\pm$ SE accuracies of participants for all modals of data, using results in Table 3.

6.1 Datasets

6.1.1 fMRI Datasets

In this paper, we use the fMRI activation datasets of Mitchell et al. (2008) and Pereira et al. (2018). The summary of the datasets is shown in Table 1.

Mitchell et al. (2008)'s fMRI activation dataset was collected from nine right-handed subjects (5 females and 4 males between 18 and 32 years old). Each time, every subject was presented with noun labels and line drawings of 60 concrete objects from 12 semantic categories with 5 exemplars per category and the corresponding fMRI activation was recorded. The 60 concrete nouns and categories are shown in Table 2. Each exemplar was presented six times with randomly permutation and each exemplar was presented 3 seconds followed by a 7 seconds rest period. During the exemplar presenting, subjects were required to think about the proprieties of it freely. For example, for the concept *'dog'*, the proprieties might be *'pet'*, *'fluffy'*, and *'labrador retrievers'*. It is not required to obtain consistency properties across subjects. Given an exemplar, the fMRI activation of each subject was recorded during the presenting each of the six times. In this paper, we create one representative fMRI activation for each exemplar by averaging six scans.

Pereira et al. (2018)'s fMRI activation dataset was collected from 16 subjects. Similarly to Mitchell et al. (2008), subjects were asked to think about the properties when they were presented with stimulus in form of words, pictures and sentences. But the exemplar words of Pereira et al. (2018) cover a broader semantic vector space and are more distinct in vector space. First, they applied 300-dimensional GloVe (Pennington et al., 2014) to obtain semantic vectors for all words in a vocabulary size of approximately 30,000 words (Brysbaert et al., 2013). They then utilized spectral clustering (Luxburg, 2007) to group the vectors into 180 regions, and hand-selected 180 representative words for each regions.

Categories	Linguistic	Visual	Auditory	L-V[1]	L-A[2]	V-A[3]	L-V-A[4]
man-made	27	24	27	26	25	26	27
building	38	31	38	31	33	32	30
build part	56	64	40	62	48	62	61
tool	44	56	40	62	44	46	50
furniture	36	47	50	47	40	44	45
animal	22	34	36	35	32	36	33
kitchen	16	17	19	12	13	12	11
vehicle	50	40	37	42	44	37	34
insect	38	34	38	34	42	33	36
vegetable	32	33	49	30	48	42	37
body part	58	30	48	33	50	28	32
clothing	44	52	39	51	44	45	47

[1] LINGUISTIC+VISUAL   [2] LINGUISTIC+AUDITORY   [3] VISUAL+AUDITORY   [4] LINGUISTIC+VISUAL+AUDITORY

MOST ERROR   LEAST ERROR

Table 4: Selected within-category error statistics.

6.1.2   Multi-Sense Dataset

We obtain **linguistic** features from the GloVe (Pennington et al., 2014), which is trained on Wikipedia 2014 and Gigaword 5. For **visual** features, We retrieve 300 to 1500 images for each concept noun from ImageNet, except human body word: *'hand'*, *'foot'*, *'arm'*, *'leg'* and *'eye'*, which are not included in the ImageNet. Thus, we retrieve these images from Google Image (Afifi, 2017). The retrieved images from ImageNet and Google are combined together as the image dataset for visual feature extraction. For **auditory** features, we use the Freesound dataset (Font et al., 2013), which is a huge collaborative database of audio snippets, samples, recordings, and bleeps.

6.1.3   Associative Word Dataset

In this paper, we use Small World of Words (SWW) (De Deyne et al., 2018) as the word association data source. SWW is a mental dictionary or lexicon in the major languages of the world. It collects associative words by inviting participants globally to play an online game of word associations[1]. The game is simple and easy to play: given a list of 18 cue words, participants are asked to give first three words that come to mind. It counts and demonstrates the human level word associations. For example, top ten forward associations of the cue word *'machine'* are *'robot'*, *'computer'*, *'engine'*, *'metal'*, *'gun'*, *'work'*, *'car'*, *'washing'*, *'factory'*, *'sewing'*; and top ten backward associations of it are *'slot'*, *'fax'*, *'pinball'*, *'mechanism'*, *'sewing'*, *'washing'*, *'xerox'*, *'contraption'*, *'cog'*, *'copier'*. Here, forward association refers to the words will come to mind when participants see the cue word *'machine'*; and backward association refers to the word *'machine'* will come to mind when participants view other cue words. And their rankings indicate the average order of the word that participants think of in the SWW game.

In our paper, we use 60 concrete words from Mitchell et al. (2008) and choose 175 words from Pereira et al. (2018) (we discard 5 words: *'argumentatively'*, *'deliberately'*, *'emotionally'*, *'tried'*, *'willingly'*, which do not present in the associative words data source) as the cue words.

6.2   Training

As mentioned in Section **Task: Predicting the fMRI Activation**, the task is to predict the fMRI activations. Following Mitchell et al. (2008), we train the encoder consisting of several estimators (500 for Mitchell et al. (2008) and 5000 for Pereira et al. (2018)). Each estimator predicts a fMRI activation value of a specific position in the brain. The estimator is trained by ridge regression where the loss function is the linear least squares function and is regularized by the L_2-norm (Eq. 1). The regularization strength α is chosen by cross-validation.

---

[1] https://smallworldofwords.org/en

6.3 Evaluation

We evaluate each encoder's performance by following the strategy of Mitchell et al. (2008) and Pereira et al. (2018). For each possible pair of fMRI activation, we compute the cosine similarity between predicted and actual one. If the predicted fMRI activation is more similar to its actual one than the alternative, we deem the classification correct. For the data of Mitchell et al. (2008), each encoder is trained on 58 words and tested on the 2 left out words. The training and testing procedure iterates 1770 times. For the data of Pereira et al. (2018), each encoder is trained within a cross-validation procedure. In each fold, the parameters are learned from 165 word vectors, and predicted fMRI activation from the 10 left out words. The overall classification accuracy is the fraction of correct pairs. The match score S is calculated as:

$$S(p_1 = i_1, p_2 = i_2) = cosine(p_1, i_1) + cosine(p_2, i_2). \tag{4}$$

6.4 Results and Discussion

6.4.1 Uni- and Multi- Modal in fMRI Prediction

The cross-validated prediction accuracies are presented in Table 3. The expected accuracy of matching the left-out words and images is 0.5 if the model was randomly matching. All learned models predict unseen words significantly above the chance level.

In terms of unimodal prediction, VISUAL based model overall outperforms others, which verifies the **picture superiority effect** — human brain is extremely sensitive to the symbolic modality of presentation. VISUAL and LINGUISTIC significantly outperform AUDITORY based model, with the mean between category accuracy drops from approximately 0.8 to 0.68.

In terms of multimodal prediction, adding visual features improves performance as LINGUISTIC+VISUAL outperforms LINGUISTIC, VISUAL+AUDITORY outperforms AUDITORY and LINGUISTIC+VISUAL+AUDITORY outperforms LINGUISTIC+AUDITORY. These results provide a new proof for the **interactive model** of brain in behaviour measures which holds that structural and semantic information interact immediately during comprehension at any point in time, and weaken the serial model which proposes that semantic aspects only come into play at later stage and do not allow overlap with previous stages. We also notice that AUDITORY weakens model's prediction ability except for $P6$ and $P7$. Together with the finding in unimodal experiments that auditory based model performs less significantly than the linguistic and visual based model, the result suggests that visual properties contribute the most in conceptual representation in conceptual representations of nouns in the human brain, while acoustic properties contribute less. The results from $P6$ and $P7$ also suggest there are individual differences in the effects of different modality data on conceptual representations in the brain.

Kiela and Clark (2015) indicate that multimodal representations enriched by auditory information perform well on relatedness and similarity on words that have auditory associations such as *instruments*. We explore if the fMRI activation can be predicted by sound features, which is generated by using the objects which do not have obvious acoustic properties such as *hand, foot*, etc. Although the prediction accuracy is lower when using auditory features than using linguistic and visual features, it is significantly above the chance level. The results suggest that acoustic properties play a less important role but are ubiquitous in cognitive processes. We may need to consider the sound factors in the conceptual representation in general.

Figure 2 shows the individual mean SE±accuracy and mean SE±accuracy of within-category and between category. From Figure 2, we can see that individual performances vary in prediction and also, the result of between category prediction is better than within category prediction. We assume that this is because the features are much different between a category but more similar within a category, which makes predictions within category more demanding. For example, for linguistic feature, *'dog'* has a very similar context with *'cat'*, such as *play, eat*, but a very different context from *'machine'*, of which the context might be *artificial, fix*. Previous research has suggested that brain may rely on enhanced perceptual processing in order to compensate for inefficient higher level semantic processing, thus the phenomena of high within-category error rate and low between category error rate reflects the **sensory compensation mechanism** of brain in language processing.

	Stimuli	Forward Association Word						Stimuli	Forward Association Word				
		1	2	3	4	5			1	2	3	4	5
s-random	0.80	0.73	0.73	0.74	0.74	0.74	s-random	0.73	0.67	0.68	0.68	0.67	0.68
s-linear		0.80	0.79	0.78	0.79	0.80	s-linear		0.71	0.71	0.71	0.71	0.71

(a) Mean accuracy on Mitchell et al. (2008) dataset. (b) Mean accuracy on Pereira et al. (2018) dataset.

Table 5: Mean **FORWARD** fMRI activation prediction accuracy on Mitchell et al. (2008) and Pereira et al. (2018) dataset.

	Stimuli	Backward Association Word						Stimuli	Backward Association Word				
		1	2	3	4	5			1	2	3	4	5
s-random	0.80	0.74	0.74	0.74	0.74	0.74	s-random	0.73	0.68	0.68	0.69	0.69	0.68
s-linear		0.77	0.78	0.80	0.79	0.78	s-linear		0.71	0.71	0.71	0.71	0.71

(a) Mean accuracy on Mitchell et al. (2008) dataset. (b) Mean accuracy on Pereira et al. (2018) dataset.

Table 6: Mean **BACKWARD** fMRI activation prediction accuracy on Mitchell et al. (2008) and Pereira et al. (2018) dataset.

Table 4 shows the within category error, and we observe that Auditory features reduce the error of some categories, for example, for *body part*, VISUAL+AUDITORY outperforms simply VISUAL, and for *building part*, LINGUISTIC+AUDITORY outperforms simply LINGUISTIC. It reflects that the brain does trigger auditory senses during the rapid visual analysis and the activation of semantic knowledge, and also supports behavioural neuroscientists on that semantic processes can strongly affect generation of **auditory imagery**.

6.4.2 Associated Concept in fMRI Prediction

We choose the top 5 forward associate words and 5 backward words in our experiments. The concept of 'associate' and associative word dataset are introduced in section 6.1.3. For example, for the word *'invention'*, the associative words that people most likely to think of are *'new'*, *'light bulb'*, *'idea'*, *'innovation'*, *'creation'*, *'patent'*, *'Edison'*, *'Einstein'*, *'science'*, *'scientist'*, *'clever'*, *'smart'*, *'creative'*, *'create'*, *'Genius'*. We use the word *'invention'*, its associative words and their combinations to predict the fMRI activation separately.

Table 5a and Table 5b are the prediction accuracy that we use stimuli and forward associative words as the input on both datasets. Tables 6a and 6b are the prediction accuracy that we use stimuli and backward associative words as input. **s-random** means using linear combination of stimuli and irrelevant word, which is randomly chosen. **s-linear** means using linear combination of stimuli and one correspondent associate word. It is important to note that, the irrelevant word is randomly chosen, and it is not associative to the stimuli. For example, for the stimuli *'invention'*, we may choose the word *'washing'*, which is not in the associative word pool of *'invention'*, as the irrelevant word. Figure 3 is the comparison of using various word association, where the original data is extracted from Table 5a, Table 5b, Table 6a and Table 6b.

Compared with (a), (b) in Figure 3, the prediction accuracy in (c), (d) is the average of 175 words. Thus, the lines in (c), (d) are more smooth. However, though the results in (a), (b) vary, they can still show the overall trend. Further, compared with using forward associative words (results from (a), (c)), using backward associative words has an equivalent performance, which means both forward and backward associative thinkings can reflect the associative conceptual representation.

We observe that all models with associative conceptual features outperform above the chance level on both datasets. Compared with using only stimuli or associate word (bottom blue line in Figure 3), we also find that the model can better predict fMRI activation by using their linear combination (top yellow line in Figure 3). Particularly, by using stimuli and their associative words, the model has the best ability to predict fMRI activations (top yellow line in Figure 3). We also observe that after added the irrelevant word, the model's performance decreases. These results show that even though both associative words and irrelevant words are not directly associated with the stimuli words and are distinct from the stimuli

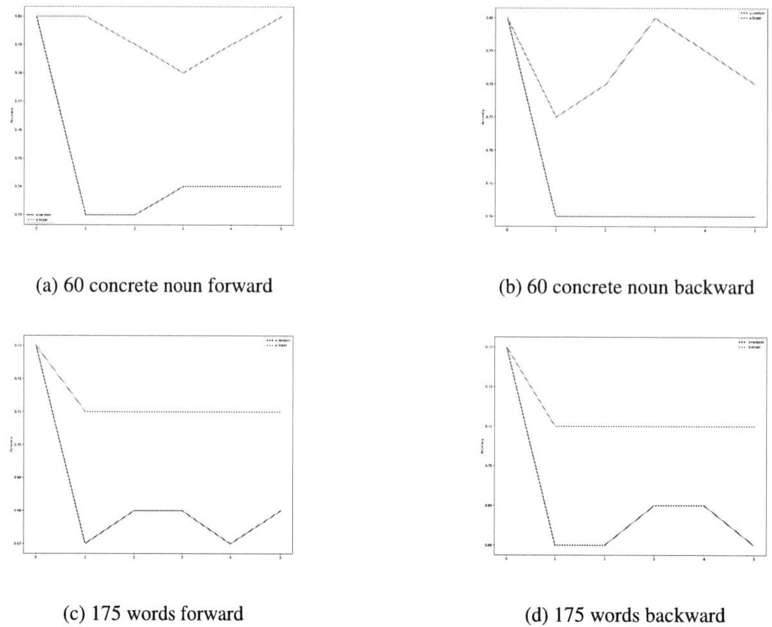

(a) 60 concrete noun forward   (b) 60 concrete noun backward

(c) 175 words forward   (d) 175 words backward

Figure 3: Comparison of various word association features. The top yellow line is corresponding to the results of *s-linear*, the below blue line is the result of *s-random*. For the point (x, y) in bottom blue line or top yellow line, x means using only the $x - th$ ranked associative word, or using linear combination of stimuli word and $x - th$ ranked associative word to predict the result. The rank tag of an associative word here means the average order of the word that participants think of in the SWW game.

words in distributed semantic representation in vector space, the associative words share some significant commonality with stimuli words in human conceptual representations while irrelevant words do not. It demonstrates that associative words serve as a complement to the stimuli words and accord with the brain activity, but the irrelevant words are noise to the conceptual representation.

In addition, there is a clear trend that the prediction accuracy decreases as the associative word rank decreases (bottom blue line in Figure 3). This result suggests that, given a stimuli, the higher ranked associate word can better reflect associative thinking related to a concept, and the subsequent associative words are less related. In other words, the rank of associative words can reflect the its weight of associative thinking in conceptual representations.

7 Conclusion and Future Work

We explored conceptual representation in human brains by evaluating the effect of multimodal data in predicting fMRI activation, observing a clear advantage in predicting brain activation for visually grounded models. This finding consistent with the neurological evidence that the word comprehension first involves activation of shallow language-based conceptual representation , which is then complemented by deeper simulation of visual properties of the concept (Louwerse and Hutchinson, 2012).

From the associative thinking perspective, we find that though the associative words might be far away in the distributed semantic vector space, we could still use them to better predict fMRI activation. We carried out more thorough and extensive work compare to the work of Bulat et al. (2017). The findings also support the hypotheses that the linguistic, conceptual and perceptual systems interplay in the human brain (Barsalou, 2008). The fMRI datasets used in our study are generated by presenting subjects with written words together with pictures. In other words, the fMRI representations are the participants' reactions to linguistic and visual input - but not acoustic. To further study human brain response representations to the acoustic stimuli, we plan to collect fMRI when presenting acoustic concepts.

References

Mahmoud Afifi. 2017. 11k hands: Gender recognition and biometric identification using a large dataset of hand images.

Lawrence Barsalou. 2008. Grounded cognition. *Annual review of psychology*, 59:617–45, 02.

Yoshua Bengio, Réjean Ducharme, Pascal Vincent, and Christian Janvin. 2003. A neural probabilistic language model. *J. Mach. Learn. Res.*, 3:1137–1155, March.

Elia Bruni, Nam Khanh Tran, and Marco Baroni. 2014. Multimodal distributional semantics. *J. Artif. Int. Res.*, 49(1):1–47, January.

Marc Brysbaert, Amy Beth Warriner, and Victor Kuperman. 2013. Concreteness ratings for 40 thousand generally known english word lemmas. *Behavior research methods*, 46, 10.

Luana Bulat, Stephen Clark, and Ekaterina Shutova. 2017. Speaking, seeing, understanding: Correlating semantic models with conceptual representation in the brain. In *Proceedings of the 2017 Conference on EMNLP*, pages 1081–1091, Copenhagen, Denmark, September. ACL.

Simon De Deyne, Danielle Navarro, Amy Perfors, Marc Brysbaert, and Gert Storms. 2018. The "small world of words" english word association norms for over 12,000 cue words. *Behavior Research Methods*, 51, 10.

Jia Deng, Wei Dong, Richard Socher, Li jia Li, Kai Li, and Li Fei-fei. 2009. Imagenet: A large-scale hierarchical image database. In *In CVPR*.

Barry Devereux, C Kelly, and A Korhonen. 2010. Using fmri activation to conceptual stimuli to evaluate methods for extracting conceptual representations from corpora. *Proceedings of First Workshop On Computational Neurolinguistics, NAACL HLT*, pages 70–78, 01.

Leonardo Fernandino, Jeffrey R. Binder, Rutvik H. Desai, Suzanne L Pendl, Colin J Humphries, William L. Gross, Lisa L. Conant, and Mark S. Seidenberg. 2016. Concept representation reflects multimodal abstraction: A framework for embodied semantics. *Cerebral cortex*, 26 5:2018–34.

John Rupert Firth. 1957. A synopsis of linguistic theory 1930-1955. *Special Volume of the Philological Society.*, page 11.

Frederic Font, Gerard Roma, and Xavier Serra. 2013. Freesound technical demo. In *ACM International Conference on Multimedia (MM'13)*, pages 411–412, Barcelona, Spain, 21/10/2013. ACM, ACM.

Jonathan T. Foote. 1997. Content-based retrieval of music and audio. In *MULTIMEDIA STORAGE AND ARCHIVING SYSTEMS II, PROC. OF SPIE*, pages 138–147.

Zellig Harris. 1954. Distributional structure. *Word*, 10(23):146–162.

Kaiming He, Xiangyu Zhang, Shaoqing Ren, and Jian Sun. 2016. Deep residual learning for image recognition. *2016 IEEE Conference on CVPR*, pages 770–778.

A. Ishai, L. G. Ungerleider, A. Martin, J. L. Schouten, and J. V. Haxby. 1999. Distributed representation of objects in the human ventral visual pathway. *Proc Natl Acad Sci U S A*, 96(16):9379–9384, Aug. 10430951[pmid].

Ahmad Babaeian Jelodar, Mehrdad Alizadeh, and Shahram Khadivi. 2010. Wordnet based features for predicting brain activity associated with meanings of nouns. In *Proceedings of the NAACL HLT 2010 First Workshop on Computational Neurolinguistics*, CN '10, pages 18–26, Stroudsburg, PA, USA. ACL.

Marcel Adam Just, Vladimir L. Cherkassky, Sandesh Aryal, and Tom M. Mitchell. 2010. A neurosemantic theory of concrete noun representation based on the underlying brain codes. *PLoS ONE*, 5(1):e8622, jan.

Douwe Kiela and Léon Bottou. 2014. Learning image embeddings using convolutional neural networks for improved multi-modal semantics. In *Proceedings of the 2014 Conference on EMNLP (EMNLP)*, pages 36–45, Doha, Qatar, October. ACL.

Douwe Kiela and Stephen Clark. 2015. Multi- and cross-modal semantics beyond vision: Grounding in auditory perception. In *Proceedings of the 2015 Conference on EMNLP*, pages 2461–2470, Lisbon, Portugal, September. ACL.

Douwe Kiela. 2016. MMFeat: A toolkit for extracting multi-modal features. In *Proceedings of ACL-2016 System Demonstrations*, pages 55–60, Berlin, Germany, August. ACL.

Max Louwerse and Sterling Hutchinson. 2012. Neurological evidence linguistic processes precede perceptual simulation in conceptual processing. *Frontiers in Psychology*, 3, 10.

Ulrike Luxburg. 2007. A tutorial on spectral clustering. *Statistics and Computing*, 17(4):395–416, December.

Alex Martin. 2007. The representation of object concepts in the brain. *Annual Review of Psychology*, 58(1):25–45. PMID: 16968210.

George A. Miller. 1995. Wordnet: A lexical database for english. *COMMUNICATIONS OF THE ACM*, 38:39–41.

Tom M. Mitchell, Rebecca Hutchinson, Radu S. Niculescu, Francisco Pereira, Xuerui Wang, Marcel Just, and Sharlene Newman. 2004. Learning to decode cognitive states from brain images. *Mach. Learn.*, 57(1-2):145–175, October.

Tom M. Mitchell, Svetlana V. Shinkareva, Andrew Carlson, Kai-Min Chang, Vicente L. Malave, Robert A. Mason, and Marcel Adam Just. 2008. Predicting human brain activity associated with the meanings of nouns. *Science*, 320(5880):1191–1195.

Brian Murphy, Partha Talukdar, and Tom Mitchell. 2012. Selecting corpus-semantic models for neurolinguistic decoding. In **SEM 2012: The First Joint Conference on Lexical and Computational Semantics – Volume 1: Proceedings of the main conference and the shared task, and Volume 2: Proceedings of the Sixth International Workshop on Semantic Evaluation (SemEval 2012)*, pages 114–123, Montréal, Canada, 7-8 June. ACL.

D. O'Shaughnessy. 1987. *Speech communication: human and machine*. Addison-Wesley series in electrical engineering: digital signal processing. Universities Press (India) Pvt. Limited.

Jeffrey Pennington, Richard Socher, and Christopher D. Manning. 2014. Glove: Global vectors for word representation. In *EMNLP (EMNLP)*, pages 1532–1543.

Francisco Pereira, Tom M. Mitchell, and Matthew Botvinick. 2009. Machine learning classifiers and fmri: A tutorial overview. *NeuroImage*, 45 1 Suppl:S199–209.

Francisco Pereira, Greg Detre, and Matthew Botvinick. 2011. Generating text from functional brain images. *Frontiers in Human Neuroscience*, 5:72.

Francisco Pereira, Matthew Botvinick, and Greg Detre. 2013. Using wikipedia to learn semantic feature representations of concrete concepts in neuroimaging experiments. *Artif. Intell.*, 194:240–252, January.

Francisco Pereira, Bin Lou, Brianna Pritchett, Samuel Ritter, Samuel J Gershman, Nancy Kanwisher, Matthew Botvinick, and Evelina Fedorenko. 2018. Toward a universal decoder of linguistic meaning from brain activation. *Nature communications*, 9(1):963.

General patterns and language variation: Word frequencies across English, German, and Chinese

Annika Tjuka
Max Planck Institute for the Science of Human History
Jena, Germany
`tjuka@shh.mpg.de`

Abstract

Cross-linguistic studies of concepts provide valuable insights for the investigation of the mental lexicon. Recent developments of cross-linguistic databases facilitate an exploration of a diverse set of languages on the basis of comparative concepts. These databases make use of a well-established reference catalog, the Concepticon, which is built from concept lists published in linguistics. A recently released feature of the Concepticon includes data on norms, ratings, and relations for words and concepts. The present study used data on word frequencies to test two hypotheses. First, I examined the assumption that related languages (i.e., English and German) share concepts with more similar frequencies than non-related languages (i.e., English and Chinese). Second, the variation of frequencies across both language pairs was explored to answer the question of whether the related languages share fewer concepts with a large difference between the frequency than the non-related languages. The findings indicate that related languages experience less variation in their frequencies. If there is variation, it seems to be due to cultural and structural differences. The implications of this study are far-reaching in that it exemplifies the use of cross-linguistic data for the study of the mental lexicon.

1 Introduction

The structure and functioning of the mental lexicon have been studied for many decades (Aitchison, 2012). The inner workings of the links and connections of the mental lexicon have been investigated in large scale studies and with non-invasive techniques such as EEG and fMRI. However, many of those studies focus solely on one language. Especially in experimental settings, creating a stimulus set across multiple languages that is controlled for the same variables such as frequency is difficult. But what if we could compare the properties of the same words in different languages to explore the similarities and differences that arise? We would need the word frequencies of translation equivalents for every word, for example, the first-person pronoun in English (*I*), German (*ich*), and Chinese (*wǒ* 我).

Although we have resources available that offer word frequencies for each of the three languages (Brysbaert and New, 2009; Brysbaert et al., 2011; Cai and Brysbaert, 2010), they lack a link between each other to make a comparison of the same word across languages possible. One solution would be to translate the words in the data set to a meta-language (e.g., English) and compare the translation equivalents. However, this comes with a risk of ignoring important information. An alternative is to link the words in the data sets to concepts. The Concepticon project (List et al., 2016) provides a list with 3,755 comparative concepts with links to elicitation glosses for various languages, including English, German, and Chinese. The decision of whether a word is mapped to a specific concept, for instance, the link between the word *tree* and the concept TREE, is based on elicitation glosses that are used in linguistic studies. Those studies often draw upon *Swadesh lists* which assess the genealogical relatedness between languages (Swadesh, 1955). The words in the list represent 'comparative concepts' (Haspelmath, 2010) that relate to basic meanings. The concept lists are linked to the concepts in Concepticon and provide the basis for the connection between a word and a concept. Tjuka et al. (2020b) used the Concepticon

Proceedings of the Workshop on Cognitive Aspects of the Lexicon, pages 23–32
Barcelona, Spain (Online), December 12, 2020

concept sets as a basis for the creation of the Database of Cross-Linguistic Norms, Ratings, and Relations for Words and Concepts (NoRaRe). This resource offers links to the Concepticon concept sets and various psycholinguistic values so that they can be easily compared across languages. The database also provides the opportunity to create and reproduce experiments on the basis of well-founded data curated by linguists.

The advantage of a cross-linguistic perspective on the mental lexicon is that we can discover general patterns and language-specific variation. The NoRaRe database promotes comparison of a shared part of the mental lexicon in different languages. The present study uses a set of three languages: English, German, and Chinese. On the one hand, English and German are related languages (both belong to the Germanic sub-branch of the Indo-European language family) and no large differences in the frequencies of the words in both languages are expected. English and Chinese, on the other hand, are genealogically different languages (Chinese belongs to the Sino-Tibetan language family). The assumption is that larger differences in the distribution of word frequencies can be found in the data of non-related languages. The aim of this study is to illustrate a database approach to language comparison on a large number of lexical items between multiple languages. The study sheds light on a cross-linguistic investigation of the mental lexicon.

Another aim of the study is to examine the variation of individual word frequencies in more detail and explore two patterns that could lead to different distributions. The first option is cultural differences in the structure of the mental lexicon. Cross-linguistic studies showed that languages vary in how they structure certain semantic domains such as color (Gibson et al., 2017) or emotion (Jackson et al., 2019). The second pattern that seems to emerge is a correlation between word frequency and the number of meanings (Zipf, 1945). If this is a valid principle, differences in frequencies of the same word in two languages might be due to differences in the number of meanings of the word in the two languages. For example, the word *back* (as a noun) seems to have more meanings in English than *Rücken* "back" in German, based on a search in the Extended Open Multilingual WordNet (Bond and Foster, 2013). A few studies demonstrated that Zipf's meaning-frequency law seems to hold across multiple languages, for instance, English, Turkish, Spanish, Dutch, among others (Ilgen and Karaoglan, 2007; Hernández-Fernández et al., 2016; Casas et al., 2019; Bond et al., 2019). Each of those studies compared the frequencies of words in different corpora with the number of meanings for the words in an individual language, which was taken from the respective WordNet (Fellbaum, 2012). They did not show particular words in each of the languages that gave rise to the correlation. Therefore, the pattern emerged on the basis of a black box. If one would analyze the words in a given data set in more detail, the Zipf's meaning-frequency law might only be true for specific words (e.g., high-frequency words) and could vary across word types (e.g., verbs, adjectives, nouns).[1]

By using the NoRaRe data (Tjuka et al., 2020b), the basis for the word frequencies can be uncovered and a well-established set of concepts in the Concepticon curated by linguists provides a solid basis for cross-linguistic comparison. The NoRaRe database facilitates a quantitative analysis in that frequency values for many concepts across languages can be correlated. Furthermore, the link to the concept sets in Concepticon offers the possibility for a qualitative analysis of outliers that show language-specific variation. The pattern of more frequent words having more meanings can thus be investigated based on individual cases to test its validity as an explanation for language specificities.

In the next section (Sect. 2), the materials and methods used for preparing the data sets of the present study are discussed. Section 3 shows the results of the correlation between the three languages as well as cases of cross-linguistic variation. Finally, in Section 4 and Section 5, the study is summarized and its implications for the investigation of the structure and functioning of the mental lexicon with cross-linguistic data are illustrated.

---

[1]For a detailed discussion of the limitations of Zipf's meaning-frequency law see Piantadosi (2014).

2 Material and Method

The foundation of this study is the concepts listed in the Concepticon resource (List et al., 2016; List et al., 2020). The Concepticon project[2] links concept sets consisting of a standardized identifier, a concept label, and a description, to elicitation glosses used in *concept lists* for research in linguistics such as Swadesh lists (Swadesh, 1955). The concept lists exist for a variety of glossing languages and the Concepticon currently supports mappings for common languages such as English, Spanish, Russian, German, French, Portuguese, and Chinese. For example, the glosses of the first-person pronoun in the languages English (*I*), German (*ich*), and Chinese (*wǒ* 我) are linked to the concept set with the ID 1209 and the label "I." The concepts in Concepticon represent comparative concepts (Haspelmath, 2010) that are commonly used to assess the relatedness of languages. The words linked to the concepts are based on elicitations from linguists either working in language documentation or historical linguistics to study basic meanings across languages. It is therefore assumed that a cross-linguistic comparison between the words that are linked to a specific Concepticon concept can be carried out. The mapping of elicitation glosses to concept sets is based on a manual workflow in which the Concepticon editors (a group of linguists) review and discuss each list that is integrated into the database. The Concepticon offers information on more than 3,500 concept sets linked to more than 300 concept lists.[3] It is also used as a reference catalog to add specialized data collections such as the NoRaRe data (Tjuka et al., 2020b) or data on colexifications (Rzymski et al., 2020).

The NoRaRe database[4] links additional information to the concept sets in Concepticon (Tjuka et al., 2020b). This information includes norms, ratings, and relations on words and concepts. The data come from studies in psychology and linguistics and currently include more than 70 data sets (Tjuka et al., 2020a). The 'norms' category consists of data on word frequencies or reaction times. The 'ratings' category provides participant judgments for psycholinguistic criteria such as age-of-acquisition, arousal, valence, among others. The category of 'relations' comprises, for instance, semantic field categorization and semantic networks. In the case of the NoRaRe data, the words *I*, *ich*, and *wǒ* 我, as well as the values for a property in a given data set, are linked to the Concepticon concept set 1209 I. The NoRaRe database also incorporates the word frequencies in subtitles for film and TV-series in English (Brysbaert and New, 2009), German (Brysbaert et al., 2011), and Chinese (Cai and Brysbaert, 2010) for several Concepticon concept sets.[5]

Another data collection that is based on the Concepticon is the Database of Cross-Linguistic Colexifications (CLICS) (Rzymski et al., 2020).[6] The term 'colexification' was established by François (2008) and refers to one lexeme having multiple meanings. It is an umbrella term for instances of vagueness, homonymy, and polysemy. The database comprises colexifications for almost 3,000 Concepticon concept sets across more than 2,000 language varieties. The colexifications are computed on the basis of the information in the concept lists by identifying whether a given elicitation gloss is mapped to multiple Concepticon concept sets. The database also offers colexification weights between concept sets. For example, the concept set 1209 I colexifies with 1212 WE in 31 language varieties compared to the colexification with the concept set 1405 NAME in 3 language varieties.[7]

All three resources are accessible online and the data can be easily retrieved. In addition, the data sets are presented in a standardized format. The workflows for the creation of each database rely on the standardization efforts of the Cross-Linguistic Data Formats initiative (CLDF) (Forkel et al., 2018).[8] The data is converted into a tabular format with an additional metadata file. This allows to instantly compare the data sets and reuse them. The Concepticon concept sets as a reference provide the further possibility for cross-linguistic comparison. The present study uses word frequencies in the SUBTLEX

---

[2]A web application of the Concepticon is available at `https://concepticon.clld.org/`

[3]The data is openly accessible on GitHub: `https://github.com/concepticon/concepticon-data`

[4]A web application of the NoRaRe database is available at `https://digling.org/norare/`

[5]The data is curated on GitHub: `https://github.com/concepticon/norare-data`

[6]A web application of the CLICS database is available at `https://clics.clld.org/`

[7]The data is available on GitHub: `https://github.com/clics/clics3`

[8]Wilkinson et al. (2016) proposed that data should be *findable*, *accessible*, *interoperable*, and *reusable* (FAIR). The CLDF initiative builds on this principle and offers standards for multiple data types.

data sets for English (Brysbaert and New, 2009), German (Brysbaert et al., 2011), and Chinese (Cai and Brysbaert, 2010) in the NoRaRe database. For information on colexifications in each of the languages, data included in CLICS from Key and Comrie (2016) as well as Haspelmath and Tadmor (2009) was selected.

The study presented in this article aims to test two hypotheses:

1. Related languages (i.e., belonging to the same language family) have more similar frequencies across a set of shared concepts than non-related languages (i.e., belonging to different language families).

2. In related languages, there are fewer concepts that have a large difference between frequencies than in non-related languages.

The hypotheses are examined on the basis of two comparisons: English–German and English–Chinese. The first language pair (English–German) was chosen because the languages represent closely related languages (both belong to the Germanic sub-branch of the Indo-European language family) while English–Chinese is the other side of the extreme, as the languages do not have a common ancestral language and therefore, are not related. To my knowledge, no study has tested either of the hypotheses with data on word frequencies before. Therefore, I assume that the correlation between word frequencies in English and German is higher than between English and Chinese. In addition, greater differences in frequency values for individual concepts between English and Chinese compared to English and German are expected. The results of the study are discussed in the next section.

3 Results

3.1 Correlations of Frequencies

The links between the Concepticon concept sets and the data in English (Brysbaert and New, 2009), German (Brysbaert et al., 2011), and Chinese (Cai and Brysbaert, 2010) are already provided in the NoRaRe database. Each data set consisted of more than 1,000 Concepticon concept sets with the respective values for word frequencies in subtitles of films and TV-series in English (2,329 concept sets), German (1,291 concept sets), and Chinese (1,644 concept sets). The language pair English–German had an overlap of 1,149 concept sets. In the language pair English–Chinese, the overlap amounted to 1,313 concept sets.[9] The shared concept sets were the basis for the correlation between each language pair.

To test the hypothesis that related languages have more similar frequencies across a set of shared concepts than non-related languages, two correlations were performed. First, the $\log_{10}$ frequencies of the 1,149 concept sets in English and German were correlated. The Pearson coefficient was 0.67 with a statistically highly significant p-value of $p < .001$. The distribution of the word frequencies is illustrated in Figure 1. Second, the $\log_{10}$ frequencies of the 1,313 concept sets in English and Chinese were compared. The Pearson coefficient was 0.55 with a statistically highly significant p-value of $p < .001$ (for the distribution see Fig. 1).

The correlation coefficients for both language pairs were not particularly high. However, there seems to be a slight difference between the data in the related languages English and German compared to English and Chinese. The next section investigates the differences between the data in more detail.

3.2 Cases of Language Variation

The mapping of the word frequency data sets to the Concepticon makes a qualitative cross-linguistic comparison possible. Tables 1 and 2 show the 15 most frequent concept sets in the two language pair data sets English–German and English–Chinese.

The logarithmic word frequencies for the concept set 1209 I across the three languages is now apparent: English *I* has a $\log_{10}$ frequency of 6.31, German *ich* has a $\log_{10}$ frequency of 5.97, and Chinese *wǒ* 我

---

[9]The overlap of the concept sets in the language pair German–Chinese was only about 700 concepts. Thus, the comparison would have been based on a much smaller data set than in the other two language pairs. The differences in the size of the data sets would most likely blur the result. For this reason, the study focused on the comparison between English–German and English–Chinese.

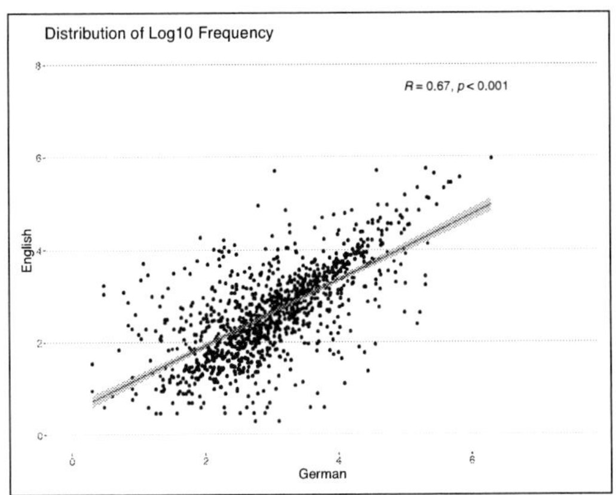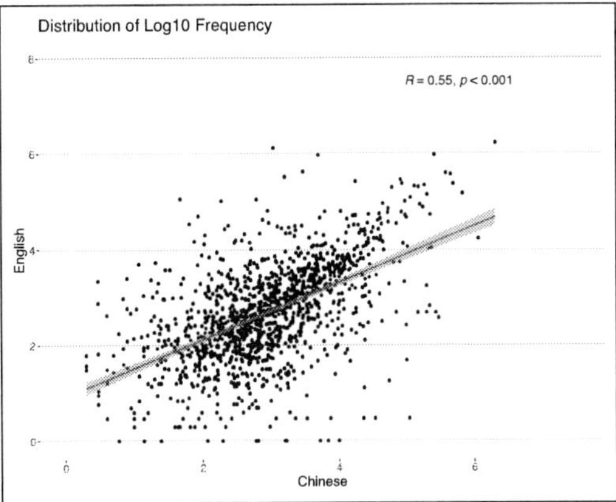

Figure 1: Distribution of the $\log_{10}$ word frequencies across the language pairs: English–German (left), English–Chinese (right). The data was taken from Brysbaert and New (2009), Brysbaert et al. (2011), and Cai and Brysbaert (2010) provided as subsets in the NoRaRe database (Tjuka et al., 2020b).

Table 1: The 15 most frequent concept sets in the overlapping data of English (Brysbaert and New, 2009) and German (Brysbaert et al., 2011) sorted by the English $\log_{10}$ word frequencies. The blue cell color indicates that the concept set does not appear in the English–Chinese language pair data set.

ID	Label	English $\log_{10}$	German $\log_{10}$
1209	I	6.31	5.97
1577	AND	5.83	5.57
1236	WHAT	5.70	5.45
1212	WE	5.66	5.45
1211	HE	5.59	5.33
1269	NO	5.48	4.97
1240	NOT	5.44	5.65
136	HERE	5.36	5.11
1937	THERE	5.35	4.13
2336	OF THIS KIND (SUCH)	5.34	5.13
817	THEY	5.32	5.75
1019	RIGHT	5.31	3.24
1117	LIKE	5.31	3.43
684	OWN	5.23	2.64
1376	NOW	5.21	4.85

has a $\log_{10}$ frequency of 6.23. The similar values indicate that the first-person pronoun occurred almost equally frequent in all three corpora. Other concept sets that are similarly common across all three data sets include 1577 AND, 1236 WHAT, 1212 WE, 1211 HE, 1937 THERE, and 817 THEY.

In contrast, some concept sets which have a high frequency in English appear to have lower frequencies in German and/ or Chinese. For example, the concept sets 1269 NO and 1240 NOT have relatively high $\log_{10}$ frequencies in English (5.48 and 5.44, respectively) and German (4.97 and 5.65, respectively), whereas the $\log_{10}$ frequencies in Chinese are considerably lower with 2.58 for the concept set 1269 NO and 2.69 for the concept set 1240 NOT. In the case of the concept set 1019 RIGHT, the English $\log_{10}$ frequency is higher (5.31) compared to German and Chinese which have the same lower $\log_{10}$ frequency of 3.24.

Some concept sets occurred only in one of the language pair data sets. On the one hand, the concept sets 2336 OF THIS KIND (SUCH), 1117 LIKE, 684 OWN, and 1376 NOW appeared in the data of the

Table 2: The 15 most frequent concept sets in the overlapping data of English (Brysbaert and New, 2009) and Chinese (Cai and Brysbaert, 2010) sorted by the English $\log_{10}$ word frequencies. The blue cell color indicates if a concept set does not appear in the English–German language pair data set.

ID	Label	English $\log_{10}$	Chinese $\log_{10}$
1209	I	6.31	6.23
2754	TOWARDS	6.06	4.24
1577	AND	5.83	5.18
1236	WHAT	5.70	5.37
1212	WE	5.66	5.57
1211	HE	5.59	5.60
1269	NO	5.48	2.58
1240	NOT	5.44	2.69
1579	BE	5.42	5.98
84	JUST	5.38	4.04
136	HERE	5.36	4.73
506	MAIZE	5.35	2.82
1937	THERE	5.35	4.01
817	THEY	5.32	5.15
1019	RIGHT	5.31	3.24

English–German language pair. The concept sets 2754 TOWARDS, 1579 BE, 84 JUST, and 506 MAIZE, on the other hand, occurred only in the English–Chinese data set.

The comparison of the 15 most frequent concept sets across the language pairs indicates that there are substantial differences in the data across the three languages. The second hypothesis of the present study was that fewer concepts have a large difference between frequencies in related languages than in non-related languages. To investigate this hypothesis, the differences in the $\log_{10}$ frequencies across the language pairs were compared. Tables 3 and 4 show the results of the comparisons for the English–German and English–Chinese data sets. Only concept sets that vary largely in their frequencies across the languages (difference greater than 3) were included for a qualitative comparison. These concept sets are extreme cases, but as discussed in the previous section, both language pair data sets share many concept sets that have similar $\log_{10}$ frequencies.

Table 3: Comparison of the differences in the $\log_{10}$ frequencies across English and German. The list includes the concept sets which vary greatly in their frequencies (difference greater than 3).

ID	Label	English $\log_{10}$	German $\log_{10}$	Difference
1301	FOOT	3.79	0.60	3.19
492	THREE	4.44	1.38	3.06

One obvious observation that becomes apparent in the comparison is the number of concept sets that have large differences between $\log_{10}$ frequencies. In the English–German data set only two concept sets vary greatly in their frequencies: 1301 FOOT and 492 THREE. Both concept sets occurred more often in English. The concept set 492 THREE refers to the natural number *three* in English and German (*drei*). The difference between the frequencies could be due to the fact that in German, the number word starts with a capital letter in some contexts, for instance, in the sentence *Sie hat eine Drei gewürfelt.* "She rolled a three." The concept set 1301 FOOT refers to the human body part. In English and German, *foot* is used also in other contexts, for instance, *foot of the mountain* or *metrical foot*. However, in German, the word *Fuß* "foot" often occurs as a compound word, as in *Versfuß* "metrical foot." This might explain the low frequency of the standalone word compared to English in which most compounds are written

Table 4: Comparison of the differences in the $\log_{10}$ frequencies across English and Chinese. The list includes the concept sets which vary greatly in their frequencies (difference greater than 3). The red row color indicates that the frequency of the concept set is higher in Chinese than in English.

ID	Label	English $\log_{10}$	Chinese $\log_{10}$	Difference
1235	WHO	5.05	0.48	4.58
1203	LONG	4.54	0.48	4.06
2483	COLD (OF WEATHER)	4.00	0.00	4.00
1417	KILL	4.36	0.48	3.89
702	CATCH	3.84	0.00	3.84
648	PAPER	3.72	0.00	3.72
1458	SAY	4.75	1.26	3.50
156	RED	3.88	0.48	3.40
705	GO UP (ASCEND)	1.68	5.06	3.38
1238	WHEN	5.02	1.69	3.33
1446	COME	4.37	1.11	3.26
1424	YELLOW	3.24	0.00	3.24
930	VILLAGE	3.23	0.00	3.23
711	TALL	3.22	0.00	3.22
1215	THOU	3.06	6.12	3.06
1208	CAT	3.53	0.48	3.05

with a space between the words, as in *three times* or *foot brake*.

The comparison between the frequencies in English and Chinese resulted in 16 concept sets with a large difference (greater than 3) in their $\log_{10}$ frequencies (see Tab. 4). A closer look at some of the concepts revealed cases of language variation which could lead to the differences in the frequencies. For example, the concept set 1235 WHO is mapped to English *who*, but Chinese has two word-forms *shuí* 谁 and *shéi* 誰 to ask about one person or people. The former is written in the simplified Chinese script, whereas the latter uses the traditional Chinese characters. Because both of them occurred in the original data, but only one word is mapped to the concept, the data set includes the frequency for *shéi* 誰 instead of *shuí* 谁 which has a $\log_{10}$ frequency of 4.72. The zero frequency of the concept set 930 VILLAGE results from a choice between two words: the concept set was mapped to the compound *cūnzhài* 村寨 instead of the more frequent word *cūnzi* 村子 ($\log_{10}$ frequency: 2.66). The expression *cūnzhài* 村寨 is used to refer to an area in which specific cultural groups live. In contrast, *cūnzi* 村子 is a more general word that can be used for all villages. In the case of the concept set 2483 COLD (OF WEATHER), the word *liáng* 凉 was mapped instead of the more frequent compound *liángshuǎng* 凉爽 with a $\log_{10}$ frequency of 1.72. The term *liángshuǎng* 凉爽 would in fact be a more accurate word for the concept set 2483 COLD (OF WEATHER) since it relates to a state of weather with low temperature. Nevertheless, in English, the concept seems to appear more frequently than in Chinese. The reason could be the climate that Chinese speakers live in. The differences in the frequencies of the concept set 1238 WHEN (English $\log_{10}$ 5.02 and Chinese $\log_{10}$ 1.69) is due to Chinese having two distinct question pronouns: *shénme shíhòu* 什么时候 and *jǐshí* 几时 of which only the latter was included in the original data set. Note that the former seems to be the default option for the concept set 1238 WHEN in everyday language, whereas *jǐshí* 几时 is used by the older generation.

Interestingly, two concept sets – 705 GO UP (ASCEND) and 1215 THOU – appear to be more frequent in Chinese compared to English. Chinese uses *shàng* 上 to indicate an upward movement. It can also occur as a compound: *shàngqù* 上去 "go up." In English, however, there is a specific verb for moving from a lower to a higher position by walking or climbing: *ascend*. The difference in the frequencies of the concept set 1215 THOU, which describes a second-person pronoun singular form, can be explained by the fact that Chinese has two forms of second-person pronoun singular *nǐ* 你 and *nín* 您, which is the formal version. Similarly, German has *Du* and *Sie* (informal and formal, respectively). English used to have *thou* to indicate the second-person pronoun singular, but in common day English, *you* refers to both forms: second-person pronoun singular and plural. Note that the concept set 1215 THOU also has the highest diversity in glossing (List, 2018). The reference to one person or more was not distinguished in the SUBTLEX data and therefore, the frequencies cannot be separated. For the other concepts sets no conclusive explanation was apparent. The implications of the results are discussed in the next section.

4 Discussion

The present article set out to study the mental lexicon from a cross-linguistic perspective. The distribution of word frequencies across three languages, namely English, German, and Chinese was investigated. The advantage of the cross-linguistic database approach of the study is that it allowed a comparison of the same property across a set of diverse languages. The NoRaRe database (Tjuka et al., 2020b) was used to correlate data sets of frequencies in subtitles (Brysbaert and New, 2009; Brysbaert et al., 2011; Cai and Brysbaert, 2010) with one another and the CLICS database (Rzymski et al., 2020) was used to search for colexifications in the languages. Both databases are built upon the same reference catalog: Concepticon (List et al., 2016). This resource is based on a link between elicitation glosses in concept lists that comprise comparative concepts. The lists are provided by linguists and are used to compare basic meanings across languages. The Concepticon offers stable identifiers for those concepts and makes a direct comparison of concepts in multiple languages possible. The elicitation glosses are the basis for the word that can be mapped to a specific concept. Thus, the Concepticon can be used for an in-depth study of cross-linguistic lexical variation.

The goal of this study was to test whether related languages have more similar frequencies across a set of shared concepts than non-related languages. In addition, I examined the hypothesis that related languages share fewer concepts with a large difference in their frequencies than non-related languages. To test the hypothesis, correlations and qualitative analysis of individual concepts were carried out across two language pairs: English–German (related) and English–Chinese (non-related). Both hypotheses were supported by the findings in Section 3. The correlation of the frequencies between the language pair English–German was slightly higher than between English–Chinese. Furthermore, the comparison of the $\log_{10}$ frequencies of the concept sets shared in each language pair revealed language-specific variation. In the case of English–German, fewer concept sets with a large difference in their $\log_{10}$ frequencies were found (2 concept sets) compared to 16 concept sets in the English–Chinese data set.

The findings of the study indicate that frequencies of the same concepts can differ greatly across languages. The detailed examination of the individual concepts showed that two processes may lead to the differences in frequencies. First, cultural diversity, for instance, different regional climates, drives the use of certain weather-related concepts such as COLD (OF WEATHER). Second, the use of two word-forms as in the case of *shuí* 谁 and *shéi* 誰 for the concept set 1235 WHO can result in varying cross-linguistic frequencies. The meaning-frequency law (Zipf, 1945) was not supported by the data. No influence of the number of colexifications for a concept on its frequency across languages was found.

When comparing frequencies across languages, it is challenging to consider the many differences that distinguish languages from one another. Nevertheless, researchers should not confine themselves to the study of single languages. The cultural differences that emerge from cross-linguistic studies offer valuable insights into the connections that languages draw between concepts in certain semantic domains, for example, emotions (Jackson et al., 2019). In addition, the study by Jackson et al. (2019) illustrated that general patterns of psycholinguistic measures, such as arousal and valency, exist independently of the family to which a given language belongs. Another advantage of the database approach used in this study is the possibility to explicitly look up comparative concepts and compare their properties across languages. Although some mappings might need refinement, the overall results prove the validity of the database. The comparison could be further improved by using frequencies in large parallel text corpora, but the data sets based on subtitles already account for a related context.

5   Conclusion

In recent years, a wealth of data for individual languages and data from cross-linguistic studies became available. The implementation of the diverse findings in databases makes a new field of exploration possible: a cross-linguistic comparison of variables such as word frequencies. Future studies can build on the hypotheses presented in this study and test other assumptions of general patterns or language variation in different areas of the mental lexicon. All data used in the present article are readily accessible and can be reused by other researchers.

Acknowledgements

Annika Tjuka was supported by a stipend from the International Max Planck Research School (IMPRS) at the Max Planck Institute for the Science of Human History and the Friedrich-Schiller-Universität Jena.

References

Jean Aitchison. 2012. *Words in the mind: An introduction to the mental lexicon.* John Wiley & Sons, 4 edition.

Francis Bond and Ryan Foster. 2013. Linking and extending an Open Multilingual WordNet. In Hinrich Schuetze, Pascale Fung, and Massimo Poesio, editors, *Proceedings of 51st Annual Meeting of the Association for Computational Linguistics*, pages 1352–1362, Sofia, Bulgaria. Association for Computational Linguistics (ACL).

Francis Bond, Arkadiusz Janz, Marek Maziarz, and Ewa Rudnicka. 2019. Testing Zipf's meaning-frequency law with wordnets as sense inventories. In Christiane Fellbaum, Piek Vossen, Ewa Rudnicka, Marek Maziarz, and Maciej Piasecki, editors, *Proceedings of the Tenth Global Wordnet Conference*, pages 342–352, Wrocław, Poland. Oficyna Wydawnicza Politechniki Wrocławskiej.

Marc Brysbaert and Boris New. 2009. Moving beyond Kučera and Francis: A critical evaluation of current word frequency norms and the introduction of a new and improved word frequency measure for American English. *Behavior Research Methods*, 41(4):977–990.

Marc Brysbaert, Matthias Buchmeier, Markus Conrad, Arthur M. Jacobs, Jens Bölte, and Andrea Böhl. 2011. The word frequency effect: A review of recent developments and implications for the choice of frequency estimates in German. *Experimental Psychology*, 58:412–424.

Qing Cai and Marc Brysbaert. 2010. SUBTLEX-CH: Chinese Word and Character Frequencies Based on Film Subtitles. *Plos ONE*, 5(6):1–8.

Bernardino Casas, Antoni Hernández-Fernández, Neus Català, Ramon Ferrer-i Cancho, and Jaume Baixeries. 2019. Polysemy and brevity versus frequency in language. *Computer Speech & Language*, 58:19–50.

Christiane Fellbaum. 2012. WordNet. *The Encyclopedia of Applied Linguistics*.

Robert Forkel, Johann-Mattis List, Simon J. Greenhill, Christoph Rzymski, Sebastian Bank, Michael Cysouw, Harald Hammarström, Martin Haspelmath, Gereon A. Kaiping, and Russell D. Gray. 2018. Cross-Linguistic Data Formats, advancing data sharing and re-use in comparative linguistics. *Scientific Data*, 5(1):1–10.

Alexandre François. 2008. Semantic maps and the typology of colexification. In Martine Vanhove, editor, *From polysemy to semantic change: Towards a typology of lexical semantic associations*, volume 106, pages 163–215. John Benjamins Publishing.

Edward Gibson, Richard Futrell, Julian Jara-Ettinger, Kyle Mahowald, Leon Bergen, Sivalogeswaran Ratnasingam, Mitchell Gibson, Steven T. Piantadosi, , and Bevil R. Conway. 2017. Color naming across languages reflects color use. *Proceedings of the National Academy of Sciences of the United States of America*, 114(40):10785–10790.

Martin Haspelmath and Uri Tadmor. 2009. *Loanwords in the world's languages. A comparative handbook.* de Gruyter, Berlin and New York.

Martin Haspelmath. 2010. Comparative concepts and descriptive categories in crosslinguistic studies. *Language*, 86(3):663–687.

Antoni Hernández-Fernández, Bernardino Casas, Ramon Ferrer-i Cancho, and Jaume Baixeries. 2016. Testing the robustness of laws of polysemy and brevity versus frequency. In Pavel Král and Carlos Martín-Vide, editors, *4th International Conference on Statistical Language and Speech Processing (SLSP)*, pages 19–29, Pilsen, Czech Republic. Springer, Cham.

Bahar Ilgen and Bahar Karaoglan. 2007. Investigation of Zipf's 'law-of-meaning' on Turkish corpora. In Ece G Schmidt, Ilkay Ulusoy, Nihan Ciçekli, and Ugur Halıcı, editors, *22nd International Symposium on Computer and Information Sciences*, pages 1–6, Ankara, Turkey. IEEE.

Joshua Conrad Jackson, Joseph Watts, Teague R. Henry, Johann-Mattis List, Peter J. Mucha, Robert Forkel, Simon J. Greenhill, and Kristen Lindquist. 2019. Emotion semantics show both cultural variation and universal structure. *Science*, 366(6472):1517–1522.

Mary Ritchie Key and Bernard Comrie. 2016. *The Intercontinental Dictionary Series*. Max Planck Institute for Evolutionary Anthropology, Leipzig.

Johann-Mattis List, Michael Cysouw, and Robert Forkel. 2016. Concepticon. A resource for the linking of concept lists. In Nicoletta Calzolari, Khalid Choukri, Thierry Declerck, Marko Grobelnik, Bente Maegaard, Joseph Mariani, Asuncion Moreno, Jan Odijk, and Stelios Piperidis, editors, *Proceedings of the Tenth International Conference on Language Resources and Evaluation*, pages 2393–2400, Luxembourg. European Language Resources Association (ELRA).

Johann-Mattis List, Christoph Rzymski, Simon J. Greenhill, Nathanael Schweikhard, Kristina Pianykh, Annika Tjuka, Mei-Shin Wu, and Robert Forkel. 2020. *Concepticon. A resource for the linking of concept lists (Version 2.4.0-rc.1)*. Max Planck Institute for the Science of Human History, Jena.

Johann-Mattis List. 2018. Towards a history of concept list compilation in historical linguistics. *History and Philosophy of the Language Sciences*, 5:1–14.

Steven T. Piantadosi. 2014. Zipf's word frequency law in natural language: A critical review and future directions. *Psychonomic Bulletin & Review*, 21(5):1112–1130.

Christoph Rzymski, Tiago Tresoldi, Simon J. Greenhill, Mei-Shin Wu, Nathanael E. Schweikhard, Maria Koptjevskaja-Tamm, Volker Gast, Timotheus A. Bodt, Abbie Hantgan, Gereon A. Kaiping, Sophie Chang, Yunfan Lai, Natalia Morozova, Heini Arjava, Nataliia Hübler, Ezequiel Koile, Steve Pepper, Mariann Proos, Briana Van Epps, Ingrid Blanco, Carolin Hundt, Sergei Monakhov, Kristina Pianykh, Sallona Ramesh, Russell D. Gray, Robert Forkel, and Johann-Mattis List. 2020. The Database of Cross-Linguistic Colexifications, reproducible analysis of cross-linguistic polysemies. *Scientific Data*, 7(13):1–12.

Morris Swadesh. 1955. Towards greater accuracy in lexicostatistic dating. *International Journal of American Linguistics*, 21(2):121–137.

Annika Tjuka, Robert Forkel, and Johann-Mattis List. 2020a. *Database of Cross-Linguistic Norms, Ratings, and Relations for Words and Concepts (Version 0.1)*. Max Planck Institute for the Science of Human History, Jena.

Annika Tjuka, Robert Forkel, and Johann-Mattis List. 2020b. Linking norms, ratings, and relations of words and concepts across multiple language varieties. PsyArXiv:10.31234. version 1.

Mark D. Wilkinson, Michel Dumontier, IJsbrand Jan Aalbersberg, Gabrielle Appleton, Myles Axton, Arie Baak, Niklas Blomberg, Jan-Willem Boiten, Luiz Bonino da Silva Santos, and Philip E. Bourne. 2016. The FAIR Guiding Principles for scientific data management and stewardship. *Scientific Data*, 3(160018):1–9.

George Kingsley Zipf. 1945. The meaning-frequency relationship of words. *The Journal of General Psychology*, 33(2):251–256.

Less is Better: A cognitively inspired unsupervised model for language segmentation

Jinbiao Yang
Max Planck Institute for Psycholinguistics
Centre for Language Studies, Radboud University
`jinbiao.yang@mpi.nl`

Antal van den Bosch
KNAW Meertens Institute
`antal.van.den.bosch`
`@meertens.knaw.nl`

Stefan L. Frank
Centre for Language Studies, Radboud University
`s.frank@let.ru.nl`

Abstract

Language users process utterances by segmenting them into many *cognitive units*, which vary in their sizes and linguistic levels. Although we can do such unitization/segmentation easily, its cognitive mechanism is still not clear. This paper proposes an unsupervised model, *Less-is-Better* (LiB), to simulate the human cognitive process with respect to language unitization/segmentation. LiB follows the principle of least effort and aims to build a lexicon which minimizes the number of unit tokens (alleviating the effort of analysis) and number of unit types (alleviating the effort of storage) at the same time on any given corpus. LiB's workflow is inspired by empirical cognitive phenomena. The design makes the mechanism of LiB cognitively plausible and the computational requirement light-weight. The lexicon generated by LiB performs the best among different types of lexicons (e.g. ground-truth words) both from an information-theoretical view and a cognitive view, which suggests that the LiB lexicon may be a plausible proxy of the mental lexicon.

1 Introduction

During language comprehension, we cannot always process an utterance instantly. Instead, we need to segment all but the shortest pieces of text or speech into smaller chunks. Since these chunks are likely the cognitive processing units for language understanding, we call them *cognitive units* in this paper. A chunk may be any string of letters, characters, or phonemes that occurs in the language, but which chunks serve as the cognitive units? Traditional studies (Chomsky, 1957; Taft, 2013, for example) often use words as the units in sentence analysis. But speech, as well as some writing systems such as Chinese, lack a clear word boundary. Even for written languages which use spaces as word boundaries, psychological evidence indicates that the morphemes, which are sub-word units, in infrequent or opaque compound words take priority over the whole word (Fiorentino et al., 2014; MacGregor and Shtyrov, 2013); at the same time, some supra-word units such as frequent phrases and idioms are also stored in our long-term mental lexicon (Arnon and Snider, 2010; Bannard and Matthews, 2008; Jackendoff, 2002). The evidence suggests that the cognitive units can be of different sizes; they can be words, or smaller than words, or multi-word expressions.

Despite the flexible size of the cognitive units, and the lack of overt segmentation clues, infants are able to implicitly learn the units in their caregivers' speech, and then generate their own utterances. Arguably, children's language intelligence allows them to build their own lexicons from zero knowledge about the basic (cognitive) units in the particular language the child is learning, and then use the lexicon to segment language sequences. Can we mimic this ability of a human language learner in a computer model? This question is often phrased as the task of unsupervised segmentation. Several types of computational models or NLP algorithms have been proposed for segmentation, taking different approaches:

Proceedings of the Workshop on Cognitive Aspects of the Lexicon, pages 33–45
Barcelona, Spain (Online), December 12, 2020

- **Model the lexicon**: A straightforward basis for segmentation is to build a lexicon. One of the lexicon-building algorithms, Byte pair encoding (BPE) (Sennrich et al., 2016), is popular for NLP preprocessing. It iteratively searches for the most common n-gram pairs and adds them into the n-gram lexicon. Some other models such as the Chunk-Based Learner (McCauley and Christiansen, 2019) and PARSER (Perruchet and Vinter, 1998) are also based on the local statistics of tokens (e.g., token frequency, mutual information, or transitional probability).

- **Model the grammar**: Some studies attempted to analyze the grammar patterns of sentences and then parse/segment the sentences based on these patterns. To find the optimal grammar, de Marcken (1996) used Minimum Description Length, and Johnson and Goldwater (2009) used the Hierarchical Dirichlet Process.

- **Model the sequences**: Recurrent neural networks and its variations are able to learn the sequential patterns in language and to perform text segmentation (Chung et al., 2017; Kawakami et al., 2019; Sun and Deng, 2018; Zhikov et al., 2013).

In general, lexicon models capture only the local statistics of the tokens so they tend to be short-sighted at the global level (e.g. long-distance dependencies). The other two types of models, in contrast, learn how the tokens co-occur globally. Yet, the ways grammar models and sequence models learn the global information makes them more complicated and computing-intensive than the lexicon models.

In this paper we propose a model that builds a lexicon, but does so by using both local and global information. Our model is not only a computational model but also a cognitive model: it is inspired by cognitive phenomena, and it needs only basic and light-weight computations which makes it cognitively more plausible than the grammar- and sequence-learning models mentioned above. We show that our model can effectively detect the cognitive units in language with an efficient procedure. We also show that our model can detect linguistically meaningful units. We further evaluate our model on traditional word segmentation tasks.

2 The Less-is-better Model

2.1 Cognitive principles

We want our system to mimic human cognitive processes of language unitization/segmentation by simulating not only the behavioral output, but also the cognitive mechanism. We designed such a computational model by emulating three cognitive phenomena: the principle of least effort, larger-first processing, and passive and active forgetting.

The principle of least effort: The essence of the model is a simple and natural cognitive principle: the principle of least effort (Zipf, 1949), which says human cognition and behavior are economic; they prefer to spend the least effort or resources to obtain the largest reward. Since a language sequence can be segmented into different sequences of language chunks, we assume the cognitive units are the language chunks in the sequence which follow the principle of least effort.

Larger-first processing: As we mentioned, any language chunk may be the cognitive unit, short or long. A broadly known finding is that global/larger processing has priority over local/smaller processing for visual scene recognition; an effect named "global precedence" (Navon, 1977). This follows from the principle of least effort: the larger the units we process, the fewer processing steps we need to take. For visual word processing, the word superiority effect (Reicher, 1969) shows the precedence of words over recognizing letters. Recent work (Snell and Grainger, 2017; Yang et al., 2020) extends global precedence to the level beyond words, and also shows that we do not process only the larger units: smaller units also have a chance to become the processing units when processing larger units does not aid comprehension. In other words, cognitive units may be of any size, but the larger have priority.

Passive and active forgetting: To mimic human cognition, the model should have a flexible memory to store and update information. Forgetting is critical to prevent the accumulation of an extremely large number of memory engrams. It has been commonly held that forgetting is merely the passive decay of the memory engram over time, but recent studies put forward that forgetting can also be an active process (Davis and Zhong, 2017; Gravitz, 2019). Passive forgetting by decay can clean up the engrams that are no longer used in our brains. However, our brains may sometimes need to suppress counter-productive engrams immediately. Active forgetting may thus be called upon to eliminate the unwanted engram's memory traces, which enhances the memory management system (Davis and Zhong, 2017; Oehrn et al., 2018).

2.2 General idea

We assume the cognitive units are the chunks in the language sequence which follow the principle of least effort (Section 2.1). In other words, the less information we need to encode the language material, the better cognitive units we have. This less-is-better assumption grounds our model, so we named it Less-is-Better, or LiB for short.

The LiB model accepts any sequence S of atomic symbols s: $S = (s_1, s_2, \ldots)$, as the input. A collection of S forms a document D and all D together form the training corpus. S can be segmented into chunk tokens $(c_1, \ldots, c_N)$, where each chunk is a subsequence of S: $c = (s_i, \ldots, s_j)$ and N is the number of chunk tokens in S. The segmentation is based on a lexicon L (Fig. 1) where all chunk types are stored in order. The ordinal number of chunk type c in L is denoted $\Theta(c)$, and $|L|$ is the number of chunk types in L.

Let $I(c)$ be the amount of information (the number of encoding bits) required to identify each chunk type in L, that is, $I(c) = \log_2 |L|$, and $I(S)$ be the amount of information required for the input S, then: $I(S) = I(c)N$. Our model aims to minimize the expected encoding information to extract the cognitive units in any S, which means minimizing $E[I(S)]$, which is accomplished by simultaneously reducing $|L|$ (smaller $|L|$ means lower $I(c)$) and $E[N]$ (the expected number of chunk tokens in S). In practice our model:

1. Starts with an empty L;
2. Randomly selects a D from the corpus and analyzes the S in D;
3. Adds previously unseen symbols s as (atomic) chunk types to L;
4. Recursively combines adjacent chunk tokens into new chunk types, reducing $E[N]$ but increasing $|L|$;
5. Removes less useful types from L, reducing $|L|$;
6. Repeats steps 2 to 5 for a predetermined number of epochs.

The LiB model can segment any string S into a sequence of chunks $(c_1, ..., c_N)$ based on the lexicon L. The chunk types in L are ordered based on their importance inferred from the segmentation. The lexicon quality and the segmentation result mutually affect each other: LiB learns from its own segmentation results and updates L accordingly, then improves its next segmentation (Figure 1). The bootstrap procedure makes the model unsupervised.

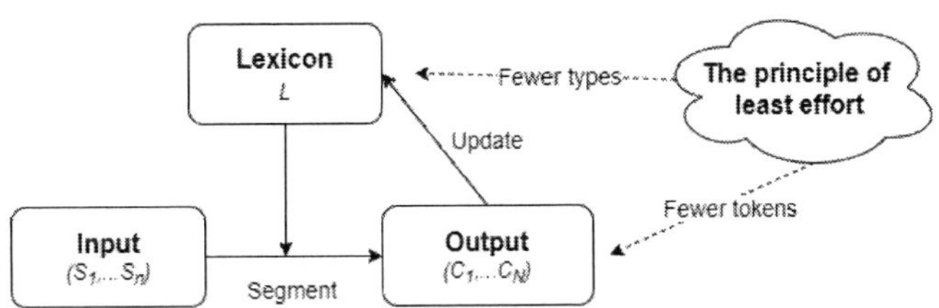

Figure 1: Information flow in the LiB model.

2.3 Implementation

2.3.1 Segmentation

Larger-first selection: An S can be segmented in different ways. For example, if both "going" and "goingto" are in L, and the given S is "goingtorain", then the first chunk token can be "going" or "goingto". The Larger-first principle (Section 2.1) dictates that LiB takes the largest substring of S that matches a chunk type in L (in the example case, it is "goingto"), i.e. greedy matching, and selects it as a chunk token (segment). If there is no chunk type in L that matches the current S, the first symbol s becomes the selected chunk token.

Chunk evaluation: In most cases, selecting larger chunk tokens will reduce the number of tokens N in S, but in some cases it will not. Let us continue the example we gave: If "goingtor", "a", "in", and "rain" are also in L, the largest chunk token becomes "goingtor", resulting in the segmentation "goingtor/a/in". If "goingto" had been selected, this would result in "goingto/rain". Hence, selecting the largest chunk type resulted in a larger N. The average chunk token sizes of the two segmentations are 5.5 and 3.6 letters, respectively.

In order to test whether the selected chunk type c reduces N, LiB compares the proposed segmentation to the segmentation that results if c is not in L, i.e., if the second largest chunk type in L is selected instead of c. In case L cannot provide a second largest chunk token, there is no evaluation and c is selected directly. Otherwise, c is evaluated as "Good" if it results in fewer chunk tokens or in the same number of tokens but with lower total ordinal numbers (i.e., chunks that are higher up in the lexicon):

$$\mathtt{segment}(S, L) : S \to (c_1, c_2, \ldots, c_N)$$
$$\mathtt{segment}(S, L - c) : S \to (c'_1, c'_2, \ldots, c'_{N'})$$

$$\mathtt{evaluate}(c) = \begin{cases} \begin{cases} \text{Good} & \text{if } N < N' \\ \text{Bad} & \text{if } N > N' \end{cases} & \text{if } N \neq N' \\[2em] \begin{cases} \text{Good} & \text{if } \sum_{i=1}^{N} \Theta(c_i) \leq \sum_{i=1}^{N'} \Theta(c'_i) \\ \text{Bad} & \text{if } \sum_{i=1}^{N} \Theta(c_i) > \sum_{i=1}^{N'} \Theta(c'_i) \end{cases} & \text{if } N = N' \end{cases}$$

If $\mathtt{evaluate}(c)$ is Good, c is selected; otherwise, the second largest chunk token is selected.

2.3.2 Lexicon update

Memorizing: LiB learns new chunks from the segmentation results. There are two types of new chunks in the results: unknown symbols $s \notin L$ and concatenations of known chunks (c_i, c_{i+1}) (with $c_i \in L$ and $c_{i+1} \in L$) that occur consecutively in S. L starts empty, learns the symbol chunks, then the smallest chunks construct larger chunks and the larger chunks construct even larger chunks. Thus, L can contain chunks in different sizes.

The number of all (c_i, c_{i+1}) in the training corpus can be enormous, and most of them are infrequent chunks. In order to reduce the lexicon size $|L|$, LiB will memorize all s, but not all (c_i, c_{i+1}). To recognize the frequent chunks, a strategy is to count all chunks' occurrences and delete the infrequent ones (Perruchet and Vinter, 1998). However, this strategy asks for storing all chunks at the beginning, which is memory inefficient for both a brain and a computer. Thus, LiB adopts a sampling strategy: The model samples from all possible (c_i, c_{i+1}) tokens in the current S and memorizes only the tokens which were sampled at least twice. The probability of sampling a chunk pair is the sampling probability α. The sampling strategy is implicitly sensitive to the chunk token frequency in the text. It makes sure that even without explicit counting, higher-frequency chunks have a higher probability to be memorized. The at-least-twice strategy is not cognitively inspired but heuristic; it helps to prevent memorization of many arbitrary chunks.

Re-ranking and active forgetting: To avoid storing the frequencies of all possible chunk types, and to be more efficient, LiB bypasses explicit frequency counting of chunk types. Instead, LiB encodes the types' importance by their ordinals $\Theta(c)$ in L – the lower the more important. The importance reflects not only the frequency but also the principle of least effort (preference for fewer tokens and fewer types). In general, newly memorized chunk types are less frequent than known chunk types, so new chunk types are appended to the tail of L. The ordinals of known chunk types also need to be adjusted after new training text data comes in. The chunk evaluation we described in Section 2.3.1 is not only for segmentation, but also for importance re-ranking. The "good" chunk types, which result in fewer chunk tokens in S, will move closer to the lexicon head (i.e., lower ordinal); The "bad" chunk types, which result in more chunk tokens in S, will move closer to the lexicon tail, i.e., they get a higher ordinal number. The updated $\Theta(c)$ of a chunk type is relative to its previous ordinal $\Theta'(c)$ in L:

$$\Theta(c) = \begin{cases} \lfloor \Theta'(c)(1 - \Delta) \rfloor & \text{if } c \text{ is good} \\ \lfloor \Theta'(c)(1 + \Delta) \rfloor & \text{if } c \text{ is bad} \end{cases}$$

where $0 < \Delta < 1$ is the re-ranking rate. In case the updated $\Theta(c) > |L|$, c will be deleted from L.

Passive forgetting: Obviously, the re-ranking also influences other chunk types whose ordinals are between $\Theta(c)$ and $\Theta'(c)$. So even though the sampling strategy of the memorizer may add a few infrequent chunk types into L, the re-ranker will move them closer to the tail of L. Those chunk types, as well as the "bad" chunk types, are "junk chunks" which increase $I(c)$. The passive forgetter removes them from L to reduce $I(c)$.

The junk chunk types tend to be at the tail of L, but the tail may also store some non-junk types. A cognitive strategy to avoid deleting them is *waiting* for more evidence. So instead of deleting these types immediately, LiB uses a soft deleting strategy: after each training epoch, LiB will select the last $\omega|L|$ (at least one) chunk types in L and assign them a probation period τ. Here, ω is the forgetting ratio and τ is the remaining time until deletion; it is initialized at τ_0 and decreases by one after each training epoch (LiB analyzes one document D in each training epoch). Once the probation time is over, when $\tau = 0$, the chunk is forgotten (i.e., removed from L). If a chunk type was evaluated as "good" during its probation period, its probation is cancelled. The c that occur in fewer documents are more likely to be forgotten.

3   Model Training

We trained the LiB model on both English and Chinese materials (Table 1). The English material is **BR-phono**, which is a branch of the Brent corpus (Bernstein-Ratner, 1987), containing phonetic transcriptions of utterances directed at children. We used it for testing segmentation of spoken language. LiB accepts the document as an input batch in each training epoch but the utterances in the BR-phono corpus have no document boundaries. We randomly sampled 200 utterances (without replacement) from BR-phono to form one document and repeated this 400 times to create 400 documents for model training. The Chinese materials are taken from Chinese Treebank 8.0 (**CTB8**) (Xue et al., 2013), which is a hybrid-domain corpus (news reports, government documents, magazine articles, conversations, web discussions, and weblogs). As preprocessing, we replaced all the Roman letters and Arabic numbers with [X], and regarded all punctuation as sequence boundaries.

In order to examine the unsupervised performance of LiB, all spaces in the corpora were removed before training. We trained LiB on BR-phono and on CTB8 separately. The parameter settings are shown in Appendix A. The example segmentations with increasing number of training epochs are shown in Appendix B. The related code and preprocessed corpora are available online[1].

---

[1] https://github.com/ray306/LiB

Corpus	Documents	Sentences	Word tokens	Word types
BR-phono	400	9,790	33,399	1,321
CTB8	3,007	236,132	1,376,142	65,410
MSR	/	18,236	89,917	11,728
PKU	/	15,492	88,327	12,422

Table 1: The training and test corpus statistics after preprocessing. MSR and PKU are the (Chinese) test corpora which are mentioned in Section 4.5. Word units are presegmented in the CTB8, MSR, and PKU corpora.

4   Model Evaluation

4.1   Subchunks

After training, we evaluated the chunk units in the training corpora from two information-theoretical views that bear a relation to cognitive processing: description length and language model surprisal. We also examined the performance of LiB on word segmentation tasks. However, since LiB can learn new chunks from the concatenation of known chunks, the learned chunks are not only words, but also possible multi-word expressions. For the word segmentation task, we want to know the words in those multi-word expressions, so we had LiB find the subchunks $c^\flat$, which are the chunks inside the original chunks (e.g., "you" and "are" inside "youare"), and regarded the subchunks as the words. LiB defines the subchunk by searching all the potential chunk sequences in the original chunk (c_{raw}) and selecting the sequence with lowest sum of ordinals unless c_{raw} has the lowest sum:

$$(c_1^\flat, \ldots, c_n^\flat) = \underset{(c_1, \ldots, c_n)}{\arg \min} \left(\sum_i \Theta(c_i) \right), \text{ where } (c_1, \ldots, c_n) = c_{raw}$$

$$\text{Subchunk(s) of } c_{raw} = \begin{cases} (c_1^\flat, \ldots, c_n^\flat) & \text{if } \max_i(\Theta(c_i^\flat)) < \Theta(c_{raw}) \\ c_{raw} & \text{otherwise} \end{cases}$$

4.2   Qualitative evaluation

Since the LiB lexicon is ordered, we may examine the head of the trained lexicons (Table 9), which are the highest-ranked chunk units. They show that LiB appears to learn common words and collocations. Among the learned units we observe some collocations (e.g., "that'sa") which are not linguistic phrases. The lexicon of LiB trained on CTB8 shows that the high-ranked Chinese chunk units are usually bigrams (Appendix C). The middle and the tail of the trained lexicons are also shown in Appendix C. We present examples of chunk and subchunk segmentation results in Table 3. The results show the chunk units include common collocations, while the subchunk units are very close to the linguistic words.

4.3   Description length evaluation

LiB provides two types of new units to segment language: **LiB chunks** are the raw segmentation result of LiB, and **LiB subchunks** are the subchunks inside LiB chunks. In order to examine the encoding efficiency of LiB chunks and LiB subchunks, we compared the description lengths (DL) on different segmentations. The DL is the number of bits required to represent the corpus; it sums the number of bits required to encode the lexicon and the number of bits required to encode the corpus when segmented by the lexicon (Zhikov et al., 2013):

$$DL(total) = DL(lexicon) + DL(corpus) = - \sum_{i=1}^{\#s} Freq(s_i) \log_2 P(s_i) - \sum_{j=1}^{\#u} Freq(u_j) \log_2 P(u_j)$$

Corpus	Top 50 entries (translated) in Lexicon
BRphono	the, yeah, you, what, wanna, can you, two, and, that's, okay, four, now, it, they're, he's, in, look, with, you want, who, he, that, all, your, here, i think, put, that's a, what's, you can, his, my, see, you wanna, no, is that, high, whose, this, good, there's, very, see the, its a, is it, alright, this is, are you, ing, have
CTB8	haven't, China, we, economics, already, kid, but, education, can, now, government, country, a, these, self, can't, if, journalist, today, they, although, require, tech, process, this, Xinhua News Agency, wish, issue, is, mainland, because, some, and, all are, so, now, may, Taiwan, should, political, development, also is, also is, society, such, via, continue, isn't, Shanghai, 's

Table 2: Transliterations/translations into English of the top 50 entries in the lexicons. The original results of BRphono are in phonemic characters, and the original results of CTB8 are the Chinese characters. For completeness, in Appendix C we repeat these results with the original results included.

Corpus	Level	Segmentation
BRphono	Input	allrightwhydon'tweputhimawaynow
	Chunks	allright·whydon't·we·puthimaway·now
	Subchunks	all·right·why·don't·we·put·him·away·now
	Words	all·right·why·don't·we·put·him·away·now
CTB8	Input	这个出口信贷项目委托中国银行为代理银行
	Chunks	这个·出口信贷·项目·委托·中国银行·为·代理·银行
	Subchunks	这个·出口·信贷·项目·委托·中国·银行·为·代理·银行
	Words	这·个·出口·信贷·项目·委托·中国·银行·为·代理·银行

Table 3: Example segmentations of strings in the two corpora. BRphono's results are transcribed into English words for ease of presentation.

Here, $\#s$ denotes the number of unique symbols s in L (either as a single-symbol chunk or as part of a larger chunk); $Freq(s_i)$ and $P(s_i)$ are the occurrence count and ratio of s_i in L; $\#u$ denotes the number of unique units u in the corpus; $Freq(u_j)$ and $P(u_j)$ are the occurrence count and ratio of u_j in the corpus.

As benchmarks, we used **Symbol** (the indivisible units; in our two corpora, phonemes and characters respectively), **Word** (the words presegmented in the corpora), and **BPE subword** (the Byte Pair generated by SentencePiece (Kudo and Richardson, 2018) with default parameters setting). The DL result (Table 4) shows that LiB chunks result in shortest DL; they minimze the information; they are the most concise encodings.

4.4 Language model evaluation

Besides the DL, which compares the information efficiencies of different lexicons, we are also interested in whether the LiB lexicon can reflect the mental lexicon. We lack a ground truth of what is in the putative mental lexicon. However, we can regard natural language material as a large-scale result of human language use and language behavior. Trained on a very large corpus, a recent study by Brown et al. (2020) shows that Language Models (LMs) can closely predict human performance on various language tasks. LMs capture the probabilistic constraints in natural language and perform the tasks by making predictions, which is a fundamental cognitive function (Bar, 2007). So, by measuring the prediction surprisal in the corpus segmented by different lexicons, we can evaluate different lexicons from a cognitive view, and we presume that the lexicon that gets the best LM performance is a better approximation of the mental lexicon.

Many studies have shown that word surprisal is positively correlated with human word-reading time (Monsalve et al., 2012; Smith and Levy, 2013) and size of the N400 component in EEG (Frank et al., 2015). From the cognitive principle of least effort, it follows that readers try to minimize reading time.

| | | Segmentation | | | | |
Corpus	Evaluation metric	Symbol	BPE subword	Word	LiB subchunk	LiB chunk
BRphono	Average length	1	2.8	2.9	2.9	3.6
	Lexicon size	50	5,574	1,321	1,119	1,869
	DL(lexicon)	<1	173	28	24	47
	DL(corpus)	490	278	262	258	**233**
	DL(total)	490	451	289	282	**281**
CTB8	Average length	1	1.4	1.7	1.7	1.9
	Lexicon size	4,697	7,980	65,410	24,763	39,320
	DL(lexicon)	**57**	133	1,767	621	1,153
	DL(corpus)	21,864	18,229	15,669	16,188	**15,602**
	DL(total)	21,921	18,362	17,436	16,809	**16,755**

Table 4: Average token lengths, lexicon sizes, and the DL results of different types of segmentation on the two corpora. The unit of Average Length is phoneme (BRphono) or Chinese character (CTB8). The unit of DL is kilobit.

| | | Segmentation | | | | |
Corpus	Model	Symbol	BPE subword	Word	LiB subchunk	LiB chunk
BRphono	2-gram	1.539	0.695	0.677	0.649	**0.548**
	3-gram	0.950	0.390	0.405	0.378	**0.335**
CTB8	2-gram	2.466	1.932	1.617	1.668	**1.452**
	3-gram	1.404	0.827	0.806	0.748	**0.626**

Table 5: Bits-per-character scores on different segmentations.

Hence, it follows that readers would try to find lexical units such that total surprisal is also minimized.

Surprisal, defined as $-\log_2(P(w|\text{context}))$, is not comparable between models with different segmentations. Instead we use bits per character (BPC) (Graves, 2013), which is average surprisal$/|c|$, where $|c|$ is the average chunk length over the whole test set. We tested the segmentations[2] on both bigram and trigram language models and the results show that the corpora represented by LiB chunks achieve the lowest surprisal (Table 5).

4.5 Word segmentation evaluation

As we already illustrated in Table 3, subchunk units tend to be close to linguistic words. We thus tested LiB subchunks as a resource for word segmentation. To evaluate LiB on English word segmentation, we compared LiB with Adaptor Grammar (AG) (Johnson and Goldwater, 2009), which achieves state-of-the-art performance on the segmentation task of BR-phono. AG requires grammar construction rules that encode prior linguistic knowledge. These rules presuppose knowledge about unigrams only, or unigrams+collocations, or unigrams+collocations+syllables. This yields three versions of AG. Table 6a shows that AG(syllable), whose rules carry extra linguistic knowledge (Johnson and Goldwater, 2009), achieves the highest score. The score of LiB is higher than AG(unigram) and slightly lower than AG(collocations), the two versions of AG comparable to our approach. AG(syllable) presumes knowledge that our model does not have (and that could possibly benefit LiB).

In the Chinese segmentation task, we compared LiB with three popular word segmentation toolboxes: Jieba[3], THULAC (Sun et al., 2016), and pkuseg (Luo et al., 2019). These toolboxes are supervised, learning the ground truth (word boundaries) during training. For comparison, we also modified a su-

---

[2] The code of the BPC calculations was modified from a Github project: `https://github.com/joshualoehr/ngram-language-model`. We kept all tokens during training.

[3] `https://github.com/fxsjy/jieba`

pervised LiB (LiB(sup)) for the word segmentation task. LiB(sup) skips the training phase. Instead, it counts all the ground-truth words in the training set and adds them as the chunk types to L. The higher the frequency of a type in the training set, the smaller its ordinal in L. We trained and tested the models on CTB8. To test the generalization performance of the models in the word segmentation task, we also test the training result on two additional corpora: MSR and PKU (Table 1) provided by the Second International Chinese Word Segmentation Bakeoff (Emerson, 2005). The segmentation rules are slightly different among MSR, PKU, and CTB8. MSR and PKU are news domain, which is different from CTB8. MSR and PKU were preprocessed in the same way as CTB8.

Table 6b shows that the scores of the unsupervised original version of LiB are lower than the supervised models[4], but the scores of the supervised version of LiB are close to the supervised models and are even higher on MSR. Due to the low out-of-vocabulary (OOV) rate of MSR (Emerson, 2005), the good performance on MSR shows that the lexicon is important for LiB. The only difference between the two versions of LiB is in their lexicons: the original LiB learned the lexicon from zero and the supervised LiB directly uses the ground-truth words in its lexicon. It shows that the segmentation module in LiB is appropriate for the word segmentation task.

[a]	Model	Scores
	AG (unigram)	56
	AG (collocations)	76
	AG (syllable)	**87**
	LiB subchunk	71

[b]	Model	CTB8	MSR	PKU
		Test set scores		
	Jieba	87.1	82.8	87.1
	THULAC	94.6	83.5	89.1
	pkuseg	**95.7**	83.7	**89.7**
	LiB subchunk	76.1	78.7	78.9
	LiB(sup) chunk	94.7	**84.5**	88.3

Table 6: Token F1 scores (%) of segmentations. [a] the scores on BR-phono by three versions of Adaptor Grammar (AG) and LiB subchunks. [b] the scores of Jieba, THULAC, PKUSEG, LiB subchunks, and LiB(sup) chunks. LiB(sup) represents the supervised adaptation of LiB.

5 Conclusions and Future Work

This paper presented an unsupervised model, LiB, to simulate the human cognitive process of language unitization/segmentation. Following the principles of least effort, larger-first processing, and passive and active forgetting, LiB incrementally builds a lexicon which can minimize the number of unit tokens (alleviating the effort of analysis) and unit types (alleviating the effort of storage) at the same time on any given corpus. Moreover, it is able to segment the corpus, or any other text in the same language, based on the induced lexicon. The computations in LiB are light-weight, which makes it very efficient. The LiB-generated lexicon shows optimal performances among different types of lexicons (e.g., ground-truth words) both in terms of description length and in terms of statistical language model surprisal, both of which are associated with cognitive processing. The workflow design and the computation requirement make LiB cognitively plausible, and the results suggest that the LiB lexicon may be a useful proxy of the mental lexicon.

Future work will be to allow skip-gram units in the lexicon. Skip-grams may help to capture longer-distance dependencies, and further lessen the cognitive effort by reducing the number of unit types/tokens. Furthermore, as the word segmentation results of the current LiB are not ideal, we hypothesize that skip-gram units may also benefit the detection of infrequent named entities (e.g., the skip-gram "Mr._said" helps to detect "Mortimer" in "Mr.Mortimersaid") and thus improve the word segmentation performance. Other future work includes a LiB variant that accepts speech input and a semi-supervised LiB variant that uses semantic knowledge (e.g., word embeddings) to enhance the language unitization.

---

[4]The scores of Jieba, THULAC, and pkuseg are provided by `https://github.com/lancopku/pkuseg-python`

References

Inbal Arnon and Neal Snider. 2010. More than words: Frequency effects for multi-word phrases. *J. Mem. Lang.*, 62(1):67–82.

Colin Bannard and Danielle Matthews. 2008. Stored word sequences in language learning: the effect of familiarity on children's repetition of four-word combinations. *Psychol. Sci.*, 19(3):241–248, March.

Moshe Bar. 2007. The proactive brain: using analogies and associations to generate predictions. *Trends Cogn. Sci.*, 11(7):280–289.

Nan Bernstein-Ratner. 1987. The phonology of parent-child speech. *Children's language*, 6(3).

Tom B Brown, Benjamin Mann, Nick Ryder, Melanie Subbiah, Jared Kaplan, Prafulla Dhariwal, Arvind Nee-lakantan, Pranav Shyam, Girish Sastry, Amanda Askell, Sandhini Agarwal, Ariel Herbert-Voss, Gretchen Krueger, Tom Henighan, Rewon Child, Aditya Ramesh, Daniel M Ziegler, Jeffrey Wu, Clemens Winter, Christopher Hesse, Mark Chen, Eric Sigler, Mateusz Litwin, Scott Gray, Benjamin Chess, Jack Clark, Christopher Berner, Sam Mc-Candlish, Alec Radford, Ilya Sutskever, and Dario Amodei. 2020. Language models are Few-Shot learners. *arXiv preprint arXiv:2005.14165*, May.

Noam Chomsky. 1957. *Syntactic Structures*. Mouton.

Junyoung Chung, Sungjin Ahn, and Yoshua Bengio. 2017. Hierarchical multiscale recurrent neural networks. In *5th International Conference on Learning Representations, ICLR 2017*, Toulon, France, April. OpenReview.net.

Ronald L Davis and Yi Zhong. 2017. The biology of forgetting — a perspective. *Neuron*, 95(3):490–503, August.

Carl de Marcken. 1996. *Unsupervised language acquisition*. Ph.D. thesis, Massachusetts Institute of Technology, Cambridge, MA, USA.

Thomas Emerson. 2005. The second international Chinese word segmentation bakeoff. In *Proceedings of the fourth SIGHAN workshop on Chinese language processing*.

Robert Fiorentino, Yuka Naito-Billen, Jamie Bost, and Ella Fund-Reznicek. 2014. Electrophysiological evidence for the morpheme-based combinatoric processing of English compounds. *Cogn. Neuropsychol.*, 31(1-2):123–146.

Stefan L Frank, Leun J Otten, Giulia Galli, and Gabriella Vigliocco. 2015. The ERP response to the amount of information conveyed by words in sentences. *Brain Lang.*, 140:1–11, January.

Alex Graves. 2013. Generating sequences with recurrent neural networks. *arXiv preprint arXiv:1308.0850*, August.

Lauren Gravitz. 2019. The importance of forgetting. *Nature*, 571:S12–S14.

Ray Jackendoff. 2002. What's in the lexicon? In Sieb Nooteboom, Fred Weerman, and Frank Wijnen, editors, *Storage and Computation in the Language Faculty*, pages 23–58. Springer Netherlands, Dordrecht.

Mark Johnson and Sharon Goldwater. 2009. Improving nonparameteric Bayesian inference: experiments on unsupervised word segmentation with adaptor grammars. In *Proceedings of Human Language Technologies: The 2009 Annual Conference of the North American Chapter of the Association for Computational Linguistics*, pages 317–325.

Kazuya Kawakami, Chris Dyer, and Phil Blunsom. 2019. Learning to discover, ground and use words with seg-mental neural language models. In *Proceedings of the 57th Annual Meeting of the Association for Computational Linguistics*, pages 6429–6441, Stroudsburg, PA, USA. Association for Computational Linguistics.

Taku Kudo and John Richardson. 2018. SentencePiece: A simple and language independent subword tokenizer and detokenizer for neural text processing. In *Proceedings of the 2018 Conference on Empirical Methods in Natural Language Processing: System Demonstrations*, pages 66–71, Brussels, Belgium, November. Association for Computational Linguistics.

Ruixuan Luo, Jingjing Xu, Yi Zhang, Xuancheng Ren, and Xu Sun. 2019. PKUSEG: A toolkit for multi-domain Chinese word segmentation. *arXiv preprint arXiv:1906.11455*, June.

Lucy J MacGregor and Yury Shtyrov. 2013. Multiple routes for compound word processing in the brain: Evidence from EEG. *Brain Lang.*, 126(2):217–229.

Stewart M McCauley and Morten H Christiansen. 2019. Language learning as language use: A cross-linguistic model of child language development. *Psychol. Rev.*, 126(1):1–51, January.

Irene Fernandez Monsalve, Stefan L Frank, and Gabriella Vigliocco. 2012. Lexical surprisal as a general predictor of reading time. In *Proceedings of the 13th Conference of the European Chapter of the Association for Computational Linguistics*, pages 398–408.

David Navon. 1977. Forest before trees: The precedence of global features in visual perception. *Cogn. Psychol.*, 9(3):353–383.

Carina R Oehrn, Juergen Fell, Conrad Baumann, Timm Rosburg, Eva Ludowig, Henrik Kessler, Simon Hanslmayr, and Nikolai Axmacher. 2018. Direct electrophysiological evidence for prefrontal control of hippocampal processing during voluntary forgetting. *Curr. Biol.*, 28(18):3016–3022.e4, September.

Pierre Perruchet and Annie Vinter. 1998. PARSER: A model for word segmentation. *J. Mem. Lang.*, 39(2):246–263, August.

Gerald M. Reicher. 1969. Perceptual recognition as a function of meaningfulness of stimulus material. *J. Exp. Psychol.*, 81(2):275–280, August.

Rico Sennrich, Barry Haddow, and Alexandra Birch. 2016. Neural machine translation of rare words with subword units. In *Proceedings of the 54th Annual Meeting of the Association for Computational Linguistics (Volume 1: Long Papers)*, pages 1715–1725, Berlin, Germany, August. Association for Computational Linguistics.

Nathaniel J Smith and Roger Levy. 2013. The effect of word predictability on reading time is logarithmic. *Cognition*, 128(3):302–319, September.

Joshua Snell and Jonathan Grainger. 2017. The sentence superiority effect revisited. *Cognition*, 168:217–221, November.

Zhiqing Sun and Zhi-Hong Deng. 2018. Unsupervised neural word segmentation for Chinese via segmental language modeling. In *Proceedings of the 2018 Conference on Empirical Methods in Natural Language Processing*, pages 4915–4920, Brussels, Belgium. Association for Computational Linguistics.

Maosong Sun, Xinxiong Chen, Kaixu Zhang, Zhipeng Guo, and Zhiyuan Liu. 2016. Thulac: An efficient lexical analyzer for Chinese.

Marcus Taft. 2013. *Reading and the mental lexicon*. Psychology Press.

Nianwen Xue, Xiuhong Zhang, Zixin Jiang, Martha Palmer, Fei Xia, Fu-Dong Chiou, and Meiyu Chang. 2013. Chinese treebank 8.0 LDC2013T21. *Linguistic Data Consortium, Philadelphia*.

Jinbiao Yang, Qing Cai, and Xing Tian. 2020. How do we segment text? two-stage chunking operation in reading. *eNeuro*, May.

Valentin Zhikov, Hiroya Takamura, and Manabu Okumura. 2013. An efficient algorithm for unsupervised word segmentation with branching entropy and MDL. *Information and Media Technologies*, 8(2):514–527.

George Kingsley Zipf. 1949. *Human behavior and the principle of least effort*, volume 573. Addison-Wesley Press, Oxford, England.

A Training parameter settings

Since BR-phono is a child-directed speech corpus, its chunk types are usually very common, and so they often have much higher document ratios than CTB8 chunks. We use a lower τ_0, which is related to document ratio, to balance the corpus difference. The number of training epochs for CTB8, which is large-scale, was set to a higher number than for BR-phono. The epochs numbers are well beyond the convergence points. α and Δ mainly affect the training speed, while ω and τ_0 mainly affect $|L|$. The current parameter settings may not be optimal for end tasks such as word segmentation; in preliminary experiments we optimized for speed[5].

Corpus	α	Δ	ω	τ_0	epochs
BR-phono				10	5,000
CTB8	0.25	0.2	0.0001	500	50,000

Table 7: The parameter settings in the training on two corpora. α is the sampling probability, Δ the re-ranking rate, ω the forgetting ratio, τ_0 the probation period.

B Segmentations with increasing number of training epochs

The progression in chunking over training epochs before convergence (Table 8) shows LiB can learn some word chunks even in the very early epochs. Also, Table 8 illustrates that convergence is reached well before the preset number of runs.

Corpus	Epoch	Segmentation
BRphono	0	Olr9tW9dontwipUthIm6wenQ
	1	O·l·r·9·t·W·9·don·t·w·i·pUt·h·I·m·6·w·e·nQ
	2	Ol·r·9t·W·9·dont·wi·pUt·h·I·m·6·we·nQ
	10	Olr9t·W9·dont·wi·pUt·hIm·6we·nQ
	100	Olr9t·W·9dont·wi·pUthIm6we·nQ
	1,000	Olr9t·W·9dont·wi·pUthIm6we·nQ
CTB8	0	这个出口信贷项目委托中国银行为代理银行
	1	这·个·出·口·信·贷·项·目·委·托·中·国·银·行·为·代·理·银·行
	2	这·个·出·口·信·贷·项·目·委·托·中·国·银·行·为·代·理·银·行
	10	这·个·出口·信·贷·项·目·委·托·中·国·银·行·为·代·理·银·行
	100	这个·出口·信·贷·项目·委·托·中·国·银·行·为·代·理·银·行
	1,000	这个·出口·信贷·项目·委·托·中国·银行·为·代·理·银行
	10,000	这个·出口信贷·项目·委托·中国银行·为·代理·银行

Table 8: Example segmentations of strings in the two corpora with increasing number of training epochs. See Table 3 for the correct word-level segementation.

---

[5]The training of BR-phone costs 57 s and the training of CTB8 costs 31 min 55 s. The code is written in pure Python 3.7 and ran on a single core of Intel Core i5-7300HQ.

C   Top, middle and tail entries in lexicon

Corpus	Entries in Lexicon
BRphono (Top 50)	D6 **the**, y& **yeah**, yu **you**, WAt **what**, wan6 **wanna**, k&nyu **can you**, tu **two**, &nd **and**, D&ts **that's**, oke **okay**, f% **four**, nQ **now**, It **it**, D* **they're**, hiz **he's**, In **in**, lUk **look**, wIT **with**, yuwant **you want**, hu **who**, hi **he**, D&t **that**, Ol **all**, y) **your**, h(**here**, 9TINk **i think**, pUt **put**, D&ts6 **that's a**, WAts **what's**, yuk&n **you can**, hIz **his**, m9 **my**, si **see**, yuwan6 **you wanna**, no **no**, IzD&t **is that**, h9 **high**, huz **whose**, DIs **this**, gUd **good**, D*z **there's**, v*i **very**, siD6 **see the**, Its6 **its a**, IzIt **is it**, Olr9t **alright**, DIsIz **this is**, #yu **are you**, IN **ing**, h&v **have**
BRphono (Middle 20)	siD&t **see that**, nik, lEtmiQt **let me out**, DIsgoz **this goes**, d&diznat **daddy's not**, 9ms%i **i'm sorry**, kIN, lUksl9k6n9s, wITDiz **with these**, hizwe **he's way**, lON **long**, h&p **happen**, lEtssiIf **let's see if**, lEtspUthIm6we **let's put him away**, diIzf%, pR, brEkf6st **breakfast**, h9c* **high chair**, lUk&tD6bUk **look at the book**, W*zD6kIti
BRphono (Tail 20)	Nkyu, T, uyuwant, * **air**, 3, (**ear**, Z, c,), M, InhIzhQs, 6mily6 **amelia**, dOghQs **doghouse**, wITt7z **with toys**, &ndsAmt9mzwi, holdh&ndz **hold hands**, tIkLmi **tickle me**, h9ke **high kay**, tekItQt, k&nyubrAShIzh*
CTB8 (Top 50)	没有 **haven't**, 中国 **China**, 我们 **we**, 经济 **economics**, 已经 **already**, 孩子 **kid**, 但是 **but**, 教育 **education**, 可以 **can**, 目前 **now**, 政府 **government**, 国家 **country**, 一个 **a**, 这些 **these**, 自己 **self**, 不能 **can't**, 如果 **if**, 记者 **journalist**, 今天 **today**, 他们 **they**, 虽然 **although**, 要求 **require**, 技术 **tech**, 进行 **process**, 这个 **this**, 新华社 **Xinhua News Agency**, 希望 **wish**, 问题 **issue**, 就是 **is**, 大陆 **mainland**, 因为 **because**, 一些 **some**, 以及 **and**, 都是 **all are**, 因此 **so**, 现在 **now**, 可能 **may**, 台湾 **Taiwan**, 应该 **should**, 政治 **political**, 发展 **development**, 也是 **also is**, 还是 **also is**, 社会 **society**, 这样 **such**, 通过 **via**, 继续 **continue**, 不是 **isn't**, 上海 **Shanghai**, 的 **'s**
CTB8 (Middle 20)	肝脏 **liver**, 军事政变推翻 **military coup overthrows**, 在其他地方 **in other places**, 在野势力 **opposition force**, 而且这个 **and this**, 泄的, 帮他 **help him**, 宝应县 **Baoying County**, 政治新闻 **political news**, 经济越 **economic more**, 塔肯, 迅速地 **rapidly**, 铅笔 **pencil**, 集体经济 **collective economy**, 起源 **origin**, 邓相扬协助 **Tang Xiangyang assisted**, 建制 **establishment**, 写完 **after writing**, 说的那样 **as said**, 后顾 **look back**
CTB8 (Tail 20)	存在主权 **there is sovereignty**, 确权 **confirm rights**, 草案还 **the draft also**, 桌会议, 第一首相 **the first prime minister**, 迪奥 **dior**, 长大了 **grown up**, 爱他 **love him**, 说他 **say him**, 子虚乌, 有没有参与 **did you participate**, 严谨的 **rigorous**, 仍然是 **is still**, 站上车, 运输署 **Transport Department**, 杀机 **murderous**, 决 **decided**, 建成通车 **completed and opened to traffic**, 主要嫌疑人赖昌星 **the main suspect Lai Changxing**, 已经向加拿大 **has to Canada**

Table 9: The top 50 entries, the middle 20 entries and the tail 20 entries in the lexicons. The original results of BRphono are in phonemic characters; we transcribed the entries containing complete words into English words (in bold font) for ease of presentation. The original results of CTB8 are the Chinese characters; we added the English translations (in bold font) with the entries containing complete words.

The CogALex Shared Task on Monolingual and Multilingual Identification of Semantic Relations

Rong Xiang
Hong Kong Polytechnic University
csrxiang@comp.polyu.edu.hk

Emmanuele Chersoni
Hong Kong Polytechnic University
emmanuelechersoni@gmail.com

Luca Iacoponi
Amazon
jacoponi@gmail.com

Enrico Santus
Bayer
esantus@gmail.com

Abstract

The shared task of the CogALex-VI workshop focuses on the monolingual and multilingual identification of semantic relations. We provided training and validation data for the following languages: English, German and Chinese. Given a word pair, systems had to be trained to identify which relation holds between them, with possible choices being synonymy, antonymy, hypernymy and no relation at all.

Two test sets were released for evaluating the participating systems. One containing pairs for each of the training languages (systems were evaluated in a monolingual fashion) and the other one proposing a surprise language to test the crosslingual transfer capabilities of the systems.

Among the submitted systems, top performance was achieved by a transformer-based model in both the monolingual and in the multilingual setting, for all the tested languages, proving the potentials of this recently-introduced neural architecture.

The shared task description and the results are available at https://sites.google.com/site/cogalexvisharedtask/.

1 Introduction

Determining whether two words are related and what kind of relations holds between them is an important task in Natural Language Processing, and it has inspired a lot of research for more than one decade (Santus, 2016). Discovering relations between words is essential also for the creation of linguistic resources, such as ontologies and thesauri (Grefenstette, 1994), and this is especially true for specialized domains.

Research on semantic relations benefited from the success of Distributional Semantic Models (Budanitsky and Hirst, 2006; Turney and Pantel, 2010), since they allow to easily generate semantic representations for words from text, in the form of semantic vectors. However, the semantic similarity measured by vector models is an underspecified relation, and it is not easy to tell, given two similar words, in which way they are similar (Baroni and Lenci, 2011; Chersoni et al., 2016; Schulte Im Walde, 2020).

In the previous edition of the CogALex workshop, co-located with COLING 2016 in Osaka, the organizers set up a shared task dedicated to the corpus-based identification of semantic relations for English (Santus et al., 2016c). For the first time, systems were being evaluated in a shared task on the classification of multiple relations at once and, not surprisingly, the task proved to be challenging for computational models. For this new edition of the workshop, we have decided to launch a new version of the same shared task, adding more languages to the evaluation and encouraging the participants to evaluate their system also in a multilingual setting. Among the three teams that submitted their systems, the top performance was achieved by a RoBERTa-based system, XLM-R, in all the four languages, and both in the monolingual and in the multilingual setting.

Proceedings of the Workshop on Cognitive Aspects of the Lexicon, pages 46–53
Barcelona, Spain (Online), December 12, 2020

2   Related Work

The earlier methods for identifying semantic relations were based on patterns. Patterns are generally very precise for identifying relations such as hypernymy-hyponymy (Hearst, 1992; Snow et al., 2004) and meronymy (Berland and Charniak, 1999; Girju et al., 2006), or even multiple relations at once (Pantel and Pennacchiotti, 2006), but their limit is that the two related words have to occur together in a corpus, and thus their recall is limited (Shwartz et al., 2016).

Distributional Models, which do not suffer from such limitations, became then the first choice for the NLP research on semantic relations. In a first phase, researchers focused on the similarity metric, proposing alternatives to cosine that can be more efficient in setting apart a specific semantic relation from the others, e.g. hypernymy (Weeds and Weir, 2003; Clarke, 2009; Lenci and Benotto, 2012; Santus et al., 2014a), synonymy (Santus et al., 2016a) or antonymy (Santus et al., 2014b), or looked for specific differences in their distributional contexts (Scheible et al., 2013). In parallel, the first large datasets for evaluating the identification of semantic relations were being released, including relations such as hypernymy, cohyponymy and antonymy (Baroni and Lenci, 2011; Lenci and Benotto, 2012; Scheible and Schulte Im Walde, 2014; Weeds et al., 2014; Santus et al., 2015).

In a second phase, following the increasing popularity of publicly-available frameworks for training word embeddings such as Word2Vec (Mikolov et al., 2013) and Glove (Pennington et al., 2014), the focus quickly shifted on the usage of these vectors as features for supervised classifiers. Some of these methods train classifiers directly on pairs of vectors (Baroni et al., 2012; Weeds et al., 2014), while others compute DSMs-based metrics first and then use them as features (Santus et al., 2016b). Late attempts to conciliate similarity metrics and word embeddings brought to proposals such as APSyn (Santus et al., 2018).

Some of the more recent contributions proposed even more sophisticated classification approaches. (Shwartz et al., 2016; Roller and Erk, 2016) aim at integrating word embeddings with information coming from lexical patterns, which proved to be extremely accurate for detecting relations. Other researchers introduced modifications to the structure of the vector spaces with the goal of identifying a specific type of semantic relation, for example by modifying the objective function of the Word2Vec training to inject external knowledge from a lexical resource (e.g. WordNet) (Nguyen et al., 2016; Nguyen et al., 2017), or by adding an extra postprocessing step that projects the word vectors into a new space, expressly specialized for modeling the target relation (Vulić and Korhonen, 2018) or even more refined techniques of vector space specialisation (e.g. adversarial specialisation) (Kamath et al., 2019).

However, these contributions mostly tried to address one relation at a time, with rare attempts of tackling the problem in a multiclass setting. The shared task organized in coincidence with CogALex 2016 (Zock et al., 2016) was one of the few exceptions, and the low results achieved by most systems (the top F-score being 0.44) showed the difficulty of distinguishing between multiple relations at once. For this reason, we have decided to propose a similar challenge, yet including another factor of complexity: multilingualism. Considering the recent approaches that have been introduced for semantic relations in multilingual (Wang et al., 2019), crosslingual (Glavaš and Vulic, 2019) and meta learning (Yu et al., 2020) settings, we provided datasets in multiple languages (English, German, Chinese and Italian) and encouraged the participants to train their systems for both monolingual and multilingual evaluation.

3   Shared Task

The CogALex-VI shared task was organized as a friendly competition: participants had access to both training and testing datasets, which were respectively released on August 1 and September 1, 2020. The scores of the participating systems were evaluated with the official scripts, and each team had to submit a short paper containing the system description. Among the three participants that submitted their systems, one only submitted results for the English data.

3.1   Task Description

The shared task was split into two main subtasks. In subtask 1, training and validation data are provided for the following languages: English, German and Chinese. Participants are required to use the given datasets to train their model and then, utilize it to identify which relation – among synonymy, antonymy, hypernymy and no relation at all – holds between two words in a testing set. Predictions are evaluated separately for each language. Subtask 2 aims at evaluating the crosslingual transfer capabilities of the participating systems by testing the already trained models on a surprise language, for which no training data was provided. The chosen evaluation language was Italian.

3.2 Datasets and Tasks

In order to build the CogALex-VI multilingual dataset, four data collections have been adopted: English (Santus et al., 2015), German (Scheible and Schulte Im Walde, 2014), Chinese (Liu et al., 2019) and Italian (Sucameli and Lenci, 2017). Data format was standardized across languages to obtain a word pair per line, followed by the semantic relation holding between the words. A description of the four semantic relations of the shared task is provided in Table 1.

Relation (label)	Description	Example
Synonymy (SYN)	$w1$ can be used with the same meaning of $w1$	new-novel
Antonymy (ANT)	$w1$ can be used as the opposite of $w2$	big-small
Hypernymy (HYP)	$w1$ is a kind of $w2$	cat-animal
Random (RANDOM)	$w1$ and $w2$ are not related	dog-fruit

Table 1: Description of the semantic relations

For each language, we tried to obtain a balanced distribution of pairs across classes. A stratified sampling is adopted for English, German and Chinese. 60% of the whole dataset is provided as training dataset, and 20% is used as validation set for above languages. Participants are expected to use the above data for model and parameter tuning. The remaining 20% is given as a test set, with no ground truth. Detailed class statistics can be found in Table 2 (no training and validation data was provided for Italian).

	English			German			Chinese			Italian
	train	valid	test	train	valid	test	train	valid	test	test
SYN	842	259	266	782	272	265	402	129	122	187
ANT	916	308	306	829	275	281	361	136	142	144
HYP	898	292	279	841	294	286	421	145	129	153
RANDOM	2554	877	887	2430	786	796	1330	428	445	523
TOTAL	5210	1736	1738	4882	1627	1628	2514	838	838	1007

Table 2: Dataset Statistics

3.3 Participating Teams

Three participants submitted their system to CogALex-VI shared task: HSemID (Colson, 2020), Text2CS (Wachowiak et al., 2020) and TransDNN (Karmakar and McCrae, 2020). All teams took part in subtask 1, while only two of them participated in subtask 2.

Text2TCS exploited a multilingual language model based on XLM-RoBERTa (Conneau et al., 2020), which is pretrained on 100 different languages using CommonCrawl data. To adapt the system to the task, the authors appended a linear layer to XLM-R, followed by a softmax for the classification. This system was fine-tuned on the three training set from different languages simultaneously.

TransDNN proposed an architecture combining BERT (Devlin et al., 2018), LSTM and CNN, in which the BERT embeddings are passed to an LSTM that helps to represent terms having multiple words, and finally reach a convolutional layer followed by a dense layer and a softmax, devised for the classification. This system was trained on the given English dataset and participated only in the first subtask.

HSemID proposed a multilayer perceptron combining 1st and 2nd order representations of semantic associations. The system was trained with default parameters and the representations were built on WaCky corpora for English, German, Italian and a translated WaCky corpus (Baroni et al., 2009) for Chinese.

The methods and corpora used are summarized in Table 3.

Team	Method	Corpus
Text2TCS	multilingual language model XLM-RoBERTa, multilingual training for English, German and Chinese simultaneously	XLM-RoBERTa is trained on 100 different languages using CommonCrawl data
TransDNN	BERT, LSTM, CNN	BERT is trained on 3.3 billion tokens using BookCorpus and English Wikipedia Data
HSemID	combination of 1st-order and 2nd-order representations of semantic associations, multilayer perceptron	WaCky corpora for English, German, Italian and a translated WaCky corpus based on similar seed words of Chinese.

Table 3: Description of the participating systems

4 Evaluation

For the evaluation, participants had to submit their predictions. The output files were expected to contain exactly the same pairs, in the same order, and using the same annotation labels of the gold standard.

Given the gold standard and the system output, our script calculates precision, recall and F1 score. The weighted performance average across the classes was calculated ignoring the RANDOM pairs, as our focus is on the system's capability of detecting actual semantic relations. To this end, only SYN, ANT and HYP were averaged in the final score. The overall ranking was based on such a weighted average.

4.1 Subtask 1

Table 4 summarizes the performance of the systems in the three languages. [1] With the only exception of Text2TCS in Chinese, the relatively low F1 scores indicate that the task of identifying semantic relations is still hard to solve and that performance would benefit from more attention by the research community. Another interesting fact is that all participating systems show a similar pattern with regard to precision and recall. These systems tend to result in higher precision, while recall remains relatively low.

System	Overall Precision	Overall Recall	Overall F1
English			
Text2TCS	0.602	0.455	0.517
TransDNN	0.563	0.355	0.428
HSemID	0.400	0.276	0.320
German			
Text2TCS	0.592	0.435	0.500
HSemID	0.395	0.258	0.312
Chinese			
Text2TCS	0.904	0.860	0.881
HSemID	0.501	0.331	0.377

Table 4: Performance of participating systems for subtask 1

The best performing system is Text2TCS. It outperforms the others in every metric for three languages, achieving 0.52 F1 score for English, 0.50 for German, and 0.88 for Chinese. Due to the lack of non-English pre-trained models, TransDNN only provided results for English, ranking second with 0.43 F1 score. The gap between Text2TCS and TransDNN is lower for precision (0.039) than for recall (0.1). HSemID performs worse in subtask 1, lagging behind the other systems by a large margin.

As described in Table 3, all the systems utilize neural networks, although they differ in the architecture complexity and corpus size. In particular, transformer-based architectures demonstrate to outperform simpler approaches, such as the HSemID one.

As for the different languages, it is unexpected that systems perform best in Chinese. In order to gain insights into this surprising result, we investigated misclassification for both English and Chinese. In English, 287 pairs out of 1738 were misclassified by all the systems. Errors concerned 79 SYN, 76 ANT and 90 HYP, which were in most cases misclassified as RANDOM. This indicates that recall still needs to

---

[1] The detailed scores by class can be found in the system description papers.

be improved. As it is shown in Table 5, RANDOM represents an important interference factor in every relation type. On the contrary, we did not find any RANDOM instance which was incorrectly classified as SYN. Another common confusion of the system was between SYN and HYP, because of the similar nature of these semantic relations (see for example the pairs "gauge-test" and "confine-constrain").

English				Chinese			
W1	W2	Gold	Pred	W1	W2	Gold	Pred
fan	blow on	SYN	RANDOM	私人(private)	公立(public)	ANT	RANDOM
workforce	loiterers	ANT	RANDOM	花(diverse)	眼花繚亂(dazed)	SYN	RANDOM
zone	reguale	HYP	RANDOM	打氣(cheer)	勉(encourage)	HYP	RANDOM
swat	hit	SYN	RANDOM	哪裏(where)	今(now)	RANDOM	SYN
misconstrue	gesture	RANDOM	HYP	貼(stick)	黏(sticky)	HYP	SYN
maze	path	ANT	HYP	狹隘(narrow)	窄(narrow)	HYP	ANT
guage	test	SYN	HYP	輕聲(whisper)	低聲(low voice)	SYN	ANT
confine	constrain	HYP	SYN	斥(blame)	使(enable)	HYP	SYN
chap	dude	SYN	ANT	醫學(medicine)	學術(academy)	HYP	SYN
arrive	rest	RANDOM	ANT	糕(cake)	糕點(cake)	HYP	SYN

Table 5: Sample of pairs that were misclassified by all systems

The common misclassified pairs for Chinese were less than for English. Only 47 instances out of 838 were wrongly classified by both Text2TCS and HSemID. It can be found in Table 5 that most errors are related to SYN and HYP. The Chinese dataset seems to show a neater distinction between semantic relations, compared to other tested languages. Moreover, it was not possible to identify any evidence for regular errors in the Chinese dataset (i.e. no relation types were more prone to be confused).

4.2 Subtask 2

Table 6 summarizes the results for the subtask 2, that is in the identification of semantic relations in Italian, proposed in the test as the surprise language. Both systems obtain metrics that are comparable to those obtained in subtask 1 for English and German. The small gap between trained models in subtask 1 and zero-shot learning approaches subtask 2 implies a certain degree of commonalities between European languages. Also in this case, Text2TCS largely outperforms HSemID. Once more, both systems retain higher precision than recall. Interestingly, however, the gap between the systems is this time higher for precision (0.192) than for recall (0.133).

System	Overall Precision	Overall Recall	Overall F1
Text2TCS	0.557	0.429	0.477
HSemID	0.365	0.296	0.325

Table 6: Performance of participating systems for subtask 2 (Italian)

5 Conclusions

In this paper, we have described the CogALex-VI shared task, which focused on monolingual and multilingual identification of semantic relations. Three teams have submitted their system. All of them have addressed subtask 1 (i.e. identifying relations in languages for which a training set was released: English, German and Chinese), while only two teams addressed subtask 2 (i.e. identifying relations in a surprise language: Italian). All the submitted systems utilized neural networks, but with different level of complexity. The evaluation shows that transformer-based approaches obtain better performance than other neural methods. These approaches, in particular, are also behind the recent developments in natural language processing, showing incredible capabilities in a large set of domains and applications. Probably because of such capabilities, traditional NLP tasks, such as the identification of semantic relations, are gradually losing traction in the community. This shared task meant to show how such core NLP tasks remain a big challenge, which would require more attention by the community to possibly generate even more powerful and robust semantic representations.

References

Marco Baroni and Alessandro Lenci. 2011. How We BLESSed Distributional Semantic Evaluation. In *Proceedings of the ACL Workshop on GEometrical Models of Natural Language Semantics*.

Marco Baroni, Silvia Bernardini, Adriano Ferraresi, and Eros Zanchetta. 2009. The WaCky Wide Web: A Collection of Very Large Linguistically Processed Web-Crawled Corpora. *Language resources and evaluation*, 43(3):209–226.

Marco Baroni, Raffaella Bernardi, Ngoc-Quynh Do, and Chung-chieh Shan. 2012. Entailment Above the Word Level in Distributional Semantics. In *Proceedings of EACL*.

Matthew Berland and Eugene Charniak. 1999. Finding Parts in Very Large Corpora. In *Proceedings of ACL*.

Alexander Budanitsky and Graeme Hirst. 2006. Evaluating Wordnet-Based Measures of Lexical Semantic Relatedness. *Computational Linguistics*, 32(1):13–47.

Emmanuele Chersoni, Giulia Rambelli, and Enrico Santus. 2016. CogALex-V Shared Task: ROOT18. In *Proceedings of the COLING Workshop on Cognitive Aspects of the Lexicon*.

Daoud Clarke. 2009. Context-Theoretic Semantics for Natural Language: An Overview. In *Proceedings of the EACL workshop on Geometrical Models of Natural Language Semantics*.

Jean-Pierre Colson. 2020. Extracting Meaning by Idiomaticity: Description of the HSemID system at CogALex VI (2020). In *Proceedings of the COLING Workshop on Cognitive Aspects of the Lexicon*.

Alexis Conneau, Alexei Baevski, Ronan Collobert, Abdelrahman Mohamed, and Michael Auli. 2020. Unsupervised cross-lingual representation learning for speech recognition. *arXiv preprint arXiv:2006.13979*.

Jacob Devlin, Ming-Wei Chang, Kenton Lee, and Kristina Toutanova. 2018. Bert: Pre-training of deep bidirectional transformers for language understanding. *arXiv preprint arXiv:1810.04805*.

Roxana Girju, Adriana Badulescu, and Dan Moldovan. 2006. Automatic Discovery of Part-Whole Relations. *Computational Linguistics*, 32(1):83–135.

Goran Glavaš and Ivan Vulic. 2019. Generalized Tuning of Distributional Word Vectors for Monolingual and Cross-lingual Lexical Entailment. In *Proceedings of ACL*.

Gregory Grefenstette. 1994. Explorations in Automatic Thesaurus Discovery. In *PubMed Abstract| Publisher Full Text OpenURL*.

Marti A Hearst. 1992. Automatic Acquisition of Hyponyms from Large Text Corpora. In *Proceedings of COLING*.

Aishwarya Kamath, Jonas Pfeiffer, Edoardo Ponti, Goran Glavaš, and Ivan Vulić. 2019. Specializing Distributional Vectors of All Words for Lexical Entailment. In *Proceedings of the ACL Workshop on Representation Learning for NLP*.

Saurav Karmakar and John P McCrae. 2020. CogALex-VI Shared Task: Bidirectional Transformer-Based Identification of Semantic Relations. In *Proceedings of the COLING Workshop on Cognitive Aspects of the Lexicon*.

Alessandro Lenci and Giulia Benotto. 2012. Identifying Hypernyms in Distributional Semantic Spaces. In *Proceedings of *SEM*.

Hongchao Liu, Emmanuele Chersoni, Natalia Klyueva, Enrico Santus, and Chu-Ren Huang. 2019. Semantic Relata for the Evaluation of Distributional Models in Mandarin Chinese. *IEEE access*, 7:145705–145713.

Tomas Mikolov, Kai Chen, Greg Corrado, and Jeffrey Dean. 2013. Efficient Estimation of Word Representations in Vector Space. *arXiv preprint arXiv:1301.3781*.

Kim Anh Nguyen, Sabine Schulte im Walde, and Ngoc Thang Vu. 2016. Integrating Distributional Lexical Contrast into Word Embeddings for Antonym-Synonym Distinction. In *Proceedings of ACL*.

Kim Anh Nguyen, Maximilian Köper, Sabine Schulte im Walde, and Ngoc Thang Vu. 2017. Hierarchical Embeddings for Hypernymy Detection and Directionality. *Proceedings of EMNLP*.

Patrick Pantel and Marco Pennacchiotti. 2006. Espresso: Leveraging Generic Patterns for Automatically Harvesting Demantic Relations. In *Proceedings of COLING-ACL*.

Jeffrey Pennington, Richard Socher, and Christopher D Manning. 2014. Glove: Global Vectors for Word Representation. In *Proceedings of EMNLP*.

Stephen Roller and Katrin Erk. 2016. Relations such as hypernymy: Identifying and exploiting hearst patterns in distributional vectors for lexical entailment. In *Proceedings of EMNLP*.

Enrico Santus, Alessandro Lenci, Qin Lu, and Sabine Schulte Im Walde. 2014a. Chasing Hypernyms in Vector Spaces with Entropy. In *Proceedings of EACL*.

Enrico Santus, Qin Lu, Alessandro Lenci, and Chu-Ren Huang. 2014b. Taking Antonymy Mask Off in Vector Space. In *Proceedings of PACLIC*.

Enrico Santus, Frances Yung, Alessandro Lenci, and Chu-Ren Huang. 2015. Evalution 1.0: An Evolving Semantic Dataset for Training and Evaluation of Distributional Semantic Models. In *Proceedings of the ACL Workshop on Linked Data in Linguistics: Resources and Applications*.

Enrico Santus, Tin-Shing Chiu, Qin Lu, Alessandro Lenci, and Chu-Ren Huang. 2016a. What a Nerd! Beating Students and Vector Cosine in the ESL and TOEFL Datasets. In *Proceedings of LREC*.

Enrico Santus, Alessandro Lenci, Tin-Shing Chiu, Qin Lu, and Chu-Ren Huang. 2016b. Nine Features in a Random Forest to Learn Taxonomical Semantic Relations. In *Proceedings of LREC*.

Enrico Santus, Anna Rogers, Stefan Evert, and Alessandro Lenci. 2016c. The CogALex-V Shared Task on the Corpus-Based Identification of Semantic Relations. In *Proceedings of the COLING Workshop on Cognitive Aspects of the Lexicon*.

Enrico Santus, Hongmin Wang, Emmanuele Chersoni, and Yue Zhang. 2018. A Rank-Based Similarity Metric for Word Embeddings. In *Proceedings of ACL*.

Enrico Santus. 2016. *Making Sense: From Word Distribution to Meaning*. Ph.D. thesis, Hong Kong Polytechnic University.

Silke Scheible and Sabine Schulte Im Walde. 2014. A Database of Paradigmatic Semantic Relation Pairs for German Nouns, Verbs, and Adjectives. In *Proceedings of the COLING Workshop on Lexical and Grammatical Resources for Language Processing*.

Silke Scheible, Sabine Schulte Im Walde, and Sylvia Springorum. 2013. Uncovering Distributional Differences Between Synonyms and Antonyms in a Word Space Model. In *Proceedings of IJCNLP*.

Sabine Schulte Im Walde. 2020. Distinguishing between Paradigmatic Semantic Relations across Word Classes: Human Ratings and Distributional Similarity. *Journal of Language Modelling*, 8:53–101.

Vered Shwartz, Yoav Goldberg, and Ido Dagan. 2016. Improving Hypernymy Detection with an Integrated Path-Based and Distributional Method. In *Proceedings of ACL*.

Rion Snow, Daniel Jurafsky, and Andrew Y Ng. 2004. Learning Syntactic Patterns for Automatic Hypernym Discovery. In *Proceedings of NIPS*.

Irene Sucameli and Alessandro Lenci. 2017. PARAD-it: Eliciting Italian Paradigmatic Relations with Crowd-sourcing. In *Proceedings of CLIC.it*.

Peter D Turney and Patrick Pantel. 2010. From Frequency to Meaning: Vector Space Models of Semantics. *Journal of Artificial Intelligence Research*, 37:141–188.

Ivan Vulić and Anna Korhonen. 2018. Injecting Lexical Contrast into Word Vectors by Guiding Vector Space Specialisation. In *Proceedings of The ACL Workshop on Representation Learning for NLP*.

Lennart Wachowiak, Christian Lang, Barbara Heinisch, and Dagmar Gromann. 2020. CogALex-VI Shared Task: Transrelation - A Robust Multilingual Language Model for Multilingual Relation Identification. In *Proceedings of the COLING Workshop on Cognitive Aspects of the Lexicon*.

Chengyu Wang, Yan Fan, Xiaofeng He, and Aoying Zhou. 2019. A Family of Fuzzy Orthogonal Projection Models for Monolingual and Cross-lingual Hypernymy Prediction. In *The World Wide Web Conference*.

Julie Weeds and David Weir. 2003. A general Framework for Distributional Similarity. In *Proceedings of EMNLP*.

Julie Weeds, Daoud Clarke, Jeremy Reffin, David Weir, and Bill Keller. 2014. Learning to Distinguish Hypernyms and Co-hyponyms. In *Proceedings of COLING*.

Changlong Yu, Jialong Han, Haisong Zhang, and Wilfred Ng. 2020. Hypernymy Detection for Low-Resource Languages via Meta Learning. In *Proceedings of ACL*.

Michael Zock, Alessandro Lenci, and Stefan Evert. 2016. Proceedings of the COLING Workshop on Cognitive Aspects of the Lexicon (CogALex-V). In *Proceedings of the 5th Workshop on Cognitive Aspects of the Lexicon (CogALex-V)*.

Extracting meaning by idiomaticity:
Description of the HSemID system at CogALex VI (2020)

Jean-Pierre Colson
University of Louvain
Louvain-la-Neuve, Belgium
jean-pierre.colson@uclouvain.be

Abstract

The HSemID system, submitted to the CogALex VI Shared Task is a hybrid system relying mainly on metric clusters measured in large web corpora, complemented by a vector space model using cosine similarity to detect semantic associations. Although the system reached rather weak results for the subcategories of synonyms, antonyms and hypernyms, with some differences from one language to another, it is able to measure general semantic associations (as being random or not-random) with an F1 score close to 0.80. The results strongly suggest that idiomatic constructions play a fundamental role in semantic associations. Further experiments are necessary in order to fine-tune the model to the subcategories of synonyms, antonyms, hypernyms and to explain surprising differences across languages.

1 Introduction

This paper is a system description of *HSemID (Hybrid Semantic extraction based on IDiomatic associations)*, presented at CogALex VI. Contrary to most models dedicated to the extraction of semantic associations, *HSemID* is based on a similar model developed for the extraction of multiword expressions, *HMSid*, presented at the Parseme 1.2. workshop of the Coling 2020 conference. From a theoretical point of view, we wished to explore the link between general meaning associations and associations based on idiomaticity, in the general sense of multiword expressions (MWEs). For instance, *beans* may display a general meaning association with food (as many of them are edible) or with coffee, but there is an idiomatic association between *spill* and *beans* because of the idiom *spill the beans* (reveal a secret). Thus, general meaning associations are mainly extralinguistic and cultural, whereas idiomatic associations are mainly intralinguistic, as they are just valid for one specific language, although similar associations may exist in other languages because they are cognate or have influenced each other.

The implicit link between semantics and idiomaticity has already been mentioned in the literature. Lapesa and Evert (2014) point out that using larger windows with statistical scores yields extraction models that can be adapted from MWEs to semantic associations. According to them, 1st-order models (based on co-occurrence statistics such as the log-likelihood, dice score or t-score) and 2nd-order models (based on similar contexts of use, as in the case of cosine similarity in a vector space model) appear to be redundant on the basis of the first experiments and do not really benefit from a combination of both approaches.

Our model for the extraction of multiword expressions (*HMSid, Hybrid Multi-layer System for the extraction of Idioms*) yielded promising results for French verbal expressions. In the official results of the Parseme 1.2. shared task, our model obtained an F1-score of 67.1, with an F1-score of 36.49 for MWEs that were unseen in the training data; in an adapted version proposed just after the workshop, we reached an even better F1-score of 71.86 in the closed track, relying only on the training data, with no external resources, and an F1-score for unseen MWEs of 40.15, which makes it by far the best score in the closed track for unseen French MWEs. It should be pointed out that the model used for the extraction of MWEs is corpus-based and derives from metric clusters used in Information Retrieval (Baeza-Yates and Ribeiro-Neto, 1999; Colson, 2017; 2018), but does not use any machine learning architecture.

We adapted this model in a deep learning approach for the CogALex VI Shared Task, as described in the following section. From a theoretical point of view, we wished to explore the performance of a model used for MWE extraction, in a related but very different context: the extraction of semantic associations. Although we realize that the main goal of the CogALex VI Shared Task was to improve the extraction of the specific categories of synonyms, antonyms and hypernyms, we did not have enough time to train our model for this subcategory distinction, and were mainly concerned with the identification of a semantic association (being random or non-random) on the basis of idiomatic patterns.

2   Methodology

Our model was tested for the different languages taking part in the CogALex VI Shared Task, using the datasets provided for English (Santus et al., 2015), Chinese (Liu et al., 2019), German (Scheible and Schulte Im Walde, 2014) and Italian (Sucameli and Lenci, 2017).

As suggested by the acronym (*HSemID, Hybrid Semantic extraction based on IDiomatic associations*), our methodology was hybrid, as we used both a vector space model (Turney and Pantel, 2010) and a co-occurrence model based on metric clusters in a general corpus (Colson, 2017; 2018). However, most features of the model were derived from the second part, so that the model mainly relies on co-occurrence and therefore on *idiomatic* meaning, as explained below.

For the vector space model, we measured cosine similarity in the Wikipedia corpora. We relied on the Wiki word vectors[1] and on the Perl implementation of Word2vec, by means of the multiword cosine similarity function[2].

For the metric cluster, we used the *cpr-score* (Colson, 2017; 2018), a simple co-occurrence score based on the proximity of the ngrams in a large corpus. In order to avoid redundancy with the Wikipedia corpora, this score was computed by using other, general-purpose web corpora: the WaCky corpora (Baroni et al., 2009) for English, German and Italian. For Chinese, we compiled our own web corpus by means of the WebBootCat tool provided by the Sketch Engine[3]. As we have only basic knowledge of Chinese, we relied for this purpose on the seed words originally used for compiling the English WaCky corpus. The English seed words were translated into Chinese by Google Translate[4]. All those corpora have a size of about 1.4 billion tokens; for Chinese (Mandarin, simplified spelling), we reached a comparable size by taking into account the number of Chinese words, not the number of Chinese characters (*hans*).

In order to train our model, we implemented a neural network (multi-layer perceptron), relying on most of the default options provided by the Microsoft Cognitive Toolkit (CNTK)[5]. We imported the CNTK library in a python script. Our neural network used minibatches, had an input dimension of just 11 features (for the 4 output classes), 2 hidden layers (dimension: 7), and we used ReLU as an activation function. For the loss, we relied on cross entropy with softmax.

Among the 11 features used for training the model, it should be noted that the vector space approach, represented by the multiple cosine similarity, only played a limited role, as it represented just one of the 11 features to be weighted by the model. The other features were based on the metric clusters. For these, the association score (*cpr-score*) was measured with a narrow window between the grams composing the pairs from the datasets, and with wider windows for a number of linguistic markers favoring semantic associations (typically *or, and, not,* and their equivalents in the different languages). The frequencies of the different grams in the WaCky corpora were also used as input features. All features were smoothened to real figures between 0 and 1. For measuring the average test error during training, we used 80 percent

---

[1] The Wiki word vectors can be downloaded from http://fasttext.cc/docs/en/pretrained-vectors.html
[2] https://metacpan.org/pod/Word2vec::Word2vec
[3] https://www.sketchengine.eu/
[4] https://translate.google.com
[5] https://www.microsoft.com/en-us/research/product/cognitive-toolkit

of the training data as the trainer, and 20 percent (with the correct labels) as the test data. The average test error when training the model was situated around 20 percent.

3   Results and discussion

Table 1 below displays the official results obtained by HSemID at the CogALex VI Shared Task for the various languages (English, Chinese, German, Italian).

HSemID			
English	**P**	**R**	**F1**
SYN	0.483	0.214	0.297
HYP	0.416	0.366	0.389
ANT	0.313	0.248	0.277
Overall	0.400	0.276	0.320
Chinese			
SYN	0.282	0.328	0.303
HYP	0.610	0.194	0.294
ANT	0.591	0.458	0.516
Overall	0.501	0.331	0.377
German			
SYN	0.374	0.219	0.276
HYP	0.386	0.273	0.320
ANT	0.422	0.281	0.338
Overall	0.395	0.258	0.312
Italian			
SYN	0.418	0.371	0.393
HYP	0.344	0.294	0.317
ANT	0.319	0.201	0.247
Overall	0.365	0.296	0.325

Table 1: Official results obtained with HSemID at the CogALex VI Shared Task

As shown in Table 1, the overall results yielded by HSemID are situated between an F1 of 0.312 and 0.377. Strangely enough, the best result was reached for Chinese, in spite of the fact that we only have basic mastery of Chinese and have assembled our web corpus, as described in the preceding section, without any feedback from native speakers or specialists of the language. It should also be noted that there is some variation as to the category that receives the best F1 score: English and German score best for hypernyms (respectively 0.389 and 0.320), Chinese for antonyms (0.516) and Italian for synonyms (0.393). Our hypothesis for explaining this phenomenon, in spite of the fact that the methodology was the same for all languages, is that the hybrid approach checked the cosine similarity in the Wikipedia corpus, but the metric cluster in the web corpora; as the word pairs from the dataset contained several technical terms, the presence or absence of those words in the web corpora was often a matter of pure chance, which may have an influence on the final score from one language to another. The fluctuating results for the Chinese dataset are also striking: not only is the overall F1 score for Chinese the best result of the model, but the model reaches surprising scores for Chinese antonyms (P=0.591, R=0.458), although this category is much more problematic for the European languages.

For lack of time, we didn't have the opportunity of fine-tuning our model to the specific subcategories SYN, HYP and ANT, as was the main goal of the CogALex VI Shared Task. As a matter of fact, our objective was to focus the training of the model on the general semantic associations (random or not-random), in the hope that this would also yield acceptable subcategories SYN, HYP and ANT. Obviously, this was not really the case, although high scores for European languages are hard to reach (the best F1 scores for English, German and Italian at the Shared Task are resp. 0.517, 0.500 and 0.477). A closer analysis of the errors produced by our model reveals that too many idiomatic associations of synonyms and antonyms are similar. For instance, *turn right* and *turn left* are equally strong idiomatic associations, and it is unclear how *right* and *left* should be considered as antonyms from this point of view. In the same way, hypernyms are very hard to discriminate from synonyms if we pay attention to their idiomatic associations. A further improvement of our model may therefore consist in a more complex neural network, in which the different contexts for SYN/ANT and SYN/HYP would be specified by additional features.

In spite of these shortcomings, our model reached pretty good scores for the general task of extracting semantic links, which does not appear in the official results but may be computed by means of the evaluation score provided in the training data, which contains the RANDOM category. If we take into consideration the F1 score obtained for the RANDOM label, we obviously get a picture of the general ability of the model to extract strong semantic associations, be they cases of synonymy, hypernymy or anything else (such as metaphors or idiomatic meaning).

For lack of space, Table 2 below just displays the results obtained in English and Chinese by our model, for the RANDOM category. The scores were computed with the official gold dataset and the original evaluation script included in the training data of the shared task.

HSemID			
English	**P**	**R**	**F1**
RANDOM	0.748	0.822	0.783
Chinese			
RANDOM	0.782	0.807	0.794

Table 2: Results obtained by HSemID for the RANDOM category

It should also be reminded that the best F1 score obtained for this task (subtask 1) at the preceding edition of the CogALex Shared Task[6], CogALex V, was 0.790. After sending the official results of the model to the Shared Task, we continued training the model for English with a more complex neural network and we can report an even better English F1 score: 0.802 (with P=0.716 and R=0.911).

In spite of the rather weak results obtained by our model for the elicitation of the subcategories SYN, HYP and ANT at the CogALex VI Shared Task, we therefore come to the conclusion that the HSemID model, relying mainly on the extraction of semantics by means of idiomatic associations, makes it possible to extract general semantic associations, with F1 figures for the RANDOM category that were rarely reached by any experiment carried out within distributional semantics. The results strongly suggest that idiomatic constructions play a key role in semantic associations. Further experiments should improve the scores obtained for synonyms, antonyms and hypernyms, which clearly remains a daunting challenge in the case of European languages.

---

[6] https://sites.google.com/site/cogalex2016/home/shared-task/results

References

Ricardo Baeza-Yates and Berthier Ribeiro-Neto. 1999. *Modern Information Retrieval*. ACM Press /Addison Wesley, New York.

Marco Baroni, Silvia Bernardini, Adriano Ferraresi and Eros Zanchetta. 2009. The WaCky Wide Web: A collection of very large linguistically processed Web-crawled corpora. *Journal of Language Resources and Evaluation*, 43: 209–226.

Jean-Pierre Colson. 2017. The IdiomSearch Experiment: Extracting Phraseology from a Probabilistic Network of Constructions. In Ruslan Mitkov (ed.), *Computational and Corpus-based phraseology, Lecture Notes in Artificial Intelligence 10596*. Springer International Publishing, Cham: 16–28.

Jean-Pierre Colson. 2018. From Chinese Word Segmentation to Extraction of Constructions: Two Sides of the Same Algorithmic Coin. In Agatha Savary et al. 2018: 41-50.

Gabriella Lapesa and Stefan Evert. 2014. A large scale evaluation of distributional semantic models: Parameters, interactions and model selection. *Transactions of the Association for Computational Linguistics*, 2:531–545.

Hongchao Liu, Emmanuele Chersoni, Natalia Klyueva, Enrico Santus, and Chu-Ren Huang. 2019. Semantic Relata for the Evaluation of Distributional Models in Mandarin Chinese. IEEE access, 7:145705–145713.

Enrico Santus, Frances Yung, Alessandro Lenci, and Chu-Ren Huang. 2015. Evalution 1.0: An Evolving Semantic Dataset for Training and Evaluation of Distributional Semantic Models. In Proceedings of the ACL Workshop on Linked Data in Linguistics: Resources and Applications.

Agata Savary, Carlos Ramisch, Jena D. Hwang, Nathan Schneider, Melanie Andresen, Sameer Pradhan and Miriam R. L. Petruck (eds.). 2018. *Proceedings of the Joint Workshop on Linguistic Annotation, Multiword Expressions and Constructions, Coling 2018*, Santa Fe NM, USA, Association for Computational Linguistics.

Silke Scheible and Sabine Schulte Im Walde. 2014. A Database of Paradigmatic Semantic Relation Pairs for German Nouns, Verbs, and Adjectives. In Proceedings of the COLING Workshop on Lexical and Grammatical Resources for Language Processing.

Irene Sucameli and Alessandro Lenci. 2017. PARAD-it: Eliciting Italian Paradigmatic Relations with Crowdsourcing. In Proceedings of CLIC.it.

Peter D. Turney and Patrick Pantel. 2010. From Frequency to Meaning: Vector Space Models of Semantics. Journal of Artificial Intelligence Research, 37:141–188.

CogALex-VI Shared Task: Transrelation - A Robust Multilingual Language Model for Multilingual Relation Identification

Lennart Wachowiak
University of Vienna / Vienna, Austria
lennartw99@univie.ac.at

Christian Lang
University of Vienna / Vienna, Austria
a0809558@univie.ac.at

Barbara Heinisch
University of Vienna / Vienna, Austria
barbara.heinisch@univie.ac.at

Dagmar Gromann
University of Vienna / Vienna, Austria
dagmar.gromann@univie.ac.at

Abstract

We describe our submission to the CogALex-VI shared task on the identification of multilingual paradigmatic relations building on XLM-RoBERTa (XLM-R), a robustly optimized and multilingual BERT model. In spite of several experiments with data augmentation, data addition and ensemble methods with a Siamese Triple Net, Translrelation, the XLM-R model with a linear classifier adapted to this specific task, performed best in testing and achieved the best results in the final evaluation of the shared task, even for a previously unseen language.

1 Introduction

Determining whether a semantic relation exists between words and which type of relation it represents is a central challenge in numerous NLP tasks, such as extracting terminological concept systems and paraphrase generation. Adding a multilingual dimension renders this task at the same time more relevant and more challenging. Recent approaches rely on aligned vector spaces for individual languages (Bojanowski et al., 2017) or meta-learning approaches (Yu et al., 2020) for hypernymy detection and a Siamese Triple Net for antonymy-synonymy distinction inherent in word embeddings (Samenko et al., 2020). However, in general a distinction of paradigmatic relations with word embeddings is difficult (im Walde, 2020). In a multilingual scenario, frequently lexical resources are utilized to reinforce the model's transfer learning abilities (Geng et al., 2020). Given relatively small training datasets and a necessity to support a previously unknown language, we decided to rely on a multilingual pretrained language model.

The CogALex-VI shared task focuses on the identification of semantic relations of the types synonymy (e.g. *chap* and *man*), antonymy (e.g. *big* and *small*), hypernymy (e.g. *screech* and *noise*), or random (e.g. *ink* and *closure*) between a given word pair. Random indicates that the word pair is unrelated. The shared task provided two subtasks. For the first subtask, participating teams were allowed to design monolingual systems being provided training and validation data for the languages Mandarin Chinese, German, and English. For the second subtask, participating teams were expected to design a single multilingual system that can correctly classify semantic relations in all three languages as well as a previously unknown surprise language, which turned out to be Italian. Additional resources were permitted with the exclusion of anything related to WordNet (Miller, 1995) or ConceptNet (Liu and Singh, 2004).

Our initial intention was to target the second subtask with a multilingual system relying on the state-of-the-art multilingual model XLM-RoBERTa (XLM-R) (Conneau et al., 2020) adapted to the task at hand utilizing a linear layer and CogALex-VI training datasets, a model we call *Transrelation* that we provided within the Text to Terminological Concept System (Text2TCS)[1] project. To support the model's ability to distinguish relations we experimented with data augmentation, data addition and ensemble methods, joining Transrelation[2] with a model trained on a Siamese Triple Net. Finally, the adapted XML-R model outperformed all other experiments as well as all other submitted models to CogALex-VI on both tasks.

[1] https://text2tcs.univie.ac.at/

[2] Code and datasets are available at https://github.com/Text2TCS/Transrelation

Proceedings of the Workshop on Cognitive Aspects of the Lexicon, pages 59–64
Barcelona, Spain (Online), December 12, 2020

2 Background

2.1 Lexico-Semantic Relations

Lexico-semantic relations, also called semantic and lexical semantic relations, represent the major organizing means for structuring lexical knowledge. A common distinction for such relations is between paradigmatic and syntagmatic relations, where the former represents relations between natural language expressions that could be found in the same position in a sentence and the latter refers to co-occurring elements. Importance of paradigmatic relations might differ by word class (im Walde, 2020), i.e, hypernymy is particularly central for the organization of nouns but less important for organizing verbs. In the CogALex VI shared task all relations are paradigmatic, which are particularly difficult to be distinguished by regular word embedding models and between different word classes (im Walde, 2020).

2.2 Relation Identification

Recent approaches trying to identify hypernym relations in a multilingual setting utilize fastText embeddings (Bojanowski et al., 2017) of different languages being aligned into a single vector space (Wang et al., 2019) or train models using different fastText embeddings in a multilingual setting with the help of meta-learning algorithms (Yu et al., 2020). Synonym and antonym differentiation has been a key problem for automatic relation identification and has in the past been tackled with partial success using word alignment over large multilingual corpora with statistical methods to determine distributional similarity (van der Plas and Tiedemann, 2006) or statistical translation to a pivot language for synonymy discovery (Wittmann et al., 2014). Samenko et al. (2020) utilize Siamese Triple Nets (Bromley et al., 1994) to train so-called contrasting maps, vector representations trained on monolingual embeddings that reinforce the distinction between antonyms and synonyms. Approaches that tackle all three relations at once in a multilingual environment frequently rely on active transfer learning and lexical resources (Geng et al., 2020) or prototypical vector representations for each type of relation (im Walde, 2020).

2.3 Language Models

Recent advances in the field of natural language processing are based on deep neural language models, which can be pretrained on large amounts of data in an unsupervised fashion and are fine-tuned afterwards on a specific task making use of the previously learned language representations. One of the most prominent example of such a model is BERT (Devlin et al., 2018) utilizing the now ubiquitous Transformer architecture. Compared to earlier approaches like word2vec (Mikolov et al., 2013) and fastText (Bojanowski et al., 2017) the word embeddings generated by these deep neural language models are context-specific, i.e., a word's embedding changes depending on its surrounding words. Language models do not have to be monolingual, but the pretraining can be extended to multiple languages at the same time, e.g. by making use of a shared subword vocabulary. Prominent examples are multilingual BERT and the more recent XLM-R (Conneau et al., 2020).

3 System Description

3.1 Architecture

Our system makes use of the multilingual language model XLM-R (Conneau et al., 2020). We use the implementation provided by the transformers library (Wolf et al., 2019), which offers the XLM-R model pretrained on 100 different languages using CommonCrawl data. We use the base model size, which uses less parameters than the large version of XLM-R, but performed equally well in our experiments. A linear layer is added on top of the pooled output in order to allow for classification into one of the four possible classes, i.e., three semantic relations or random.

3.2 Datasets

The CogALex VI shared task provided training and validation datasets in English (Santus et al., 2015), German (Scheible and Im Walde, 2014) and Mandarin Chinese (Liu et al., 2019). The test data for the surprise language Italian were taken from Sucameli and Lenci (2017). Word pair counts for the training datasets are provided in Table 1.

Language	ANT	HYP	SYN	RANDOM
English	916	998	842	2554
German	829	841	782	2430
Chinese	361	421	402	1330

Table 1: Word pair counts of training sets

Language	ANT	HYP	SYN	Weighted
English	0.587	0.483	0.473	0.517
German	0.534	0.535	0.427	0.500
Chinese	0.914	0.876	0.849	0.881
Italian	0.447	0.462	0.513	0.477

Table 2: F1-score on test set

3.3 Input and Preprocessing

The input provided to the model consists of a word pair labeled with a relation surrounded by XLM-R specific classification and sequence separation tokens, as well as additional padding tokens, which guarantee that all inputs have the same length. For instance, the input pair *tiger* and *animal* is encoded as '<s>', '_tiger', '</s>', '</s>', '_animal', '</s>', excluding the padding tokens.

3.4 Training and Hyperparameters

This model was then trained on the training datasets (see Table 1) in three languages simultaneously. Hyperparameters were fine-tuned manually and via gridsearch on the given validation sets. The best results were achieved with the following hyperparameters: Optimizer: AdamW, Learning rate = 2e-5, Epsilon = 1e-8, Weight Decay = 0, Warm-up steps = 0, Epochs = 7, Batch size = 32.

4 Results and Analysis

Table 2 shows the results of our model on the four provided test sets. The computed score is a weighted F1-score excluding unrelated words labeled with RANDOM. The strongest performance can be observed in Chinese with a weighted F1-score of 0.881. English and German are far behind with scores of 0.517 and 0.500 respectively. Interestingly, the model performs nearly as well on the Italian test set with a score of 0.477, although the model had not been trained on this language, thus showing the remarkable zero-shot-learning abilities of XLM-R.

Fig. 1 shows the normalized confusion matrix based on the joined results on all four test sets. Besides confusing meaningful relations with RANDOM, which can be explained by the fact that RANDOM is the majority class, the highest confusion exists between hypernyms and synonyms. For Chinese, for instnace, 19 HYP/SYN labeled test examples were confused. From these examples, in 11 pairs some characters in one sequence are present in the other, such as 海水- 水(sea water - water) (label: HYP) and 船- 船舶(ship/boat - ship) (label: SYN). This also occurred in four SYN/ANT labeled examples, e.g. 無線- 有線(wireless - wired) (gold: ANT). For the remainder of wrongly classified SYN/ANT examples, our model frequently selected RANDOM, e.g. 私人- 公立(private individual - public) (gold: ANT).

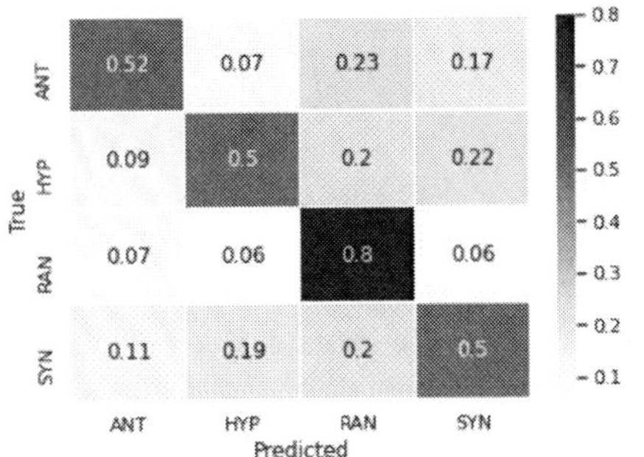

Figure 1: Normalized Confusion Matrix

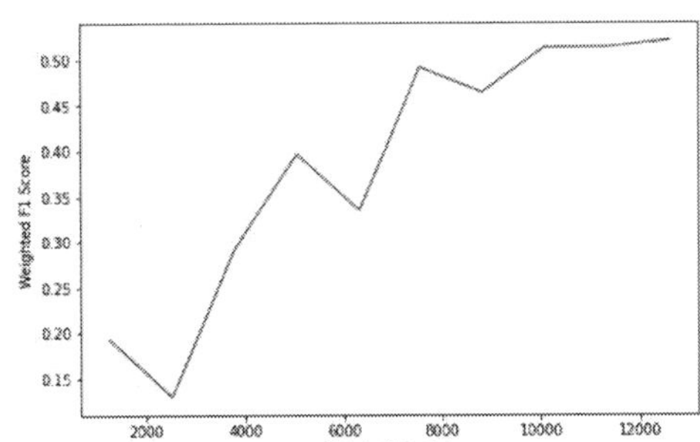

Figure 2: Learning Curve

The learning curve shown in Fig. 2 plots the achieved weighted F1 score in relation to the number of samples in the training set. For each training set size we trained four models and reported the highest observed score. The model greatly benefits from additional training samples when the training set size is below 8,000. However, the usefulness of adding more data diminishes quickly as the learning curve seems to plateau towards the end. This was confirmed when we tried to add additional training data to data provided by CogALex-VI observing the WordNet/ConceptNet exclusion.

5   Discussion

In additional experiments we trained a Siamese Triplet Net (Bromley et al., 1994) to learn meta-embeddings that contrast synonyms and antonyms, which we also tried for hypernym and synonym distinction. However, an ensemble method combining this model and XLM-R performed worse than XLM-R on its own. Due to our model's strong performance in Chinese we also experimented with data augmentation by machine translating the training and validation sets from Chinese to the other languages. The model's performance on these translated datasets was, however, considerably worse than solely on the original untranslated datasets. Additionally, performance of both models trained for individual languages or consecutively one language after another lagged considerably behind our final model.

Given the vast differences in model performance on the different languages, we briefly analyzed the data quality. In the confusion matrix in Fig. 1 it becomes evident that our model tended to confuse hypernyms and synonyms a well as random and antonyms. A brief check on the German data where the model performed worse showed that some word pairs labeled as hypernyms might be understood as synonyms by human classifiers, e.g. *fett* (fat) - *dick* (plump), *unruhig* (anxious/restless) - *erregt* (excited/aroused), and *radikal* (radical) - *drastisch* (radical/extreme) could instead be labeled as synonyms. Additional training data not related to WordNet or ConceptNet we experimented with (e.g. Kober et al. (2020)) had similar issues and data addition did not improve performance of both the tested models. So on the one hand we attribute this confusion problem of our model to word pairs that might easily be confused by human users. On the other hand, the number of training examples was rather low and data augmentation/addition with high-quality data might have considerably improved performance.

Depending on the fact that the semantics of these examples change with context, we believe that providing words in context could be one way to alleviate this misclassification problem. One curious example underlining this issue was the result we got for the surprise language Italian not seen during training, where *farfalla* (butterfly) and *coccinella* (ladybug) are labeled as antonyms, while our system labeled the pair as a synonym. Since both can be used to lovingly refer to a young female person in Italian, the result of our system could be regarded as correct if the words are understood in this sense. Further such examples can be found in great number in the training, validation and test datasets. Curiously, performance on Mandarin Chinese did not seem to be impacted as heavily by this problem, which might be due to the fact that the training datasets were compiled from a different source of different quality.

6   Conclusion

In this paper, we present our system Transrelation for the CogALex VI shared task on multilingual relation identification called Transrelation. We experimented with data addition, data augmentation and ensemble methods joining pretrained transformer-based models with a Siamese Triple Net. The final system is based on the multilingual pretrained language model XLM-R, which turned out to be the winning system and delivered a strong performance on all four languages, including one previously unknown and unseen additional language.

In the future, it would be interesting to apply ideas from curriculum learning (Bengio et al., 2009) or meta-learning, as already done for simpler models in the case of hypernymy detection (Yu et al., 2020) to improve the learning process of our model. This would especially apply to similar scenarios of few available training datasets. Furthermore, it would be interesting to evaluate the model's performance on different lexico-semantic relations as well as languages from different language families, e.g. Slavic.

Acknowledgements

This work has been supported by the project Text2TCS funded by the European Language Grid H2020 (grant number 825627).

References

Yoshua Bengio, Jérôme Louradour, Ronan Collobert, and Jason Weston. 2009. Curriculum learning. In *Proceedings of the 26th annual international conference on machine learning*, pages 41–48.

Piotr Bojanowski, Edouard Grave, Armand Joulin, and Tomas Mikolov. 2017. Enriching word vectors with subword information. *Transactions of the Association for Computational Linguistics*, 5:135–146.

Jane Bromley, Isabelle Guyon, Yann LeCun, Eduard Säckinger, and Roopak Shah. 1994. Signature verification using a" siamese" time delay neural network. In *Advances in neural information processing systems*, pages 737–744.

Alexis Conneau, Kartikay Khandelwal, Naman Goyal, Vishrav Chaudhary, Guillaume Wenzek, Francisco Guzmán, Edouard Grave, Myle Ott, Luke Zettlemoyer, and Veselin Stoyanov. 2020. Unsupervised cross-lingual representation learning at scale. pages 8440–8451, July.

Jacob Devlin, Ming-Wei Chang, Kenton Lee, and Kristina Toutanova. 2018. Bert: Pre-training of deep bidirectional transformers for language understanding. *arXiv preprint arXiv:1810.04805*.

ZhiQiang Geng, GuoFei Chen, YongMing Han, Gang Lu, and Fang Li. 2020. Semantic relation extraction using sequential and tree-structured lstm with attention. *Information Sciences*, 509:183–192.

Sabine Schulte im Walde. 2020. Distinguishing between paradigmatic semantic relations across word classes: human ratings and distributional similarity. *Journal of Language Modelling*, 8(1):53–101.

Thomas Kober, Julie Weeds, Lorenzo Bertolini, and David Weir. 2020. Data augmentation for hypernymy detection. *ArXiv e-prints*.

Hugo Liu and Push Singh. 2004. Conceptnet—a practical commonsense reasoning tool-kit. *BT technology journal*, 22(4):211–226.

Hongchao Liu, Emmanuele Chersoni, Natalia Klyueva, Enrico Santus, and Chu-Ren Huang. 2019. Semantic relata for the evaluation of distributional models in mandarin chinese. *IEEE access*, 7:145705–145713.

Tomas Mikolov, Ilya Sutskever, Kai Chen, Greg S Corrado, and Jeff Dean. 2013. Distributed representations of words and phrases and their compositionality. In *Advances in neural information processing systems*, pages 3111–3119.

George A Miller. 1995. Wordnet: a lexical database for english. *Communications of the ACM*, 38(11):39–41.

Igor Samenko, Alexey Tikhonov, and Ivan P. Yamshchikov. 2020. Synonyms and Antonyms: Embedded Conflict. *arXiv:2004.12835v1 [cs]*.

Enrico Santus, Frances Yung, Alessandro Lenci, and Chu-Ren Huang. 2015. Evalution 1.0: an evolving semantic dataset for training and evaluation of distributional semantic models. In *Proceedings of the 4th Workshop on Linked Data in Linguistics: Resources and Applications*, pages 64–69.

Silke Scheible and Sabine Schulte Im Walde. 2014. A database of paradigmatic semantic relation pairs for german nouns, verbs, and adjectives. In *Proceedings of Workshop on Lexical and Grammatical Resources for Language Processing*, pages 111–119.

Irene Sucameli and Alessandro Lenci. 2017. Parad-it: Eliciting italian paradigmatic relations with crowdsourcing. *CLiC-it 2017 11-12 December 2017, Rome*, page 310.

Lonneke van der Plas and Jörg Tiedemann. 2006. Finding synonyms using automatic word alignment and measures of distributional similarity. (July):866–873.

Chengyu Wang, Yan Fan, Xiaofeng He, and Aoying Zhou. 2019. A family of fuzzy orthogonal projection models for monolingual and cross-lingual hypernymy prediction. In *The World Wide Web Conference*, pages 1965–1976.

Moritz Wittmann, Marion Weller, and Sabine Schulte Im Walde. 2014. Automatic extraction of synonyms for German particle verbs from parallel data with distributional similarity as a re-ranking feature. *Proceedings of the 9th International Conference on Language Resources and Evaluation, LREC 2014*, (1998):1430–1437.

Thomas Wolf, Lysandre Debut, Victor Sanh, Julien Chaumond, Clement Delangue, Anthony Moi, Pierric Cistac, Tim Rault, Rémi Louf, Morgan Funtowicz, et al. 2019. Huggingface's transformers: State-of-the-art natural language processing. *ArXiv*, pages arXiv–1910.

Changlong Yu, Jialong Han, Haisong Zhang, and Wilfred Ng. 2020. Hypernymy detection for low-resource languages via meta learning. In *Proceedings of the 58th Annual Meeting of the Association for Computational Linguistics*, pages 3651–3656.

CogALex-VI Shared Task: Bidirectional Transformer based Identification of Semantic Relations

Saurav Karmakar
Insight Centre for Data Analytics
Data Science Institute
National University of Ireland Galway
Galway, Ireland
`saurav.karmakar@insight-centre.org`

John McCrae
Insight Centre for Data Analytics
Data Science Institute
National University of Ireland Galway
Galway, Ireland
`john@mccr.ae`

Abstract

This paper[1] presents a bidirectional transformer based approach for recognising semantic relationships between a pair of words as proposed by CogALex VI[2] shared task in 2020. The system presented here works by employing BERT embeddings of the words and passing the same over tuned neural network to produce a learning model for the pair of words and their relationships. Afterwards the very same model is used for the relationship between unknown words from the test set. CogALex VI[2] provided Subtask 1 as the identification of relationship of three specific categories amongst English pair of words and the presented system opts to work on that. The resulted relationships of the unknown words are analysed here which shows a balanced performance in overall characteristics with some scope for improvement.

1 Introduction

Predicting the relationship between two words in terms of semantics has become a quintessential problem to be solved in the present day NLP world and reflect great impacts on the theoretical psycholinguistic modeling of the mental lexicon as well. The field of NLP finds many useful applications through tackling this direction, such as thesaurus generation (Grefenstette, 1994), ontology learning (Zouaq and Nkambou, 2008), paraphrase generation and identification (Madnani and Dorr, 2010), question answering and recognizing textual entailment (Dagan et al., 2013), as well as drawing inferences (Martínez-Gómez et al., 2016). Many NLP applications make use of handcrafted resources such as WordNet (Fellbaum, 1998). As a matter of fact, WordNet came from a similar direction with a substantial manual effort. Creating such resources is expensive and time consuming; thus efforts of this sort do not cover the variety of languages equally. Practically, coverage of a wide range of languages through such manual initiatives also far from completion. Many organizations and institutes, who are interested in creating knowledge bases on the field of their practice have attempted to classify such word pairs to shape taxonomies (Pereira et al., 2019).

Lately distributional or corpus based approaches came into popularity for investigating the semantic linkage between words; this approach utilizes the usage and appearance of the words in the corpus. These methods have been able to reflect potential in pattern-recognition-based exploration for word to word semantic mapping through distributional parameters. Exploring and connecting semantic relationships are quite difficult and variety of approaches have been tried yet.

Cognitive Aspects of the Lexicon VI (CogALex VI)[2] has arranged a shared task in 2020; it was looking to explore different efforts to figure out paradigmatic semantic relations, specifically synonymy, antonymy and hypernymy. In the field of NLP these type of relations are notoriously difficult to be distinguished between word pairs given a distribution.

To tackle this problem, we employ a deep learning framework to develop training models and test their performances through semantic link prediction between unknown word set. In this paper, we demonstrate our bidirectional transformer based approach to classify whether a given pair of words are semantically

---

[2]https://sites.google.com/view/cogalex-2020/home/shared-task

Proceedings of the Workshop on Cognitive Aspects of the Lexicon, pages 65–71
Barcelona, Spain (Online), December 12, 2020

connected with one of the three relationships just mentioned above or some other random ones: as asked by this shared task. In the following Section 2 we describe the related work, Section 3 provides the system description; following that Section 4 describes the experimental set up, while Section 5 describes the results and Section 6 lays out the conclusion and future direction.

2 Related Work

2.1 Identifications of semantic relations

Recognizing the semantic meaning of words in terms of connecting them with semantic relationships has become a key direction to grow knowledge base and many further practices in NLP. This connects to a wide range of applications, such as textual entailment, text summarization, sentiment analysis, ontology learning, and so on. Following this, several supervised and unsupervised approaches have been initiated and for reference the works of (Lenci and Benotto, 2012) and (Shwartz et al., 2016). (Mohammad et al., 2013) and (Santus et al., 2014) on antonymy are of relevance here. One key commonality amongst these were that these approaches targeted one semantic relationship discovery at once amongst the words rather multiple. There were pattern based multiclass classification task carried out by (Turney, 2008) on similarity, antonymy and analogy, and by (Pantel and Pennacchiotti, 2006) on generic pattern recognition and filtering. These approaches resulted in higher precision and lower recall compared to distributional-semantic-model-based methods due to their sole dependency on patterns. The later mentioned method has been explored in an unsupervised manner (Weeds and Weir, 2003); (Lenci and Benotto, 2012); (Santus et al., 2015) and didn't measure up in terms of efficacy. Thereafter supervised methods have been adopted (Kruszewski et al., 2015); (Roller and Erk, 2016); (Nguyen et al., 2016); (Shwartz et al., 2016) in the very same direction aiming for classifying the multiclass relationships better. Count-based vectors have been substituting the prediction based ones in some recent approaches, which apparently performed better in some task, such as similarity estimation (Baroni et al., 2014), even though (Levy et al., 2015) demonstrated that these improvements were most likely due to the optimization of hyper-parameters that were instead left unoptimized in count based models. (Shwartz et al., 2016) had an approach combining patterns and distributional information reflected promising parameters in hypernymy recognition.

2.2 Shared Task regarding Semantic Relations Identification

Several shared tasks has been emerged from the NLP related conferences in this decade and the following covers a brief survey on such tasks. Seven "encyclopedic" semantic relations between nouns (cause-effect, instrument-agency, product-producer, origin-entity, content-container, theme-tool, part-whole) were asked for exploration in the SemEval-2007 shared task 4 (Girju et al., 2007). The participants were allowed to use WordNet synsets on the sentences in which the noun pairs could be observed for this task. There were fifteen participants and the best one achieved 76.3% average accuracy. Entity-destination, component-whole, member-collection and message-topic relations were added for exploration along with the first five semantic relations of SemEval-2007 (Girju et al., 2007) shared task 4 in the SemEval-2010 shared task 8 (Hendrickx et al., 2009). Given a sentence and two tagged nominals, the task was to predict the relation between those nominals and its direction towards which these nominals were pointing to the relationships. Twenty-eight participants explored this with the freedom of using semantic, syntactic and morphological resources and the best system produced 82% accuracy. SemEval-2015 (Bordea et al., 2015) and SemEval-2016 (Bordea et al., 2016) were the initiative to find participation and exploration on taxonomy generation through a specific lexical semantic relation identification of hypernymy (and its inverse, hyponymy). A list of domain terms were provided as the test data and formation of taxonomy (a list of pairs: [term, hypernym]) is asked with possible addition of intermediate terms when needed. The participating systems experimented using dictionary definitions, Wikipedia, knowledge bases, lexical patterns and vector space models. Related to this SemEval-2016 Task 14 (Jurgens and Pilehvar, 2016) asked participants to enrich WordNet taxonomy by augmenting new words to the existing synsets (thus combining detection of hypernyms with word sense disambiguation). The last CogALex shared task (CogALex V)[3] is different in terms of the relationship explorations

---

[3]https://sites.google.com/site/cogalex2016/

from the earlier mentioned shared tasks. CogALex V[3] asked for the detection of synonymy, antonymy, hypernymy, part-whole meronymy, and random or "semantically unrelated" relationships between word pairs. Unlike the above tasks, the CogALex-V[3] shared task forbade the use of any thesauri, knowledge bases, or semantic networks (particularly WordNet and ConceptNet), forcing the participating systems to rely on the merit of of the corpus data and their developing system. This CogALex shared task (CogALex VI)[2] has asked for finding synonymy, antonymy and hypernymy relationships amongst word pairs along with undetectable relations as random ones. This one also blocked the usage of of any thesauri, knowledge bases, or semantic networks (particularly WordNet and ConceptNet) so that the system merit should reflect its capability without augmented help. This shared task brought a variant of English only relationship mapping in the Subtask 1 and as well multilingual word mapping as in the Subtask 2.

3   System Description

The system first reads the training data and preprocess it to a structure consumable further in the process flow. We use BERT (Devlin et al., 2018) embeddings to represent each words. BERT adopts the transformer architecture to learn embeddings for words. Since each term can have one or more words, we use an LSTM layer to track the context of the terms. Each of the two terms is first sent into a BERT embedding layer providing the embeddings of the two terms. Afterword each embedding is individually sent into an LSTM layer. The output of the two LSTM layers are concatenated and sent to a convolutional layer. The output of the convolutional layer is then flattened and sent to dense layer and further into a softmax output layer of the model as final phase of training. System produced model trained on training data is used for predicting on test data.

Cross entropy loss has been chosen as the loss function for this solution and a softmax output layer is chosen since multiple semantic relationship classes have to be learnt and predicted.

Figure 1 shows the system architecture deployed for our experimentation.

3.1   Experimental Setup

This section specifies the system specific parameters chosen for experimentation in the model settings section and then the description of the data follows.

3.1.1   Model Settings:

In the deployed BERT (Devlin et al., 2018) model for this experiment, each word is represented by an embedding space of 768 dimensions. The embeddings of the two input terms are concatenated along the row to produce an output of dimension 2 times 768. Further on the concatenated output 2Dconvolution is applied with 9 filters, kernel size of 2 times 2, strides as 1 along each direction and the activation function is chosen as "relu". The output of the convolution layer is flattened and then passed through a dense layer with 256 nodes and then sent to the final output layer.The learning rate for the model is kept at 0.005 after tuning and the batch size for training is kept at 256. The above parameters were chosen after tuning on this experiment keeping in mind of overfitting and underfitting.

3.1.2   Data Description:

For the Subtask 1, an English training data set as well test data set has been provided (Santus et al, 2015), where each data set came in tab separated text file with each row having two words and corresponding relationships in abbreviations of "SYN" (synonymy), "ANT" (antonymy), "HYP" (hypernymy) and "RANDOM". Table 1 shows the distribution of relationship counts in the English dataset.

3.2   Results and Analysis

The participants of CogALex VI[2] were provided with a Python script for the evaluation. The system produced relationship labeled output file from the test data file and was tested with gold standard test file with respect to their precision, recall and F1 score. All these metrics were tested individually and as well as whole and Table 2 depicts them all.

Looking at these result from Table 2 we can see the system did an overall balanced job for synonymy category in terms of precision, recall and F1 score. Noticeably for the other two categories of relation-

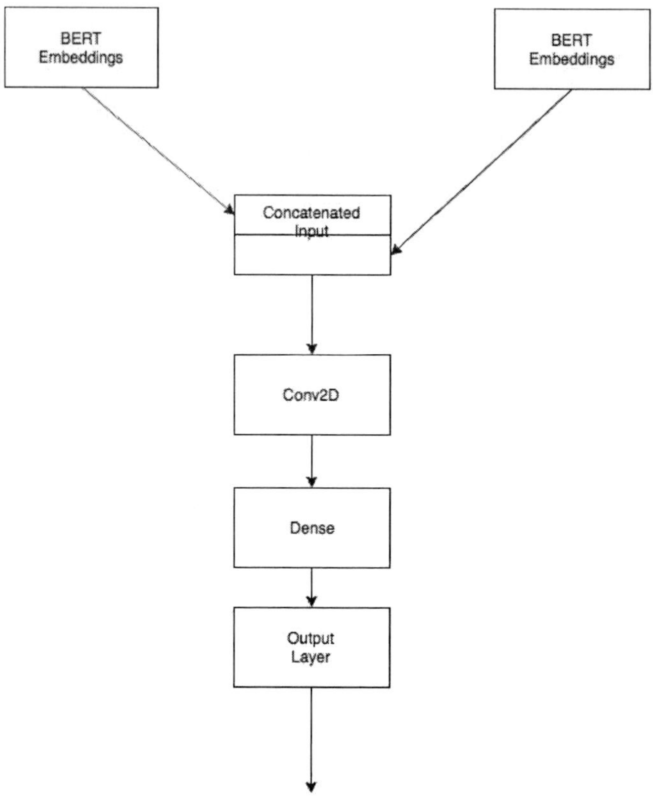

Figure 1: System (Model Training) Architecture

Relationship	Train(Count)	Test-Gold(Count)
SYN	842	266
ANT	916	306
HYP	898	279
RANDOM	2554	887
Total	5210	1738

Table 1: Relationship Distribution of English Data

ships (antonymy and hypernymy) the system had higher precision but lower recall while Table 1 reflects that the support for these two types were higher than synonymy in both the training and gold test set. These numbers reflect that the system does not detect the antonymy and hypernymy as greatly as compared to the synonymy ones. That being said, it has been noticed that for antonymy and hypernymy it doesn't mis-classify as much through false positives. As the system is based on bidirectional transformer model BERT (Devlin et al., 2018), so maybe with BERT embeddings it finds higher support for synonymous words compared to the other two types but whenever it founds any such it grasps well.

The system output shows highest recall for synonyms while the lowest for the hypernyms, whereas the highest precision shows up for antonyms and lowest for synonyms.

We looked into the system-produced relationships with the gold-test-set data for tallying and analysing some error spectrum. For example the implemented system correctly related the word "fiscal" with "commercial" as hypernym and "non financial" as antonym, but it produced synonymy relationship with the word "financial" in place of hypernymy: I believe such intricate examples are pointers for further deep diving. Another example to mention is the relationship between the words "elephant" and "goliath": our

Relationship	Precision	Recall	F1 Score
SYN	0.472	0.417	0.443
ANT	0.654	0.402	0.498
HYP	0.548	0.244	0.337
Overall	0.563	0.355	0.428

Table 2: Precision, Recall and F1 Score for Subtask 1

implemented approach couldn't find any specific kind of relationship and marked as random while in actual it is synonymy. In this last example the word "goliath" is quite of rare use and as our system was primarily depended on the BERT embeddings, therefore the support might have been very less or null in terms of the embedding: this calls for learning using further balanced and rich resources for reference.

4   Conclusion

The current BERT based system demonstrates here a prominent approach for recognizing semantical classes between word pairs. This approach has been applied to the Shared task proposed by CogALex VI[2] on their Subtask 1 for English data to identify synonymy, antonymy, hypernymy or random semantic relationship amongst provided words. These relationships are paradigmatic ones and quite hard for discovering them together. The approach employed here through bidirectional transformer based deep learning network BERT handles this task quite well and produce reasonable precision and recall for each category.

Looking at the difference between the evaluation parameters observed amongst the relationship classes on testing it seems like a thorough investigation should be guided further for better outcomes. To improve the outcomes, introducing variability in deep learning models as well as tuning inside of the model could well have potential. Some specific example based error analysis showed there is ample scope of improvement in the identification of closely related word relationships as well relationship prediction for rarely used words. The exploration of the multiclass semantic relationship mappings could be further interesting if the classes for the experimentation are closely connected ones and many in numbers. Different distributional training data should be exploited further to train model for evaluating the efficacy of such models on predicting such semantic relationships.

References

Marco Baroni, Georgiana Dinu, and Germán Kruszewski. 2014. Don't count, predict! A systematic comparison of context-counting vs. context-predicting semantic vectors. In *Proceedings of the 52nd Annual Meeting of the Association for Computational Linguistics (Volume 1: Long Papers)*, pages 238–247, Baltimore, Maryland. Association for Computational Linguistics.

Georgeta Bordea, Paul Buitelaar, Stefano Faralli, and Roberto Navigli. 2015. SemEval-2015 Task 17: Taxonomy Extraction Evaluation (TExEval). In *Proceedings of the 9th International Workshop on Semantic Evaluation (SemEval 2015)*, pages 902–910, Denver, Colorado. Association for Computational Linguistics.

Georgeta Bordea, Els Lefever, and Paul Buitelaar. 2016. SemEval-2016 Task 13: Taxonomy Extraction Evaluation (TExEval-2). In *Proceedings of the 10th International Workshop on Semantic Evaluation (SemEval-2016)*, pages 1081–1091, San Diego, California. Association for Computational Linguistics.

Ido Dagan, Dan Roth, Mark Sammons, and Fabio Massimo Zanzotto. 2013. Recognizing Textual Entailment: Models and Applications. *Synthesis Lectures on Human Language Technologies*, 6(4):1–220, July.

Jacob Devlin, Ming-Wei Chang, Kenton Lee, and Kristina Toutanova. 2018. BERT: pre-training of deep bidirectional transformers for language understanding. *CoRR*, abs/1810.04805.

Christiane Fellbaum, editor. 1998. *WordNet: an electronic lexical database*. Language, speech, and communication. MIT Press, Cambridge, Mass.

Roxana Girju, Preslav Nakov, Vivi Nastase, Stan Szpakowicz, Peter Turney, and Deniz Yuret. 2007. SemEval-2007 task 04: classification of semantic relations between nominals. In *Proceedings of the 4th International*

Workshop on Semantic Evaluations - SemEval '07, pages 13–18, Prague, Czech Republic. Association for Computational Linguistics.

Gregory Grefenstette. 1994. *Explorations in Automatic Thesaurus Discovery*. Springer US, Boston, MA.

Iris Hendrickx, Su Nam Kim, Zornitsa Kozareva, Preslav Nakov, Diarmuid Ó Séaghdha, Sebastian Padó, Marco Pennacchiotti, Lorenza Romano, and Stan Szpakowicz. 2009. SemEval-2010 task 8: multi-way classification of semantic relations between pairs of nominals. In *Proceedings of the Workshop on Semantic Evaluations: Recent Achievements and Future Directions - DEW '09*, page 94, Boulder, Colorado. Association for Computational Linguistics.

David Jurgens and Mohammad Taher Pilehvar. 2016. SemEval-2016 Task 14: Semantic Taxonomy Enrichment. In *Proceedings of the 10th International Workshop on Semantic Evaluation (SemEval-2016)*, pages 1092–1102, San Diego, California. Association for Computational Linguistics.

German Kruszewski, Denis Paperno, and Marco Baroni. 2015. Deriving Boolean structures from distributional vectors. *Transactions of the Association for Computational Linguistics*, 3:375–388, December.

Alessandro Lenci and Giulia Benotto. 2012. Identifying hypernyms in distributional semantic spaces. In *Proceedings of the First Joint Conference on Lexical and Computational Semantics-Volume 1: Proceedings of the main conference and the shared task, and Volume 2: Proceedings of the Sixth International Workshop on Semantic Evaluation*, pages 75–79.

Omer Levy, Steffen Remus, Chris Biemann, and Ido Dagan. 2015. Do Supervised Distributional Methods Really Learn Lexical Inference Relations? In *Proceedings of the 2015 Conference of the North American Chapter of the Association for Computational Linguistics: Human Language Technologies*, pages 970–976, Denver, Colorado. Association for Computational Linguistics.

Nitin Madnani and Bonnie J. Dorr. 2010. Generating Phrasal and Sentential Paraphrases: A Survey of Data-Driven Methods. *Computational Linguistics*, 36(3):341–387, September.

Pascual Martínez-Gómez, Koji Mineshima, Yusuke Miyao, and Daisuke Bekki. 2016. ccg2lambda: A Compositional Semantics System. In *Proceedings of ACL-2016 System Demonstrations*, pages 85–90, Berlin, Germany. Association for Computational Linguistics.

Saif M. Mohammad, Bonnie J. Dorr, Graeme Hirst, and Peter D. Turney. 2013. Computing lexical contrast. volume 39, page 555–590.

Kim Anh Nguyen, Sabine Schulte im Walde, and Ngoc Thang Vu. 2016. Integrating Distributional Lexical Contrast into Word Embeddings for Antonym-Synonym Distinction. In *Proceedings of the 54th Annual Meeting of the Association for Computational Linguistics (Volume 2: Short Papers)*, pages 454–459, Berlin, Germany. Association for Computational Linguistics.

Patrick Pantel and Marco Pennacchiotti. 2006. Espresso: leveraging generic patterns for automatically harvesting semantic relations. In *Proceedings of the 21st International Conference on Computational Linguistics and the 44th annual meeting of the ACL - ACL '06*, pages 113–120, Sydney, Australia. Association for Computational Linguistics.

Bianca Pereira, Cecile Robin, Tobias Daudert, John P. McCrae, Pranab Mohanty, and Paul Buitelaar. 2019. Taxonomy extraction for customer service knowledge base construction. In Maribel Acosta, Philippe Cudré-Mauroux, Maria Maleshkova, Tassilo Pellegrini, Harald Sack, and York Sure-Vetter, editors, *Semantic Systems. The Power of AI and Knowledge Graphs*, pages 175–190, Cham. Springer International Publishing.

Stephen Roller and Katrin Erk. 2016. Relations such as Hypernymy: Identifying and Exploiting Hearst Patterns in Distributional Vectors for Lexical Entailment. In *Proceedings of the 2016 Conference on Empirical Methods in Natural Language Processing*, pages 2163–2172, Austin, Texas. Association for Computational Linguistics.

Enrico Santus, Qin Lu, Alessandro Lenci, and Chu-Ren Huang. 2014. Unsupervised antonym-synonym discrimination in vector space. In *Atti della Conferenza di Linguistica Computazionale Italiana*.

Enrico Santus, Frances Yung, Alessandro Lenci, and Chu-Ren Huang. 2015. EVALution 1.0: an Evolving Semantic Dataset for Training and Evaluation of Distributional Semantic Models. In *Proceedings of the 4th Workshop on Linked Data in Linguistics: Resources and Applications*, pages 64–69, Beijing, China. Association for Computational Linguistics.

Vered Shwartz, Yoav Goldberg, and Ido Dagan. 2016. Improving Hypernymy Detection with an Integrated Path-based and Distributional Method. In *Proceedings of the 54th Annual Meeting of the Association for Computational Linguistics (Volume 1: Long Papers)*, pages 2389–2398, Berlin, Germany. Association for Computational Linguistics.

Peter D. Turney. 2008. A uniform approach to analogies, synonyms, antonyms, and associations. In *Proceedings of the 22Nd International Conference on Computational Linguistics - Volume 1*, COLING '08, pages 905–912, Stroudsburg, PA, USA. Association for Computational Linguistics.

Julie Weeds and David Weir. 2003. A general framework for distributional similarity. In *Proceedings of the 2003 conference on Empirical methods in natural language processing -*, volume 10, pages 81–88, Not Known. Association for Computational Linguistics.

A. Zouaq and R. Nkambou. 2008. Building Domain Ontologies from Text for Educational Purposes. *IEEE Transactions on Learning Technologies*, 1(1):49–62, January.

Leveraging Contextual Embeddings and Idiom Principle for Detecting Idiomaticity in Potentially Idiomatic Expressions*

Reyhaneh Hashempour
University of Essex
rh18456@essex.ac.uk

Aline Villavicencio
The University of Sheffield
a.villavicencio@sheffield.ac.uk

Abstract

The majority of studies on detecting idiomatic expressions have focused on discovering potentially idiomatic expressions overlooking the context. However, many idioms like ***blow the whistle*** could be interpreted idiomatically or literally depending on the context. In this work, we leverage the Idiom Principle (Sinclair et al., 1991) and contextualized word embeddings (CWEs), focusing on Context2Vec (Melamud et al., 2016) and BERT (Devlin et al., 2019) to distinguish between literal and idiomatic senses of such expressions in context. We also experiment with a non-contextualized word embedding baseline, in this case Word2Vec (Mikolov et al., 2013) and compare its performance with that of CWEs. The results show that CWEs outperform the non-CWEs, especially when the Idiom Principle is applied, as it improves the results by 6%. We further show that the Context2Vec model, trained based on Idiom Principle, can place potentially idiomatic expressions into distinct 'sense' (idiomatic/literal) regions of the embedding space, whereas Word2Vec and BERT seem to lack this capacity. The model is also capable of producing suitable substitutes for ambiguous expressions in context which is promising for downstream tasks like text simplification.

1 Introduction

The task of determining whether a sequence of words (a Multiword Expression - MWE) is idiomatic has received lots of attention (Fazly and Stevenson, 2006; Cook et al., 2007). Especially for MWE type idiomaticity identification (Constant et al., 2017), where the goal is to decide if an MWE can be idiomatic regardless of context, high agreement with human judgments has been achieved, for instance, for compound nouns (Reddy et al., 2011; Cordeiro et al., 2016). However, as this task does not take context into account, these techniques have limited success in the case of ambiguous MWEs where the same expression can be literal or idiomatic depending on a particular context. For example, such models would always classify ***hit the road*** as idiomatic (or conversely always as literal) while the expression could be idiomatic in one context and literal in another. As a consequence, for practical NLP tasks, especially Machine Translation and Information Retrieval, token idiomaticity identification is needed, with the classification of a potential idioms as literal (or idiomatic) in context. For example, ***hit the road*** must be translated differently in "The bullets were ***hitting the road*** and I could see them coming towards me a lot faster than I was able to reverse", and "The Ulster Society are about to ***hit the road*** on one of their magical history tours" (Burnard, 2000).

We argue that successful classification of potentially idiomatic expressions as idiomatic/literal is not possible without taking the context into account. Recently introduced Contextualized Word Embeddings (CWEs) are ideal for this task as they can provide different embeddings for each instance of the same word type. CWEs such as Context2Vec (Melamud et al., 2016) and BERT (Devlin et al., 2019) proved successful in the task of Word Sense Disambiguation (WSD) (Huang et al., 2019; Hadiwinoto et al., 2019). We also argue that disambiguation of potentially idiomatic expressions is analogous to WSD in a sense that it also tries to assign the most appropriate sense to an idiom, i.e. literal, or idiomatic depending on its respective context.

Proceedings of the Workshop on Cognitive Aspects of the Lexicon, pages 72–80
Barcelona, Spain (Online), December 12, 2020

Moreover, we hypothesize that in order to fully exploit the capacity of CWEs, an idiom should be treated as a single token both in training and testing. This hypothesis is inspired by the evidence from psycholinguistic studies which support the idea that the idiomatic expressions are stored and retrieved as a whole from memory at the time of use (Siyanova-Chanturia and Martinez, 2014). It is also rooted in the idea that different types of information are captured in vectors depending on the type of input, i.e. word, character, phrase to the model (Schick and Schütze, 2019). Moreover, this method proved successful in other tasks. For instance, Carpuat and Diab (2010) conducted a study for integrating MWEs in Statistical Machine Translation (SMT) and improved the BLEU score by treating MWEs as single tokens in training and testing.

Contribution: We show that CWEs can be utilized directly to detect idiomaticity in potentially idiomatic expressions due to their nature of providing distinct vectors for the same expression depending on its context. We also apply the Idiom Principle (Sinclair et al., 1991) when training the models which improves the results as expected and supports our hypothesis that an MWE should be treated as a single token both in training and testing the models. We further show that Context2Vec trained based on Idiom Principle is able to provide suitable replacement for MWEs in both the idiomatic and literal senses. To the best of our knowledge, this is the first attempt to integrate Idiom Principle into CWEs and directly use them for the task of identification idiomaticity in MWEs at the token level.

2   Related work

Distributional Semantic Models (DSM) are computational models based on the Distributional Hypothesis (Harris, 1954) and the idea that words occurring in similar contexts tend to have a similar meaning. Recently, two flavours of Distributional Models have been introduced and utilized which are known as contextualized and non-contextualized embedding models. The former produces different embeddings for a word depending on the context and the latter offers only one embedding for a word regardless of the context. Researchers have leveraged DSMs along with linguistic knowledge to deal with identifying MWEs at type (Cook et al., 2007; Cordeiro et al., 2016; Nandakumar et al., 2019) and token level (King and Cook, 2018; Rohanian et al., 2020).

For instance, the degree of linguistic fixedness was used as the basis for Fazly and Stevenson (2006) to apply an unsupervised method to distinguish between idiomatic and literal tokens of verb-noun combinations (VNCs). They argue that idiomatic VNCs come in fixed syntactic forms in terms of passivation, determiner, and noun pluralization. They extracted these forms using known idiomatic/literal VNC patterns and among all variations they determined which were the canonical form(s). Then they classified new tokens as idiomatic if they appeared in their canonical forms.

Cook et al. (2007) leveraged the idea of canonical forms and the Distributional Hypothesis and built co-occurrence vectors representing the idiomatic and literal meaning of each expression based on their context and (canonical) forms. The problem with this model is relying solely on the canonical form to label an expression as idiomatic/literal which is not enough as there are many MWEs, e.g. *kick the bucket* that can be in their canonical form and yet have a literal meaning depending on the context they appear in. Hence, each MWE should be disambiguated in its own individual context.

Cordeiro et al. (2016) also built their work based on Distributional Hypothesis and the Principle of Compositionality to classify MWEs as idiomatic/literal. Their idiomaticity identification model at the type level works well for MWEs that are either idiomatic or literal but falls short for idiomaticity identification at the token level when the MWE is ambiguous.

Nandakumar et al. (2019) used different types of contextualized and non-contextualized word embeddings from character-level to word-level models to investigate the capability of such models in detecting nuances of non-compositionality in MWEs. When evaluating the models, they considered the MWEs out of their context which is problematic especially in case of utilizing CWEs as the reason behind the success (Peters et al., 2018; Devlin et al., 2019; Akbik et al., 2019) of these models is in their ability to produce context-specific embeddings for each token.

The main drawback of above-mentioned works is that they do not take the context of each individual expression into account when classifying them. However, there have been some attempts to detect idiomaticity in MWEs in context (at token level) using Distributional Models.

Peng et al. (2015) exploited contextual information captured in word embeddings to automatically recognize idiomatic tokens. They calculate the inner product of the embeddings of the context words with the embedding of target expression. They argue that since the literal forms can predict the local context better, their inner product with context words is larger than that of idiomatic ones, hence they tell apart literals from idiomatic forms.

Salton et al. (2016) exploited Skip-Thought Vectors (Kiros et al., 2015) to represent the sentential context of an MWE and used SVM and K-Nearest Neighbours to classify MWEs as idiomatic or literal in their context. They compared their work against a topic model representation that include the full paragraph as the context and showed competitive results.

King and Cook (2018) proposed a model based on distributed representations, non-CWE to classify VNC usages as idiomatic/literal. First, they represented the context as the average embeddings of context words and trained a Support Vector Machines (SVM) classifier on top of that. They further showed that incorporating the information about the expressions canonical forms boosted the performance of their model.

A related task of metaphor token detection has seen successful results with the combination of CWEs and non-CWEs, along with linguistic features (Gao et al., 2018; Mao et al., 2019). For instance, Gao et al. (2018) used Word2Vec and ELMo (Peters et al., 2018) as embeddings, with a bidirectional LSTM to encode sentences, and a feed-forward neural network for classifying them as literal or metaphoric.

Rohanian et al. (2020) presented a neural model and BERT, to classify metaphorical verbs in their sentential context using information from the dependency parse tree and annotations for verbal MWEs. They showed that incorporating the knowledge of MWEs can enhance the performance of a metaphor classification model.

We follow the intuition that CWEs can be directly used for the task of token level identification of idiomaticity in MWEs due to their ability to produce different embeddings for the different tokens of the same MWE. Our work is also inspired by the Idiom Principle which explains how human distinguish idiomatic expressions.

3 Distributional Models and Idiom Principle

In this work, we use Word2Vec as non-CWEs and leverage the Context2Vec and BERT as CWEs in combination with the Idiom Principle to detect idiomaticity in potentially idiomatic expressions. The embedding models and Idiom Principle are briefly described here.

3.1 Word2Vec

For Word2Vec we use CBOW (Mikolov et al., 2013) which represents the context around a target word as a simple average of the embeddings of the context words in a window around it. For example, for the window size of two, two words before and two words after the target word are considered as the context of the target word whose embeddings are averaged to represent context embeddings. To train our Word2Vec model, we use Gensim (Řehůřek and Sojka, 2010) with window size of 5 and 300 dimensions. We ignore all words that occur less than fifteen times in the training corpus. We perform negative sampling and set the number of training epochs to five as in King and Cook (2018).

3.2 Context2Vec

Context2Vec (Melamud et al., 2016) uses a bidirectional LSTM recurrent neural network, where one LSTM is fed with with the sentence words from left to right, and the other from right to left. Then right-to-left and left-to-right context embeddings are concatenated and fed into a multi-layer perceptron to capture dependencies between the two sides of the context. We consider the output of this layer as the embedding of the entire joint sentential context around the target word. This is a better representation of the context compared to that of Word2Vec, as it takes the order of words into account. To train our Context2Vec model, we use the code provided by the authors[1] having the same configuration for the

---

[1] https://github.com/orenmel/context2vec

hyper-parameters.

3.3 BERT

Contrary to the Context2Vec, BERT (Devlin et al., 2019) does not rely on the merging of two unidirectional recurrent language models, but using the transformer (Vaswani et al., 2017) encoder, it reads the entire sequence of words at once. It also benefits from the next sentence prediction feature which helps capture more contextual information. To train our BERT model, we use BERT-Base keeping the configuration of the hyper-parameters intact.

3.4 Idiom Principle

The principle of idiom is that a language user has available to him or her a large number of semi-preconstructed phrases that constitute single choices, even though they might appear to be analyzable into segments (Sinclair et al., 1991). In other words, MWEs are treated as single tokens in mental lexicon when stored in or retrieved from memory. One of the highly cited definitions of MWEs is also supports the Idiom Principle; Wray (2002) defines MWEs as a sequence, continuous or discontinuous, of words or other elements, which is, or appears to be, prefabricated:that is, stored, retrieved whole from memory at the time of use, rather than being subject to generation or analysis by the language grammar.

Model	Idiomatic			Literal			Ave.F
	P	R	F	P	R	F	
Original Models							
Word2Vec	0.75	0.80	0.77	0.51	0.51	0.51	0.64
Context2Vec	0.76	0.78	0.77	0.62	0.61	0.61	0.70
BERT	0.80	0.81	0.80	0.60	0.61	0.60	**0.71**
Idiom-Principle-inspired							
Word2Vec	0.70	0.73	0.72	0.56	0.60	0.58	0.65
Context2Vec	0.80	0.82	0.81	0.71	0.72	0.71	**0.76**
BERT	0.77	0.79	0.78	0.66	0.63	0.64	0.71
King and Cook (2018)							
W2V-CF	0.82	0.88	0.83	0.63	0.54	0.56	0.69
W2V+CF	0.83	0.89	0.85	0.76	0.68	0.69	**0.77**

Table 1: Precision (P), recall (R), and F1 score (F), for the idiomatic and literal classes, as well as average F1 score (Ave.F) for the original and the Idiom-Principle-Inspired models. The results of King and Cook (2018) are also reported for comparison.

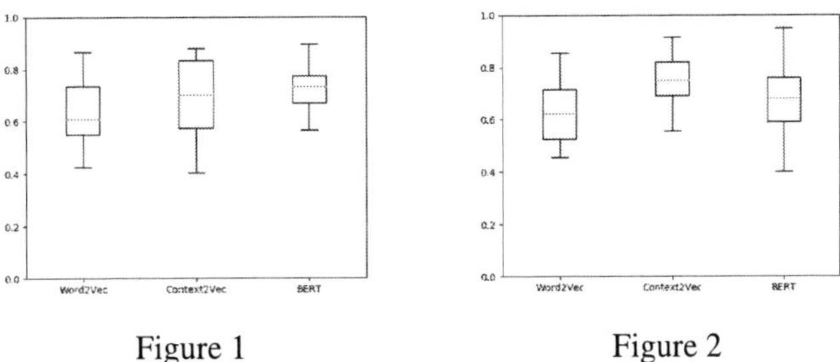

Figure 1   Figure 2

Table 2: Box plot for average F-score for the original (Figure 1) and Idiom-Principle-inspired (Figure 2) models.

4   Experimental Setup

To test the hypothesis, we build 6 different context representations using three embedding models: Word2Vec, Context2Vec and BERT in two different settings: 1- Their original models where each expression is not treated as a single token 2- Our own models, which we call Idiom-Principle-Inspired models, where each expression is treated as a single token.

For the first setting, we use the original pre-trained models, Word2Vec, Context2Vec and BERT-base-uncased. For the second setting, we use BNC corpus (Burnard, 2000) and first lemmatize it using spaCy (Honnibal and Johnson, 2015). Then, we tokenize it where each MWE is treated as a single token with an underline between the first and the second part (e.g. ***blow the whistle*** is mapped to ***blow_whistle***). Finally, we build three semantic spaces, using Word2Vec, Context2Vec, and BERT. Our goal is to determine the correct sense of an MWE in context, based on a manually tagged dataset, VNC (Cook et al., 2008). Following Melamud et al. (2016), we use the simple non-parametric version of the kNN classification algorithm (Cover and Hart, 1967) with k = 1 and for the distance measure, we rely on cosine distance of the vectors. As we do not do any extra training on the dataset, we divide it into evaluation and test sets. To classify a test MWE instance in context, we consider all the instances of the same MWE in the evaluation set and find the instance whose context embedding is the most similar to the context embedding of the test instance using the context-to-context similarity measure. Finally, we use the label of that instance as the correct label for the MWE in the test set. The rationale behind such a simple classification model is to make the comparison between the representations easy so that each model's success can be attributed directly to the input representations.

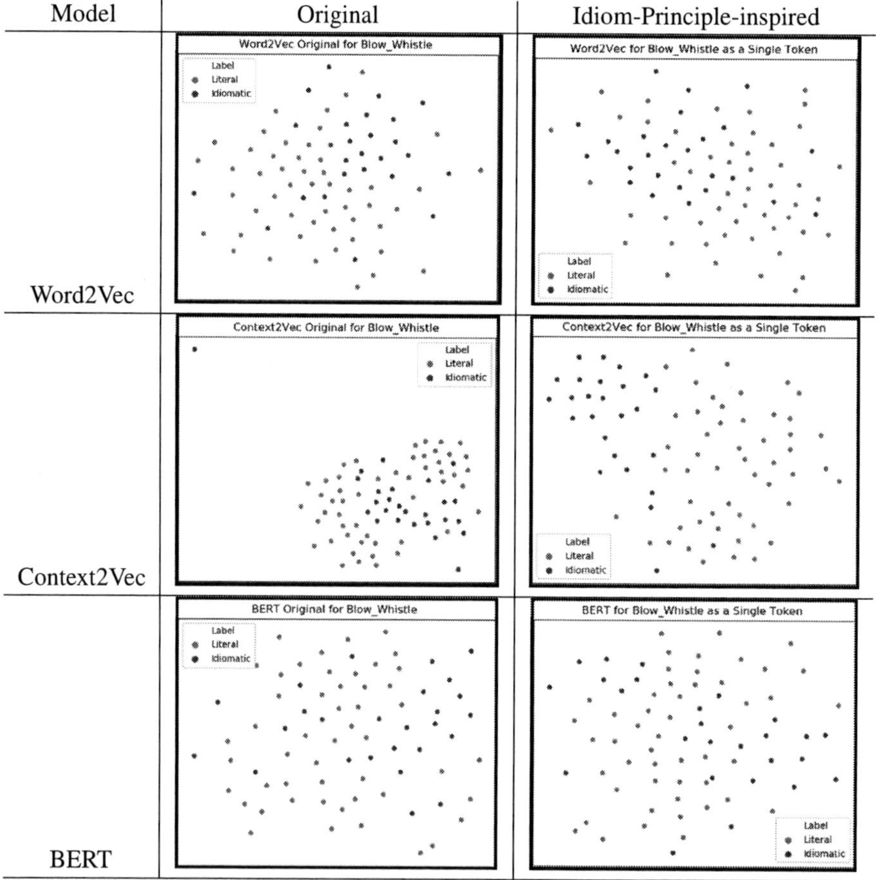

Table 3: t-SNE plots of different senses of 'blow the whistle' and their contextualized embeddings. The literal sense is in red and the idiomatic sense is in blue. Here, the VNC dataset is used.

5   Dataset and Evaluation

We use VNC-Tokens dataset (Cook et al., 2008) to evaluate our models. The dataset includes sentences containing Verb-Noun Combinations (VNC) tokens labelled as either idiomatic (I) / literal (L) (or "unknown"). For our experiments, we only use VNCs that are annotated as I or L as in King and Cook (2018). We evaluate the models using five-fold cross-validation and calculate the precision, recall, and F-score per each expression and then report the average scores as in King and Cook (2018), the results are reported per sense.

We also investigate to see how well different models encode information such as distinguishable senses in their vector space.

6   Experimental Results

In this section, we report the results of the first set of experiments where we create context representation using the original pre-trained models and then we present the results of the second set of experiments in which inspired by the Idiom Principle, we train our own models by treating each MWE as a single token. Then context embeddings are inferred using these trained models. Table 1 shows the results for the original pre-trained embeddings. As it can be seen the CWE, i.e. Context2Vec and BERT outperform the non-CWE, i.e. Word2Vec, up to 7% higher average F-score. In the next rows, Table 1 shows the results for Idiom Principle-inspired models along with those reported by King and Cook (2018). As it can be seen, the average F-score is the same for BERT and 1% higher for Word2Vec compared to the original models. However, both models achieved higher F-scores in detecting literal sense of MWEs. As for Context2Vec, the results improved by 6% on average and up to 10% in detecting literal sense of MWEs. We used an ANOVA test to check the statistical significance of the results of our models and found all our results to be significant at p <0.05.

We did not expect the results to improve for Word2Vec as it always conflates the senses so it will not be able to learn different embeddings for different senses no matter how MWEs are treated in pre-processing step. In regard to BERT, we cannot see the improvement observed for Context2Vec. We speculate this might be due to the models inability to provide quality embeddings for rare words (Schick and Schütze, 2019) as treating each MWE as a single token turns it into a rare word for which the models need to learn an embedding. We will be investigating this in our future work. Nevertheless, the improvement on the results are noticeable (even for BERT) as we used a much smaller corpus to train our models compared to those used by the original models. We used BNC which contains 100 million words whereas the original models were trained on the corpora of much bigger size, namely Google News dataset with 100 billion words for Word2Vec, ukWaC (Ferraresi et al., 2008) with 2 billion words for Context2Vec, and the entire Wikipedia with about 2,500 million words and a book corpus with 800 million words for BERT.

King and Cook (2018) reported 0.69 F-score for the same dataset and then they used extra feature, the expression being in its canonical form or not, and increased the F-score to 0.77. However, this method is limiting as it requires feature engineering while our model of Context2Vec is capable of producing on par results, 0.75, without any external knowledge and by only relying on the features extracted by the model itself. We also used much smaller corpus to train our model in comparison with what they used, which was a snapshot of Wikipedia from September 2015, consisting of approximately 2.6 billion tokens (King and Cook, 2018). Moreover, they did extra training on the dataset after extracting the embeddings from their model whereas we did not do any training on the dataset.

To see how robust the models are across different expressions, we created the box plot for the models using the average F-scores of the models per expression. This is illustrated in Figure 1 and Figure 2 of Table 2 which shows the most robust model is BERT in the first setting and Context2Vec in the second setting. The robustness of a model is important as we do not want a model to work well for one MWE and poor for the other.

We are also curious to see whether the models are capable of placing different senses of an expression in different segments of their semantic space. For this, we use t-SNE (van der Maaten and Hinton, 2008) to map these high-dimensional spaces into two dimensional spaces. Table 3 shows t-SNE plots of two different senses of the expression ***blow the whistle*** in the VNC dataset encoded by the six different models in two settings: Original and Idiom-Principle-inspired.

As you can see, the Word2Vec and BERT embeddings hardly allow to distinguish any clusters as the senses are scattered across the entire plot, both in the original and Idiom-Principle-inspired settings. However, in Context2Vec embedding space, senses are placed in clearly separable clusters especially in the Idiom-Principle-inspired setting. This made us dig deeper into the Context2Vec model and probe its level of understanding through a lexical substitution task. In the lexical substitution task, the goal is to find a substitute word for a given target word in sentential context. To do so, we remove the MWE from a sentence and then get the embeddings of the remaining sentence which is in fact the context of the MWE. Then we find the embeddings of which words have the highest cosine similarity with the embeddings of the context. Table 4 shows the list of lexical substitutes proposed by the model for three MWEs per their literal/idiomatic senses. As you can see the model seems to be able to distinguish well between literal and idiomatic senses as it suggest suitable substitute for the removed MWE. The sentences are listed in Table 5.

MWE	Sense	Sentence #	Proposed Substitute
Kick heel	I	1	**wait**, stay, stop
	L	2	**Clap**, barefoot, **kick**
Hit road	I	3	go, **start, embark**
	L	4	**smash**, drop, shoot

Table 4: The lexical substitutes proposed by Context2Vec to replace MWEs in their literal or idiomatic senses.

Sentence #	Sentence
1	The man won't step foot outside his castle without myself as escort so I have to *[kick my heels]* until his business with Queen Matilda is done
2	I could see I was going to get warmer still because the bullock was beginning to enjoy the game *[kicking up his heels]* and frisking around after each attempt
3	The Ulster Society are about to *[hit the road]* on one of their magical history tours
4	The bullets were *[hitting the road]* and I could see them coming towards me a lot faster than I was able to reverse.

Table 5: List of sentences that are referred to in Table 4 by their number.

7   Conclusion and Future Work

In this work, we used Contextualized Word Embeddings (CWE), i.e. Context2Vec and BERT to include contextual information for distinguishing between the idiomatic and literal senses of an idiom in context. Moreover, inspired by the Idiom Principle, we hypothesized that to fully exploit the capacity of CWE, an idiom should be treated as a single token both in training and testing; The results showed that by applying Idiom Principle to CWE, especially Context2Vec, we can build a model to distinguish between literal and idiomatic senses of a potentially idiomatic expression in context. Through dimensionality reduction and lexical substitution, we further showed that Context2Vec is capable of placing literal and idiomatic senses in distinct regions of semantic space; Besides, the model has a good level of understating of the meaning as it suggests suitable replacement for both literal and idiomatic senses of set of MWEs. In our future work, we are interested in improving the results for BERT. We also would like to train the Idiom-Principle-inspired models on a bigger corpus to investigate how the results compare to what were achieved here.

References

Alan Akbik, Tanja Bergmann, Duncan Blythe, Kashif Rasul, Stefan Schweter, and Roland Vollgraf. 2019. FLAIR: An easy-to-use framework for state-of-the-art NLP. In *Proceedings of the 2019 Conference of the North American Chapter of the Association for Computational Linguistics (Demonstrations)*, pages 54–59, Minneapolis, Minnesota. Association for Computational Linguistics.

Lou Burnard. 2000. The British National Corpus Users Reference Guide. Library Catalog: www.natcorp.ox.ac.uk.

Marine Carpuat and Mona Diab. 2010. Task-based evaluation of multiword expressions: a pilot study in statistical machine translation. In *Human Language Technologies: The 2010 Annual Conference of the North American Chapter of the Association for Computational Linguistics*, pages 242–245, Los Angeles, California. Association for Computational Linguistics.

Mathieu Constant, Gülşen Eryiğit, Johanna Monti, Lonneke van der Plas, Carlos Ramisch, Michael Rosner, and Amalia Todirascu. 2017. Multiword expression processing: A survey. *Computational Linguistics*, 43(4):837–892.

Paul Cook, Afsaneh Fazly, and Suzanne Stevenson. 2007. Pulling their weight: exploiting syntactic forms for the automatic identification of idiomatic expressions in context. In *Proceedings of the Workshop on a Broader Perspective on Multiword Expressions - MWE '07*, pages 41–48, Prague, Czech Republic. Association for Computational Linguistics.

Paul Cook, Afsaneh Fazly, and Suzanne Stevenson. 2008. The VNC-tokens dataset. In *Proceedings of the LREC Workshop Towards a Shared Task for Multiword Expressions (MWE 2008)*, pages 19–22.

Silvio Cordeiro, Carlos Ramisch, Marco Idiart, and Aline Villavicencio. 2016. Predicting the compositionality of nominal compounds: Giving word embeddings a hard time. In *Proceedings of the 54th Annual Meeting of the Association for Computational Linguistics (Volume 1: Long Papers)*, pages 1986–1997, Berlin, Germany. Association for Computational Linguistics.

T. Cover and P. Hart. 1967. Nearest neighbor pattern classification. *IEEE Transactions on Information Theory*, 13(1):21–27.

Jacob Devlin, Ming-Wei Chang, Kenton Lee, and Kristina Toutanova. 2019. BERT. In *Proceedings of the 2019 Conference of the North*, pages 4171–4186, Minneapolis, Minnesota. Association for Computational Linguistics.

Afsaneh Fazly and Suzanne Stevenson. 2006. Automatically Constructing a Lexicon of Verb Phrase Idiomatic Combinations. page 9.

Adriano Ferraresi, Eros Zanchetta, Marco Baroni, and Silvia Bernardini. 2008. Introducing and evaluating ukwac , a very large web-derived corpus of english.

Ge Gao, Eunsol Choi, Yejin Choi, and Luke Zettlemoyer. 2018. Neural metaphor detection in context. In *Proceedings of the 2018 Conference on Empirical Methods in Natural Language Processing*, pages 607–613, Brussels, Belgium. Association for Computational Linguistics.

Christian Hadiwinoto, Hwee Tou Ng, and Wee Chung Gan. 2019. Improved word sense disambiguation using pre-trained contextualized word representations. In *Proceedings of the 2019 Conference on Empirical Methods in Natural Language Processing and the 9th International Joint Conference on Natural Language Processing (EMNLP-IJCNLP)*, pages 5297–5306, Hong Kong, China. Association for Computational Linguistics.

Zellig S. Harris. 1954. Distributional Structure. *WORD*, 10(2-3):146–162.

Matthew Honnibal and Mark Johnson. 2015. An improved non-monotonic transition system for dependency parsing. In *Proceedings of the 2015 Conference on Empirical Methods in Natural Language Processing*, pages 1373–1378, Lisbon, Portugal. Association for Computational Linguistics.

Luyao Huang, Chi Sun, Xipeng Qiu, and Xuanjing Huang. 2019. GlossBERT: BERT for word sense disambiguation with gloss knowledge. In *Proceedings of the 2019 Conference on Empirical Methods in Natural Language Processing and the 9th International Joint Conference on Natural Language Processing (EMNLP-IJCNLP)*, pages 3509–3514, Hong Kong, China. Association for Computational Linguistics.

Milton King and Paul Cook. 2018. https://doi.org/10.18653/v1/P18-2055 Leveraging distributed representations and lexico-syntactic fixedness for token-level prediction of the idiomaticity of English verb-noun combinations. In *Proceedings of the 56th Annual Meeting of the Association for Computational Linguistics (Volume 2: Short Papers)*, pages 345–350, Melbourne, Australia. Association for Computational Linguistics.

Ryan Kiros, Yukun Zhu, Ruslan Salakhutdinov, Richard S. Zemel, Raquel Urtasun, Antonio Torralba, and Sanja Fidler. 2015. Skip-thought vectors. *ArXiv*, abs/1506.06726.

Laurens van der Maaten and Geoffrey Hinton. 2008. Visualizing data using t-SNE. *Journal of Machine Learning Research*, 9:2579–2605.

Rui Mao, Chenghua Lin, and Frank Guerin. 2019. End-to-end sequential metaphor identification inspired by linguistic theories. In *Proceedings of the 57th Annual Meeting of the Association for Computational Linguistics*, pages 3888–3898, Florence, Italy. Association for Computational Linguistics.

Oren Melamud, Jacob Goldberger, and Ido Dagan. 2016. context2vec: Learning Generic Context Embedding with Bidirectional LSTM. In *Proceedings of The 20th SIGNLL Conference on Computational Natural Language Learning*, pages 51–61, Berlin, Germany. Association for Computational Linguistics.

Tomas Mikolov, Kai Chen, Greg Corrado, and Jeffrey Dean. 2013. Efficient Estimation of Word Representations in Vector Space. *arXiv:1301.3781 [cs]*. ArXiv: 1301.3781.

Navnita Nandakumar, Timothy Baldwin, and Bahar Salehi. 2019. How well do embedding models capture non-compositionality? a view from multiword expressions. In *Proceedings of the 3rd Workshop on Evaluating Vector Space Representations for NLP*, pages 27–34, Minneapolis, USA. Association for Computational Linguistics.

Jing Peng, Anna Feldman, and Hamza Jazmati. 2015. Classifying idiomatic and literal expressions using vector space representations. In *Proceedings of the International Conference Recent Advances in Natural Language Processing*, pages 507–511.

Matthew Peters, Mark Neumann, Mohit Iyyer, Matt Gardner, Christopher Clark, Kenton Lee, and Luke Zettlemoyer. 2018. Deep contextualized word representations. In *Proceedings of the 2018 Conference of the North American Chapter of the Association for Computational Linguistics: Human Language Technologies, Volume 1 (Long Papers)*, pages 2227–2237, New Orleans, Louisiana. Association for Computational Linguistics.

Siva Reddy, Diana McCarthy, and Suresh Manandhar. 2011. An empirical study on compositionality in compound nouns. In *Proceedings of 5th International Joint Conference on Natural Language Processing*, pages 210–218, Chiang Mai, Thailand. Asian Federation of Natural Language Processing.

Radim Řehůřek and Petr Sojka. 2010. Software Framework for Topic Modelling with Large Corpora. In *Proceedings of the LREC 2010 Workshop on New Challenges for NLP Frameworks*, pages 45–50, Valletta, Malta. ELRA.

Omid Rohanian, Marek Rei, Shiva Taslimipoor, and Le An Ha. 2020. Verbal multiword expressions for identification of metaphor. In *Proceedings of the 58th Annual Meeting of the Association for Computational Linguistics*, pages 2890–2895, Online. Association for Computational Linguistics.

Giancarlo Salton, Robert Ross, and John Kelleher. 2016. Idiom token classification using sentential distributed semantics. In *Proceedings of the 54th Annual Meeting of the Association for Computational Linguistics (Volume 1: Long Papers)*, pages 194–204, Berlin, Germany. Association for Computational Linguistics.

Timo Schick and Hinrich Schütze. 2019. Rare Words: A Major Problem for Contextualized Embeddings And How to Fix it by Attentive Mimicking. *arXiv:1904.06707 [cs]*. ArXiv: 1904.06707.

J. Sinclair, L. Sinclair, and R. Carter. 1991. *Corpus, Concordance, Collocation*. Describing English language. Oxford University Press.

Anna Siyanova-Chanturia and Ron Martinez. 2014. The Idiom Principle Revisited. *Applied Linguistics*, page amt054.

Ashish Vaswani, Noam Shazeer, Niki Parmar, Jakob Uszkoreit, Llion Jones, Aidan N Gomez, Ł ukasz Kaiser, and Illia Polosukhin. 2017. Attention is all you need. In I. Guyon, U. V. Luxburg, S. Bengio, H. Wallach, R. Fergus, S. Vishwanathan, and R. Garnett, editors, *Advances in Neural Information Processing Systems 30*, pages 5998–6008. Curran Associates, Inc.

A. Wray. 2002. https://books.google.sc/books?id=h2kpuAAACAAJ *Formulaic Language and the Lexicon*. Cambridge University Press.

Definition Extraction Feature Analysis:
From Canonical to Naturally-Occurring Definitions

Mireia Roig Mirapeix   **Luis Espinosa-Anke**   **Jose Camacho-Collados**
School of Computer Science and Informatics
Cardiff University, United Kingdom
`{roigmirapeixm,espinosa-ankel,camachocolladosj}@cardiff.ac.uk`

Abstract

Textual definitions constitute a fundamental source of knowledge when seeking the meaning of words, and they are the cornerstone of lexical resources like glossaries, dictionaries, encyclopedia or thesauri. In this paper, we present an in-depth analytical study on the main features relevant to the task of definition extraction. Our main goal is to study whether linguistic structures from canonical (the Aristotelian or *genus et differentia* model) can be leveraged to retrieve definitions from corpora in different domains of knowledge and textual genres alike. To this end, we develop a simple linear classifier and analyze the contribution of several (sets of) linguistic features. Finally, as a result of our experiments, we also shed light on the particularities of existing benchmarks as well as the most challenging aspects of the task.

1   Introduction

Definition Extraction (DE) is the task to extract textual definitions from naturally occurring texts (Navigli and Velardi, 2010). The development of models able to identify definitions in freely occurring text has many applications such as the automatic generation of dictionaries, thesauri and glossaries, as well as e-learning materials and lexical taxonomies (Westerhout, 2009; Del Gaudio et al., 2014; Jurgens and Pilehvar, 2015; Espinosa-Anke et al., 2016). Moreover, definitional knowledge has proven to be a useful signal for improving language models in downstream NLP tasks (Joshi et al., 2020). The task of DE is currently approached almost unanimously as a supervised classification problem, and the latest methods have demonstrated an outstanding performance, to the point of reducing the error rate to less than 2% in some datasets (Veyseh et al., 2019). However, the high performance of these models could be mainly due to artifacts in the data, and thus they may not generalize to different domains.

The main aim of this paper is to analyze to what extent is possible to learn a universal definition extraction system from canonical definitions, and to understand the core differences that currently exist in standard evaluation testbeds. In particular, we propose experiments where we develop a machine learning model able to distinguish definitions with high accuracy in a corpus of canonical definitions, and later evaluate such model in different (pertaining to different domains and genres) datasets. Our evaluation datasets are two, namely: the Word-Class Lattices (WCL) dataset from Navigli et al. (2010), and DEFT, from the SemEval 2020 Task 6 - Subtask 1 (Spala et al., 2019). The former provides an annotated set of definitions and non-definitions with syntactic patterns similar to those of definition sentences from Wikipedia (what the authors call *syntactically plausible false definitions*). The latter presents a robust English corpus that explores the less straightforward cases of term-definition structures in free and semi-structured text from different domains (i.e., biology, history and government), and which is not limited to well-defined, structured, and narrow conditions.

We include a detailed descriptive analysis of both corpora that identifies similarities and differences between definitions and non-definitions, later used for feature selection and analysis. We come to conclusions regarding the discriminative power of certain linguistic features. Interestingly, these features alone

Proceedings of the Workshop on Cognitive Aspects of the Lexicon, pages 81–91
Barcelona, Spain (Online), December 12, 2020

do not have a strong effect on the results, but, the combining feature sets of different nature can improve performance, even in target corpora having heterogeneous domains and non-canonical definitions.

To train and first evaluate the model, we use the annotated WCL dataset. This dataset contains sentences from a sample of the WCL corpus that includes both definitions and non-definitions with syntactic patterns very similar to those found in definitions (e.g. "Snowcap is unmistakable"). The syntactic patterns are simple and represent what we could refer to as canonical definitions. We will test the performance of a model trained on this dataset, and evaluate on the DEFT dataset, which contains a set of definitions and non-definitions from various topics such as biology, history and government.

2 Related Work

Over the last years, DE has received notorious attention for its applications in Natural Language Processing, Computational Linguistics and Computational Lexicography (Espinosa-Anke and Saggion, 2014), as it has been proven to be applicable to glossary generation (Muresan and Klavans, 2002; Park et al., 2002), terminological databases (Nakamura and Nagao, 1988) or question answering systems (Saggion and Gaizauskas, 2004; Cui et al., 2005), among many others.

Research on DE has seen contributions where the task is typically proposed as a binary classification problem (whether a sentence is a definition or not), although with exceptions (Jin et al., 2013). DE has also been studied in languages other than English, e.g., Slavic languages (Przepiórkowski et al., 2007), Spanish (Sierra et al., 2008) or Portuguese (Del Gaudio et al., 2014). Many of these approaches use symbolic methods depending on manually crafted or semi-automatically learned lexico-syntactic patterns (Hovy et al., 2003; Westerhout and Monachesi, 2007) such as 'refers to' or 'is a'.

A notable contribution to DE is the Word Class Lattices model (Navigli and Velardi, 2010), which explores DE on the WCL dataset, a set of encyclopedic definitions and distractors, and which we use in this paper. In a subsequent contribution, Espinosa-Anke and Saggion (2014) present a supervised approach in which only syntactic features derived from dependency relations are used, and whose results are reported higher to the WCL method. For identifying definitions with higher linguistic variability, a weakly supervised approach is presented in Espinosa-Anke et al. (2015). And finally, models based on neural networks have been leveraged for exploiting both long and short-range dependencies, either combining CNNs and LSTMS (Espinosa-Anke and Schockaert, 2018) or BERT (Veyseh et al., 2019), and which are currently the highest performing models on WCL.

3 Data

In this section we present the datasets utilized for our analysis, namely WCL (Section 3.1) and DEFT (Section 3.2), and provide a descriptive analysis comparing both datasets (Section 3.3).

3.1 WCL dataset

The WCL dataset (Navigli et al., 2010) contains 1,772 definitions and 2,847 non-definitions. Each instance is extracted from Wikipedia, and definitions follow a canonical structure following the *genus et differentia* model (i.e., 'X is a Y which Z'). A preliminary (and shallow) analysis that can be performed without any linguistic detail revolves around comparing the length of definitions vs non definitions. Specifically, definitions have 27.5 words on average, while non-definitions have an average length of 27.2 words. The median for definitions and non-definitions, respectively, is 25 and 24. Although the difference is quite small, it seems that encyclopedic definitions are in general slightly longer.

A particular feature of the WCL dataset is that each candidate is composed of a sentence with part-of-speech and phrase chunking annotation. For definitional sentences, an additional set of tags is provided, which identify core components in definitions such as DEFINIENDUM (term defined), DEFINITOR (definition trigger), DEFINIENS (cluster of words that define the definiendum) and REST (rest of the sentence).

Let us look now at the average length of each of these definition components (see Table 1). The DEFINIENS is typically the most important part of definition sentences (where the definition actually happens), however, it is also the shortest one, followed by the DEFINIENDUM. Moreover, REST is generally the longest but also the one with the highest variance, which fits in with the fact that it is a non-essential part of the definition that can contain varying amounts of information. These results seem to suggest that the part of the sentence that actually makes it a definition (definiens and definiendum) is, in many occasions, quite short compared to the overall length of the sentence.

	Mean	25% Quartile	Median	75% Quartile	Standard deviation
Definiendum	7.03	2.0	4.0	9.0	7.70
Definiens	4.47	3.0	4.0	5.0	2.94
Rest	14.4	7.0	13.0	20.0	11.66

Table 1: Summary statistics of the length of definiendum, definiens and rest.

The original annotation of the WCL dataset also identifies the main verb of the definition, i.e. that are not in the REST part (Table 1(a) lists the frequent ones). As expected, the verb "to be" tops the list, with four different conjugations taking up the top 5 verbs. Note that these 5 verbs together appear in 1,670 of the 1,772 definitions in the WCL corpus, which could be a sign that the appearance of one of these verbs is a relevant feature to identify definitions. We can also find the most common hypernyms in Table 1(b), although their counts are significantly lower, matching the fact that they are related to the term defined.

Verb	**Counts**		**Hypernym**	**Counts**
is	1405		instrument	28
was	114		person	22
are	58		plants	19
refers	58		device	14
were	35		mammal	12

Table 2: 5 most common main verbs and hypernyms in definitions in the WCL dataset.

3.2 DEFT dataset

The DEFT dataset (Spala et al., 2019) contains 853 sentences, of which 279 are definitions and 574 are non-definitions. It presents a corpus of natural language term-definition pairs embracing different topics such as biology, history, physics, psychology, economics, sociology and government. Sentences have been classified following a new schema that explores how explicit in-text definitions and glosses work in free and semi-structured text, especially those whose term-definition pairs span crosses a sentence boundary and those lacking explicit definition phrases. Thus, they identify as definitions sentences where the relation between a term and a definition requires more deduction than finding a definition verb phrase. Their focus is to identify terms and definitions, but not necessarily the verb that may or may not connect them two, which identifies as definitions a broather variety of structures.

In this case, the average length of definitions is 27.38 and non-definitions have an average length of 23.84. The median length for definitions and non-definitions is 26 and 22 respectively.

3.3 Descriptive analysis

In this section we perform a short descriptive analysis comparing the two datasets. Continuing with the instance length analysis, Table 3 shows statistics for both datasets, this time comparing length of positive (definition) and negative (non definition) sentences. As can be observed, definitions generally tend to be longer than non-definitions, although the main part of the definition is quite short compared to its overall length. Moreover, while the distribution of definitions/non-definitions is similar, the number of instances is considerably larger in the WCL corpus, which is improtant to note, as we will use it as our training set in our experiments (cf. Section 4.1.)

Regarding frequency of specific POS tags, in Section 3.1 we have seen how some verbs are extremely abundant in definitions in the WCL corpus. However, these are quite common verbs in general in these datasets, as Figures 1(a) and 1(b) show. Note that, for instance, 'is' is more frequent in definitions in both datasets, with an average frequency greater than 1 in both datasets (1.4% and 1.1% in WCL and DEFT, respectively). However, 'was' is actually the opposite and is more frequent in non-definitions while the others are much less common and do not seem to be as present in both types of sentences.

		Instances	Mean Length	Median Length
WCL	Definitions	1772 (38.36%)	27.5	25
	Non-Definitions	2847 (61.64%)	27.2	24
DEFT	Definitions	279 (32.71%)	27.38	26
	Non-Definitions	574 (67.29%)	23.84	22

Table 3: Number of instances, mean and median length for definitions and non-definitions from both WCL and DEFT datasets.

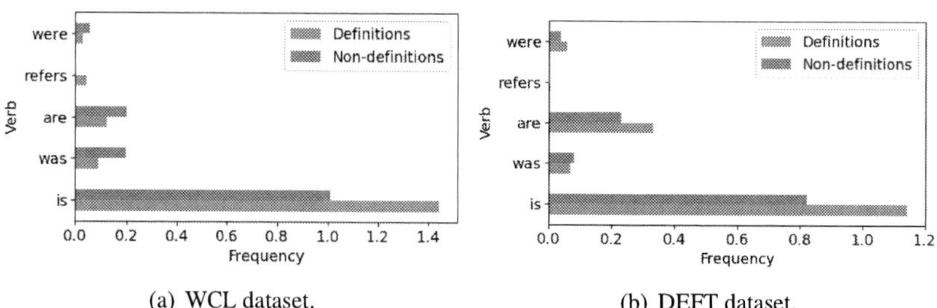

(a) WCL dataset.   (b) DEFT dataset.

Figure 1: Frequency of common verbs in definitions and non-definitions.

Concerning hypernyms (a.k.a `genus` in Aristotelian definitions), although the counts are much lower for hypernyms than for verbs (Table 2), in Figure 2 we illustrate how the hypernyms that appear at least 5 times in the WCL dataset are usually more common in definitions in both datasets. The presence of such hypernyms is likely to be more related to the topics defined than the structure of the sentence, but having any kind of hypernym is probably a relevant feature of definitions, as canonical or lexicographic definitions have (or should have) at least one.

We observed that definitions and non-definitions present different frequencies of POS and chunk patterns. In the WCL dataset it seems that definitions have a higher frequency of noun phrases (denoted as 'NP' or 'NP NN', for instance), while non-definitions have more prepositional phrases ('PP' or 'PP IN'). However, we do not observe these similarities in the DEFT dataset.

Finally, we computed the most PoS-based patterns structures[1] (occurring at least 5 times) in the main part of definitions from the WCL dataset. We have observed that these structures are much more common in definitions than in non-definitions in both corpora, which seems to indicate definitions tend to use a particular morphosyntactic set of structures which can be strong indicators of definitional knowledge.

4 Evaluation

In this section we explain our experiments in definition extraction. In particular, we train a supervised model on the WCL corpus of canonical definitions, and tested on the same corpus (via cross-validation) and the DEFT corpus. With this experiment we aim at understanding relevant features for definition extraction and whether features from canonical definitions can be extrapolated to other domains.

Section 4.1 describes the experimental settings and Section 4.2 presents the main results.

4.1 Experimental setting

In the following we explain the experimental setting for our definition extraction experiments. In Section 4.1.1 we explain our supervised definition extraction model and its features inspired by our descriptive analysis. Then, we explain the data preprocessing (Section 4.1.2) and training details (Section 4.1.3).

4.1.1 Model and features

As supervised model we made use of a Support Vector Machine (SVM) given its efficiency and effectiveness in handling a large set of linguistic features. The model uses an RBF kernel and a combination of different features. The main one is based on n-grams of range 1 to 3 from the tagged sentences, i.e. each word contains chunk tag, PoS tag and word separated by an underscore.

---

[1]PoS-based patterns are any ordered sequences of tags (PoS or chunk) such as 'NP DT' (noun phrase followed by a determiner).

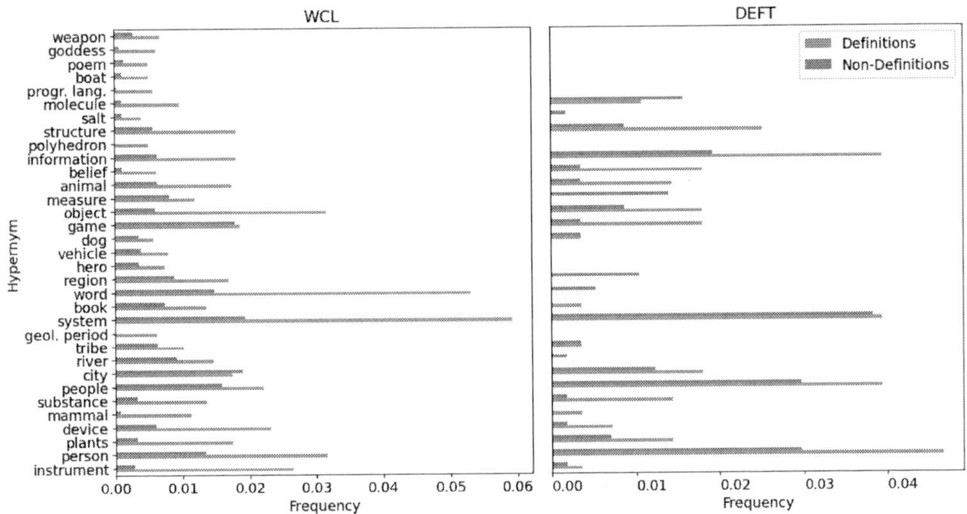

Figure 2: Average frequency of common hypernyms in definitions and non-definitions.

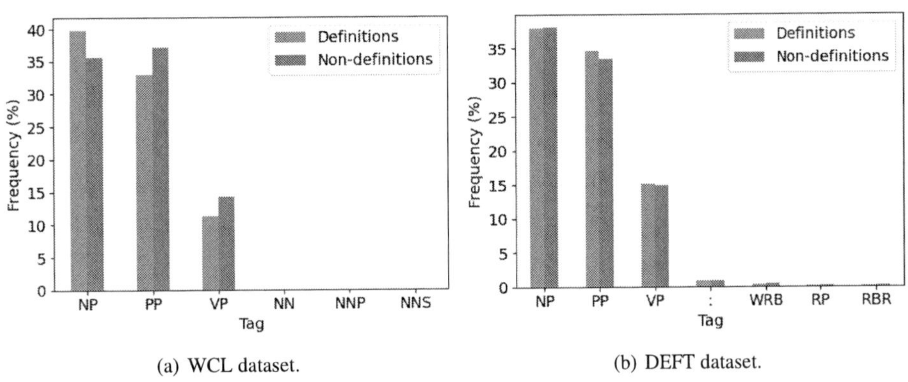

(a) WCL dataset.　　　　　　　　(b) DEFT dataset.

Figure 3: Presence of chunk and PoS tags in definitions and non definitions.

The other features are based on the findings from Section 3.3. For each training set, the model computes the 5 most common definition verbs, i.e. in the main part of the definition, the 20 most common hypernyms, the 10 most common composition of chunk and PoS tags, the 6 most common chunk tags[2], the 10 most common structures of chunk and PoS tags combined, the 10 most common structures of chunk tags and the maximum length of definitions. Using this, we obtain the following new features:

- VERB: Count of common verbs present in the sentence.
- HYP: Count of common hypernyms present in the sentence.
- CT-Ch, CT-Ch&PoS: For each of the 6 most common chunk tags and the 10 most common combinations of chunk and PoS, number of occurrences divided by total number of tags in the sentence.
- STR-Ch, STR-Ch&PoS: For each of the 10 most common structures (chunk and combination of chunk and PoS respectively), a binary variable indicating if the structure is present in the sentence.
- LEN: The length of the sentence divided by the maximum length of a definition.

4.1.2 Data preprocessing

As each corpus contains different information and has a different structure, their preprocessing is slightly different, although the output has the same format: a matrix where the features are obtained from.

---

[2]After the 6th most common, the appearances are significantly lower and hardly relevant.

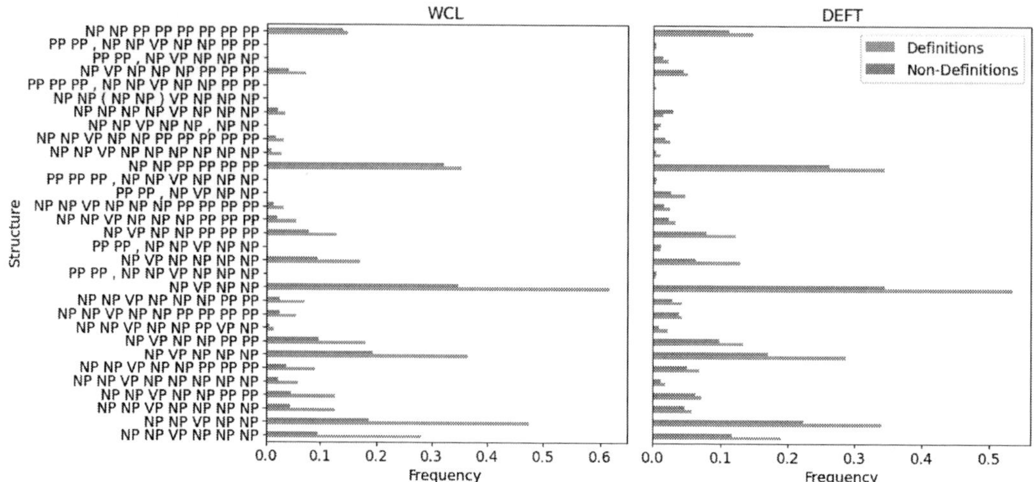

Figure 4: Presence of structures of chunk tags in definitions and non-definitions.

As the WCL dataset contains all the definitions' annotations, we classify each part in a different column and also the verbs and hypernyms annotated. We later retag the sentences with PoS tags and chunk, using, respectively, the NLTK[3] pos_tag function and the RegexpParser with the following grammar:

```
parser = RegexpParser('''
    VP: {<MD>?<RB.?>?<V.*>+(<CC><V.*>+)*} {<TO>?<V.*>+(<CC><V.*>+)*}
    PP: {<TO|IN>+<DT>*<CD>*<JJ.?>*<N.*>*<CC>*<N.*>*} {<TO|IN>+<WDT|EX|WP.?|PP.?|RB>*}
    NP: {<DT>*<CD>*<JJ.?>*<N.*|P.*>*<CC>*<N.*|PP.?>*} {<WDT|EX|WP.?|P.*|RB>*}''')
```

It distinguishes 3 phrases: verb phrases (contain a verb sometimes preceded by a modal or 'to', with possible adverbs and another verb after a coordinating conjunction), prepositional phrases (starting with a preposition and followed by determinants, cardinal numbers, nouns or pronouns) and noun phrases (including a noun or pronoun sometimes preceded by determiners, cardinal numbers or adjectives).

The output is a matrix where each row corresponds to a sentence and each column has different information such as the sentence (tagged and not), the term being defined, the hypernyms annotated in the sentence, the main verb of the definition, the label and different columns that contain the tags (both PoS tags and chunk or only chunk) for the whole sentence and for the main part of the definition (definiendum and definiens). For non-definitions, some columns such as the verb, hypernym and tags of the main part of the definition contain NaN values, as they only exist for definitions.

The preprocessing for the DEFT corpus is simpler: we tag the sentences using the same rules and save the sentences, tags and label in different columns. Numbers at the beginning of sentences have removed.

4.1.3 Training procedure

As mentioned earlier, the model was trained on the WCL dataset. We used sklearn[4] for training and evaluating the SVM model. For the experiments, the SVM hyperparameters were chosen after testing the following values: $[0.0001, 0.001, 0.1, 1, 5, 10, 50, 100]$ for C, and $[0.0001, 0.001, 0.1, 1, 5, 10, 50, 100]$ for gamma, both in a validation set. Finally, the evaluation on the WCL dataset is performed through 10-fold cross-validation, with 10% of the corpus used for validation in each fold. Then, the model is trained on the whole WCL corpus and evaluated on the DEFT corpus. The final hyperparameters of the SVM were $C = 5$ and gamma= 0.1. In addition to the SVM model, as a baseline we trained a Naive Bayes with the same features. This model was trained with its standard implementation in sklearn.

4.2 Results

The results on the WCL dataset are displayed in Table 4. As a naive baseline we include the results of a system that would identify all sentences as definitions (referred to as *Naive(all defs)* in the table).

---

[3] https://www.nltk.org/
[4] https://scikit-learn.org/stable/

As can be observed, all metrics are above 0.97 and the average metrics are all close to 0.98. This proves the reliability of the SVM model with all our proposed linguistic features, which attains the highest performance of any non-linear model in the task. As a point of comparison, recent works have reported slightly worse results using highly parametrized models such as convolutional and recurrent neural networks (Espinosa-Anke and Schockaert, 2018).

Fold	Accuracy	Precision	Recall	F1-Score
1	0.9805	0.9820	0.9776	0.9797
2	0.9762	0.9755	0.9761	0.9758
3	0.9827	0.9838	0.9796	0.9816
4	0.9870	0.9872	0.9847	0.9859
5	0.9740	0.9756	0.9667	0.9710
6	0.9740	0.9748	0.9717	0.9731
7	0.9892	0.9901	0.9876	0.9888
8	0.9784	0.9767	0.9732	0.9750
9	0.9827	0.9828	0.9810	0.9819
10	0.9805	0.9784	0.9796	0.9790
Average	0.9805	0.9807	0.9778	0.9792
Naive Bayes	0.8837	0.8849	0.8686	0.8743
Naive(all defs)	0.3836	0.1918	0.5000	0.2768

Table 4: Results of the SVM model on the WCL dataset using 10-fold cross validation. Precision, recall and F1 are macro metrics. The last two rows include the average results of the two baselines considered.

When testing the model on the DEFT corpus, the results are not close to being as satisfactory as they are in the WCL dataset, as we can see in Table 5. The model trained on the WCL dataset performs significantly worse than other recent models (Spala et al., 2020), which could be expected given the different nature of the definitions. In the following section we provide a more extensive analysis that also attempts at explaining the performance difference between the two datasets.

Model	Accuracy	Precision	Recall	F1-Score
SVM	0.7011	0.6573	0.5900	0.5872
Naive Bayes	0.5909	0.5626	0.5689	0.5611
Naive(all defs)	0.3271	0.1635	0.5000	0.2465

Table 5: DEFT results of the SVM and baselines trained on the WCL corpus.

5 Analysis

5.1 Feature analysis

Figure 5 shows the features of the model with highest χ^2. Some of them are compositions extremely common in definitions such as 'is a', 'is an' or 'refers', but we also find others more topic related such as 'mythology' or 'greek', which would probably be artifacts from the WCL dataset.

For a detailed view of each additional feature's significance, we ran the model removing one or more features at a time. Morever, we also ran the model using the n-gram features only, with different combinations of words and tags. We can find this feature analysis in Table 6. Although the accuracy in the 10-fold cross-validation setting does not change significantly when removing only one feature, and even improves slightly in the case of hypernyms, they do show changes when evaluating on the DEFT corpus. We observe significantly lower accuracy when removing more than one feature at a time (last two rows), decreasing regularly when removing more features and obtaining between $0.93 - 0.94$ using only n-gram features, which indicates that these features rely on and interact with each other to improve accuracy. The differences are more significant when evaluating the model on the DEFT corpus, the accuracy goes from around 0.70 when using all features to 0.55 when removing some of them. This proves that the

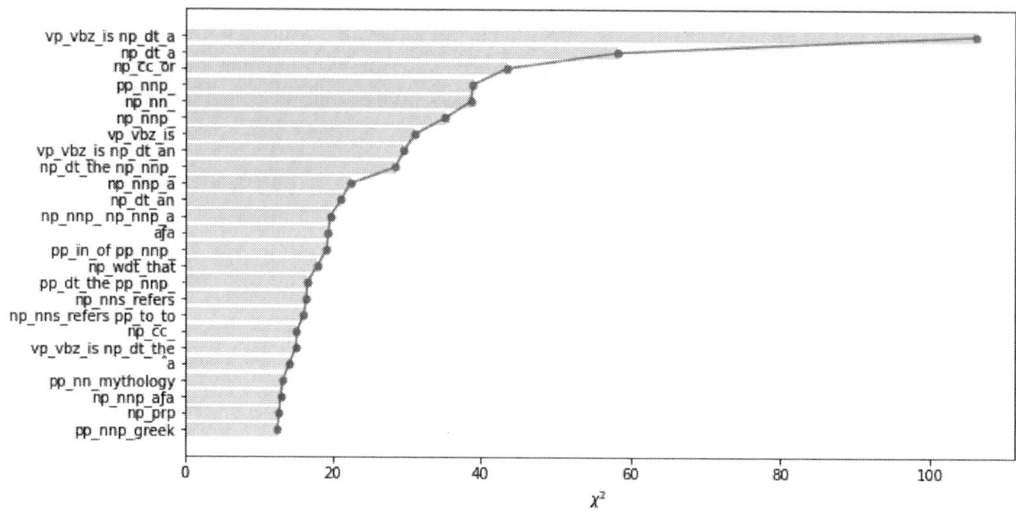

Figure 5: Features from the SVM model trained on WCL with highest χ^2.

additional features are relevant to identify definitions and improve the metrics significantly, especially in unseen corpora. In fact, the performance of using n-grams features only achieves a performance of 0.934 F1 in the in-domain WCL corpus, and a significantly lower 0.575 performance on the DEFT corpus.

Features Removed	Average of 10-fold cross validation				Evaluation of model on DEFT corpus			
(Number of features)	Accuracy	Precision	Recall	F1	Accuracy	Precision	Recall	F1
None (0)	0.9805	0.9807	0.9778	0.9792	0.7011	0.6573	0.5900	0.5872
VERB (1)	0.9805	0.9807	0.9778	0.9792	0.7011	0.6573	0.5900	0.5872
HYP (1)	0.9812	0.9818	0.9781	0.9799	0.7046	0.6626	0.5972	0.5968
LEN (1)	0.9801	0.9803	0.9773	0.9787	0.7022	0.6599	0.5909	0.5881
CT-Ch&PoS (10)	0.9803	0.9803	0.9777	0.979	0.6928	0.6395	0.5894	0.5889
CT-Ch (5)	0.9799	0.9795	0.9775	0.9785	0.6928	0.6398	0.6088	0.6132
STR-Ch&PoS (10)	0.9805	0.9807	0.9778	0.9792	0.7011	0.6573	0.5900	0.5872
STR-Ch (10)	0.9805	0.9807	0.9778	0.9792	0.7011	0.6573	0.5900	0.5872
CT (15)	0.9706*	0.9697	0.9673	0.9684	0.5557*	0.5842	0.5934	0.5515
STR (20)	0.9719	0.9707	0.9691	0.9699	0.6131	0.5951	0.6066	0.5918
CT and STR (35)	0.9706	0.9697	0.9673	0.9684	0.5662	0.5907	0.6013	0.5612
All except n-grams (38)	0.9379	0.9349	0.9336	0.934	0.5885	0.5875	0.5994	0.5754

Table 6: Results of the SVM model (trained on the WCL dataset) using different sets of features. For accuracy, * indicates when the results start to show differences that are statistically significant (p-value$<$ 0.05 according to a t-test) with respect to the model using all features (first row).

Furthermore, we can see in Table 7 how the n-gram model is significantly more accurate when using both PoS and chunk tags and words rather than only some of them, which indicates that both words and structure of the sentence determine whether it is a definition or not.

5.2 Error analysis

In Table 8 we can see some examples of predictions from the model that provide a more in-depth view. We observe how the model is successful in correctly predicting sentences with unorthodox structures, such as non-definitions using the verb "is", and syntactically complex definitions. Moreover, some of sentences that have been predicted wrongly as definitions could be considered as definitions, but they are not defining the target word. The false negatives present complex structures probably unseen for the model. Thus, evidence suggests the model succeeds most of the times at identifying definitions and non-definitions, and has incorporated satisfactorily the distinctive characteristics of each kind of sentence.

As for the DEFT dataset, as expected from the obtained accuracy, the model makes numerous mistakes.

Terms used for n-gram	Average of 10-fold cross validation				Evaluation of model on DEFT corpus			
	Accuracy	Precision	Recall	F1	Accuracy	Precision	Recall	F1
Chunk, PoS, words	0.9379	0.9349	0.9336	0.934	0.5885	0.5875	0.5994	0.5754
PoS tags, words	0.8809	0.8841	0.8624	0.8705	0.687	0.6383	0.551	0.5251
Words	0.8326	0.8249	0.8182	0.8206	0.6729	0.6009	0.5562	0.5452
Chunk, PoS tags	0.8465	0.8459	0.8259	0.8329	0.6917	0.6433	0.6433	0.5674

Table 7: Results of the SVM model using different types of n-gram features only.

It has a large number of false negatives (23.9 %), making its predictions less reliable in this setting. The model does a good job at detecting true negatives (91.1% of all negative instances), also due to the fact that most sentences are predicted as non-definitions. However, some false negatives do not seem to contain definitional information. Something similar happens with false positives, as some of them would most likely be considered definitions under more flexible criteria. Thus, although the performance of the model on this data set seems to be relatively low overall, this is probably because of the different tagging criteria, as many sentences that appeared as incorrectly predicted, could be labelled correctly under the annotation criteria used in the WCL dataset. For instance, the sentence "Elimination blackjack is a tournament format of blackjack." could be considered a definition with the criteria used in the DEFT dataset as it presents a *direct-defines* relation, while "It carries the correct amino acid to the site of protein synthesis" would not be considered a definition in the WCL corpus as it is not an actual textual definition.

		Predicted nodef⋆	Predicted def⋆
WCL	nodef	His death is deeply mourned by Alleycats fans as seen in the press and media. Covering the head is respectful in Sikhism and if a man is not wearing a turban, then a rumāl must be worn before entering the Gurdwara. The following are links to pictures of Myddfai taken by the club.	The term "carbonate" is also commonly used to refer to one of these salts or carbonate minerals. Elimination blackjack is a tournament format of blackjack. Balderton Old Boys also are a local football team.
	def	The Callitrichinae form one of the four families of New World monkeys now recognised In everyday usage, risk is often used synonymously with the probability of a known loss. Both equivocation and amphiboly are fallacies arising from ambiguity.	The Aurochs or urus (Bos primigenius) was a very large type of cattle that was prevalent in Europe until its extinction in 1627. In the 19th century the term anglicanism was coined to describe the common religious tradition of these churches. The term biotic refers to the condition of living organisms.
		Predicted nodef⋆	Predicted def⋆
DEFT	nodef	Living things are highly organized and structured , following a hierarchy that can be examined on a scale from small to large. At its most fundamental level , life is made up of matter. It consists of a nucleus surrounded by electrons.	Transfer RNA (tRNA) is one of the smallest of the four types of RNA , usually 70 – 90 nucleotides long. A microphyll is small and has a simple vascular system. An individual with dyslexia exhibits an inability to correctly process letters.
	def	It carries the correct amino acid to the site of protein synthesis. The rays themselves are called nuclear radiation. Herbivores eat plant material , and planktivores eat plankton.	The atom is the smallest and most fundamental unit of matter. A prokaryote is a simple, mostly single-celled (unicellular) organism that lacks a nucleus, or any other membrane-bound organelle. Matter is any substance that occupies space and has mass.

Table 8: Definition (def⋆) and non-definition (nodef⋆) predictions on both WCL and DEFT ground truth (for def and nodef classes).

6 Conclusion and Future Work

In conclusion, extracting definitions from texts is a challenging research task, which is highly dependant on the distribution and scope of the application. Nonetheless, in this paper we have shown that a simple SVM model trained on a dataset with canonical definitions using linguistic features can provide high performance while helping us understand the task better. This model has also been evaluated on a corpus with heterogeneous domains, which also provided us with insights on the qualitative difference among definitions in each setting.

Our descriptive analysis discovered interesting differences and similarities between definitions and non-definitions that can be used to differentiate them automatically. The inclusion of linguistic features based on our analysis improved significantly the performance of the model. As future work it would be interesting to extend the analysis to corpora of different characteristics and languages. As an straightforward application, a model with accurate performance across corpora would allow the automatic creation of dictionaries from general or specialized domains, as well as to better understand certain topics.

Acknowledgements

We thank the reviewers for their feedback and Emrah Ozturk for his help in the early stages of this paper.

References

Hang Cui, Min-Yen Kan, and Tat-Seng Chua. 2005. Generic soft pattern models for definitional question answering. In *Proceedings of the 28th Annual International ACM SIGIR Conference on Research and Development in Information Retrieval*, SIGIR '05, page 384–391, New York, NY, USA. Association for Computing Machinery.

Rosa Del Gaudio, Gustavo Batista, and António Branco. 2014. Coping with highly imbalanced datasets: A case study with definition extraction in a multilingual setting. *Natural Language Engineering*, 20(3):327–359.

Luis Espinosa-Anke and Horacio Saggion. 2014. Applying dependency relations to definition extraction. In *Natural Language Processing and Information Systems, NLDB 2014*, pages 63–74. Springer International Publishing Switzerland 2014, Montpellier, France, 06.

Luis Espinosa-Anke and Steven Schockaert. 2018. Syntactically aware neural architectures for definition extraction. In *Proceedings of the 2018 Conference of the North American Chapter of the Association for Computational Linguistics: Human Language Technologies, Volume 2 (Short Papers)*, pages 378–385.

Luis Espinosa-Anke, Horacio Saggion, and Francesco Ronzano. 2015. Weakly supervised definition extraction. In *Proceedings of the International Conference Recent Advances in Natural Language Processing*, pages 176–185, Hissar, Bulgaria, September. INCOMA Ltd. Shoumen, BULGARIA.

Luis Espinosa-Anke, Horacio Saggion, Francesco Ronzano, and Roberto Navigli. 2016. Extasem! extending, taxonomizing and semantifying domain terminologies. In *Thirtieth AAAI Conference on Artificial Intelligence*.

Eduard Hovy, Andrew Philpot, Judith Klavans, Ulrich Germann, and Peter T. Davis. 2003. Extending metadata definitions by automatically extracting and organizing glossary definitions. In *Proceedings of the 2003 Annual National Conference on Digital Government Research*, dg.o '03, page 1. Digital Government Society of North America.

Yiping Jin, Min-Yen Kan, Jun Ping Ng, and Xiangnan He. 2013. Mining scientific terms and their definitions: A study of the acl anthology. In *Proceedings of the 2013 Conference on Empirical Methods in Natural Language Processing*, pages 780–790.

Mandar Joshi, Kenton Lee, Yi Luan, and Kristina Toutanova. 2020. Contextualized representations using textual encyclopedic knowledge. *arXiv preprint arXiv:2004.12006*.

David Jurgens and Mohammad Taher Pilehvar. 2015. Reserating the awesometastic: An automatic extension of the wordnet taxonomy for novel terms. In *Proceedings of the 2015 Conference of the North American Chapter of the Association for Computational Linguistics: Human Language Technologies*, pages 1459–1465.

Smaranda Muresan and Judith Klavans. 2002. A method for automatically building and evaluating dictionary resources. In *Proceedings of the Third International Conference on Language Resources and Evaluation (LREC'02)*, Las Palmas, Canary Islands - Spain, May. European Language Resources Association (ELRA).

Jun-ichi Nakamura and Makoto Nagao. 1988. Extraction of semantic information from an ordinary english dictionary and its evaluation. In *Proceedings of the 12th Conference on Computational Linguistics - Volume 2*, COLING '88, page 459–464, USA. Association for Computational Linguistics.

Roberto Navigli and Paola Velardi. 2010. Learning word-class lattices for definition and hypernym extraction. In *Proceedings of the 48th Annual Meeting of the Association for Computational Linguistics*, pages 1318–1327, Uppsala, Sweden, July. Association for Computational Linguistics.

Roberto Navigli, Paola Velardi, and Juana Maria Ruiz-Martínez. 2010. An annotated dataset for extracting definitions and hypernyms from the web. In *Proceedings of the Seventh International Conference on Language Resources and Evaluation (LREC'10)*, Valletta, Malta, May. European Language Resources Association (ELRA).

Youngja Park, Roy J Byrd, and Branimir K Boguraev. 2002. Automatic glossary extraction: Beyond terminology identification. In *Proceedings of the 19th International Conference on Computational Linguistics - Volume 1*, COLING '02, page 1–7, USA. Association for Computational Linguistics.

Adam Przepiórkowski, Łukasz Degórski, Miroslav Spousta, Kiril Simov, Petya Osenova, Lothar Lemnitzer, Vladislav Kubon, and Beata Wójtowicz. 2007. Towards the automatic extraction of definitions in slavic. In *Proceedings of the Workshop on Balto-Slavonic Natural Language Processing*, pages 43–50.

Horacio Saggion and Rob Gaizauskas. 2004. Mining on-line sources for definition knowledge. In *In Proceedings of the 17th FLAIRS 2004, Miami Bearch*, 01.

Gerardo Sierra, Rodrigo Alarcón, César Aguilar, and Carme Bach. 2008. Definitional verbal patterns for semantic relation extraction. *Terminology. International Journal of Theoretical and Applied Issues in Specialized Communication*, 14(1):74–98.

Sasha Spala, Nicholas A. Miller, Yiming Yang, Franck Dernoncourt, and Carl Dockhorn. 2019. DEFT: A corpus for definition extraction in free- and semi-structured text. In *Proceedings of the 13th Linguistic Annotation Workshop*, pages 124–131, Florence, Italy, August. Association for Computational Linguistics.

Sasha Spala, Nicholas A Miller, Franck Dernoncourt, and Carl Dockhorn. 2020. Semeval-2020 task 6: Definition extraction from free text with the deft corpus.

Amir Pouran Ben Veyseh, Franck Dernoncourt, Dejing Dou, and Thien Huu Nguyen. 2019. A joint model for definition extraction with syntactic connection and semantic consistency. *arXiv preprint arXiv:1911.01678*.

Eline Westerhout and Paola Monachesi. 2007. Extraction of dutch definitory contexts for elearning purpose. In Peter Dirix, Ineke Schuurman, Vincent Vandeghinste, and Frank Van Eynde, editors, *Proceedings of the 17th Meeting of Computational Linguistics in the Netherlands (CLIN 2007)*, pages 219–34. CLIN, Nijmegen, Netherlands.

Eline Westerhout. 2009. Definition extraction using linguistic and structural features. In *Proceedings of the 1st Workshop on Definition Extraction*, pages 61–67.

Speech Disfluencies occur at Higher Perplexities

Priyanka Sen

Amazon Alexa

`sepriyan@amazon.com`

Abstract

Speech disfluencies have been hypothesized to occur before words that are less predictable and therefore more cognitively demanding. In this paper, we revisit this hypothesis by using OpenAI's GPT-2 to calculate predictability of words as language model perplexity. Using the Switchboard corpus, we find that 51% of disfluencies occur at the highest, second highest, or within one token of the highest perplexity, and this distribution is not random. We also show that disfluencies precede words with significantly higher perplexity than fluent contexts. Based on our results, we offer new evidence that disfluencies are more likely to occur before less predictable words.

1 Introduction

Speech disfluencies occur naturally in spontaneous speech. Disfluencies such as filled pauses ('uh', 'um'), repetitions ('<u>about</u> about eight months ago'), and repairs ('about eight <u>days I mean</u> months ago') are estimated to occur in 6% of words in spoken English (Kasl and Mahl, 1965; Tree, 1995). In 1954, Lounsbury (1954) hypothesized a relationship between disfluencies and the likelihood of the next word. He proposed that speakers have habitual ways of speaking, and the more unexpected a word given the context, the greater the likelihood of a disfluency. Lounsbury did not test this hypothesis, saying that calculating the probability of every word in every context was, at the time, "an impossible task" (Lounsbury, 1954). Since then, several studies have found that disfluencies occur before less predictable words (Tannenbaum et al., 1965; Beattie and Butterworth, 1979; Siu and Ostendorf, 1996; Arnold et al., 2007).

In this short paper, we revisit Lounsbury (1954)'s hypothesis with newer NLP technology. Using OpenAI's GPT-2 (Radford et al., 2019), a neural language model, we calculate the predictability of words in disfluent sentences using language model perplexity. On the Switchboard corpus (Godfrey et al., 1992), a large-scale spoken language dataset, we find that 22% of disfluencies precede the word with the highest perplexity (i.e. the lowest probability), 51% of disfluencies occur either at the highest, second highest, or within one token of the highest perplexity, and this distribution is not random. We also find that words preceded by a disfluency have significantly higher perplexity than words in fluent contexts. Based on these findings, we offer new evidence of a relationship between disfluencies and less predictable words and conclude with suggested applications in NLP.

2 Related Works

Cognitive load has often been studied as a factor that affects disfluencies (Corley and Stewart, 2008). Disfluencies are found more often before longer sentences (Shriberg, 1994), in new or unfamiliar contexts (Barr, 2001; Merlo and Mansur, 2004), and when speakers are performing more challenging tasks (Oviatt, 1995). Lounsbury (1954) suggested that the likelihood of a word also affects disfluencies. Early studies evaluating disfluencies and the probability of a word used the Shannon guessing technique (Shannon, 1951) or the Cloze procedure (Taylor, 1953). In these techniques, a spoken text was transcribed and given to judges with missing words. In the Shannon guessing technique, judges guessed each word given the preceding context. In the Cloze procedure, every *n*th word was deleted, so judges had both left and

Proceedings of the Workshop on Cognitive Aspects of the Lexicon, pages 92–97
Barcelona, Spain (Online), December 12, 2020

right context. The probability of a word was based on how many judges could correctly guess it. With the Shannon guessing technique, Goldman-Eisler (1958) found that words preceding a silent pause had lower probability than words without a pause. Using the Cloze procedure, studies found that disfluencies occurred before words with lower probability than fluent contexts (Tannenbaum et al., 1965; Cook, 1969). Beattie and Butterworth (1979) compared word frequency and contextual probability and found that disfluencies were more likely to occur before words with lower contextual probability, even when word frequency was held constant.

With the release of larger-scale datasets, contextual probability no longer needed to be hand-annotated but could be calculated in a large enough corpus. The probability of a word given its previous word was estimated by counting the number of times both words occurred together divided by the number of times the first word occurred. This could be extended to the first n words in an n-gram language model. Using large corpora and n-gram language models, studies again found that disfluencies occur before words with significantly lower probability (Shriberg and Stolcke, 1996), probability varies for different disfluency types and positions (Siu and Ostendorf, 1996), and disfluencies tend to be longer before lower probability words (Harmon and Kapatsinski, 2015).

In related psychology works, eye-tracking studies have shown that listeners are primed to anticipate low frequency words when hearing a disfluency (Arnold et al., 2007; Watanabe et al., 2008) and speakers are more likely to hesitate before low frequency words (Hartsuiker and Notebaert, 2009; De Jong, 2016). Many psychology studies, however, focus more on word frequency rather than contextual probability.

3 Method

To calculate the probability of a word, we use OpenAI's GPT-2 (Radford et al., 2019), a large-scale neural language model that has achieved state-of-the-art results on various NLP tasks. GPT-2 uses a transformer-based architecture with 1.5 billion parameters and is trained on 8M documents. To our knowledge, we are the first to evaluate the relationship between disfluencies and contextual probability with a language model of this scale. To calculate probability, we use the perplexity returned by GPT-2. Perplexity is the inverse probability of a sequence normalized by the number of words. Due to the inverse, the lower the probability of a sequence, the higher the perplexity. The perplexity of a sequence of words W is calculated with the joint probabilities P of each word w using the formula:

$$Perplexity(W) = P(w_1, w_2..w_N)^{-1/N}$$

We use the implementation of GPT-2 available from HuggingFace (Wolf et al., 2019). Since GPT-2 is trained on written text and we experiment with spoken language, we fine-tune our GPT-2 model with the objective of predicting the next word given the previous words on 150K examples from Switchboard (Godfrey et al., 1992) for 2 epochs. This prevents our language model from predicting high perplexities for phrases that are common in spoken language but not in written language (e.g. "bye bye").

4 Dataset

For our experiemnts, we use the Switchboard corpus (Godfrey et al., 1992), which was built by asking volunteers to speak to each other on the telephone about a topic assigned by a computer operator. We use the version released by Zayats et al. (2019)[1]. We modify this dataset by including 'uh' and 'um' as disfluencies, which are included in the transcriptions but not labeled as disfluencies. From this dataset, we use 150K examples to fine-tune our GPT-2 model. We hold out 10,000 disfluent sentences from the model for our experiments. We filter this held-out disfluent set by: 1) Removing sentences that are fewer than 5 words or longer than 15 words long (excluding disfluencies), as these are often incomplete (e.g. "oh uh") or run-on sentences, 2) Removing sentences where the disfluency is the first or last word of the sentence since our experiments require left and right context to measure perplexity, and 3) Removing sentences with non-consecutive disfluencies. This is done for simplicity and because a majority (70%) of sentences contain consecutive disfluencies. Statistics about our disfluent set are shown in Table 1.

---

[1] https://github.com/vickyzayats/switchboard_corrected_reannotated

Count	10,000
Word Count (excl disfl)	9.5 ($\pm$3.0)
Word Count (incl disfl)	12.1 ($\pm$3.6)
Disfluency Length	2.6 ($\pm$1.8)
Disfluency Position	3.3 ($\pm$2.8)

Table 1: Statistics on the set of 10,000 disfluent utterances from Switchboard used in our experiments. Values are reported as means ($\pm$ standard deviation)

Sequence	Perplexity
i'd be	80.63
i'd be very	63.12
i'd be very very	68.47
i'd be very very careful	70.90
————DISFL————	
i'd be very very careful checking	167.04
i'd be very very careful checking them	120.38
i'd be very very careful checking them out	76.44

Table 2: An example of perplexity calculated for the consecutive substrings of: "i'd be very very careful {and uh you know} checking them out".

5 Experiments

For each utterance in our disfluent set, we create a fluent version by removing the disfluencies. Using the fluent versions, we calculate the perplexity of each substring starting with the first two tokens of the sentence and adding one token at a time until the sentence is complete. An example is shown in Table 2. We expect the word following the disfluency to be the most unpredictable, so in our example, we would expect highest perplexity at the word "checking".

First, we evaluate how often disfluencies occur at the most unpredictable word. Given the list of perplexities for each sentence, we measure how often the maximum perplexity occurs at the word following the disfluency. We find that only 22% of disfluencies occur before the highest perplexity. We next calculate two more lenient measures of highest perplexity. We measure both how many disfluencies occur before the second highest perplexity and how many occur within one token of the highest perplexity. We find that 15% of disfluencies occur before the second highest perplexity, and 23% occur within one token of the highest perplexity. Taken together, 51% of disfluencies occur either before the highest perplexity, the second highest perplexity, or within one token of the highest perplexity.

The histogram in Figure 1 shows the distribution of disfluencies by rank in terms of perplexity (i.e. disfluencies at 1 occur at the highest perplexity, 2 at the second highest perplexity, etc.). This figure shows that disfluencies occur most often at the highest perplexity and trend downward for lower ranks. The histogram in Figure 2 shows the disfluency distribution by distance from the highest perplexity (i.e. disfluencies at 0 are at the highest perplexity, disfluencies at 1 are 1 token away from the highest perplexity, etc.). Here we see that disfluencies occur most often between 0 to 1 tokens from the highest perplexity and this also trends downward as distance increases. Finally, the graph in Figure 3 plots by number of words how often a disfluency occurs at the maximum perplexity compared to how often we would expect it given random chance. The error bars are calculated as a binomial proportion confidence interval based on the number of examples at that word length. For example, for all 5-word sentences,

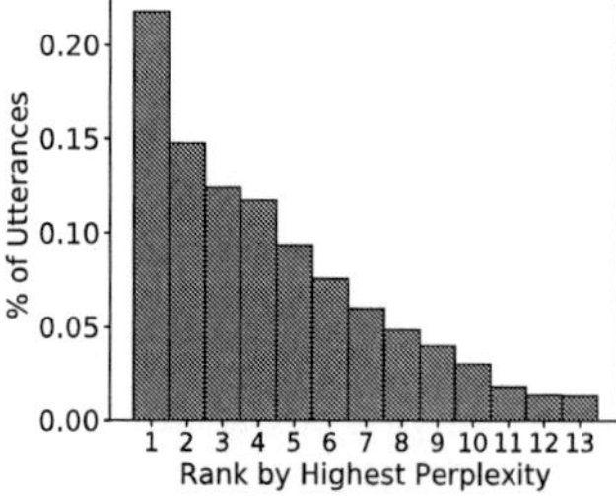

Figure 1: The distribution of disfluencies by rank in terms of highest perplexity

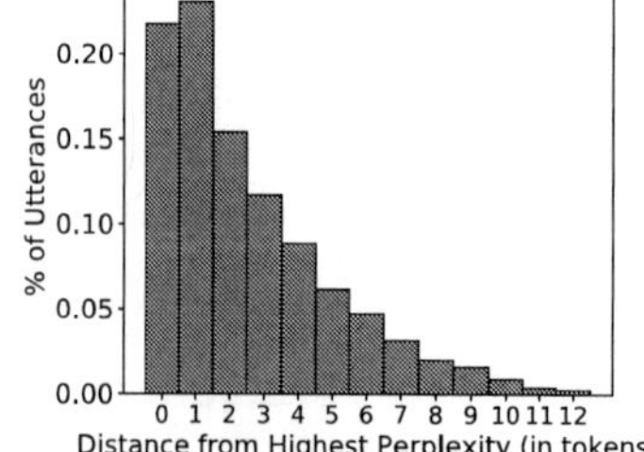

Figure 2: The distribution of disfluencies by distance from the highest perplexity

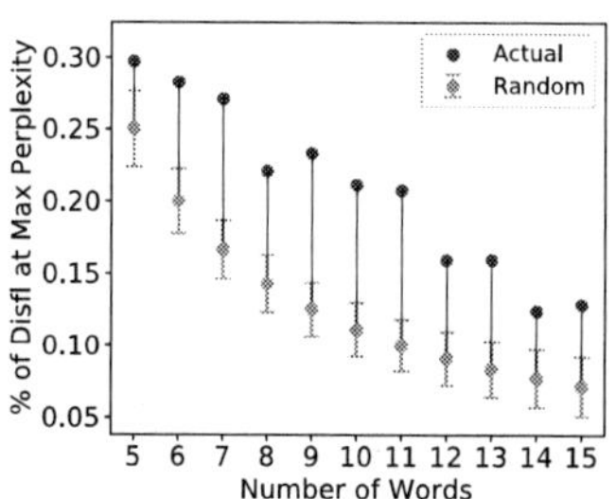

Figure 3: The occurrence of disfluencies at max perplexity compared to random chance

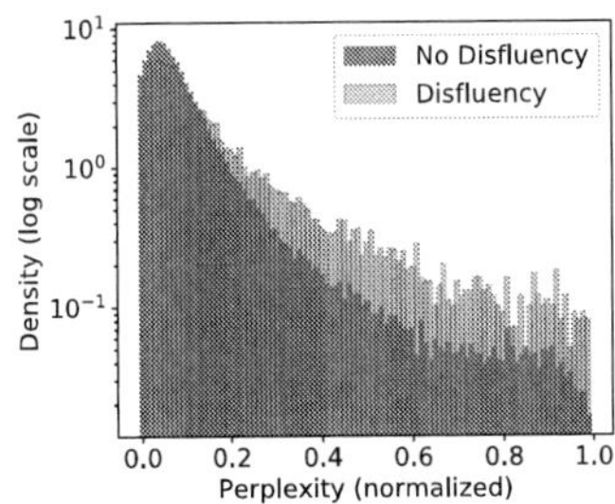

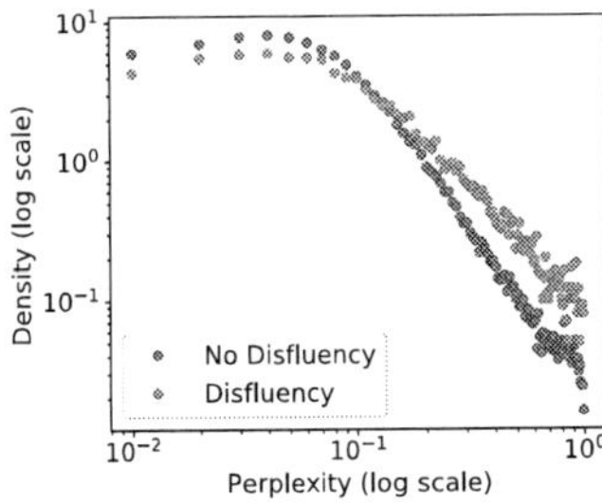

	No Disfl	Disfl
Mean	0.11	0.17
Median	0.07	0.10
Q1	0.04	0.05
Q3	0.13	0.21
IQR	0.09	0.16

Figure 4: A histogram of the distribution of perplexities

Figure 5: A log-log plot of the distribution of perplexities

Table 3: Statistics on the distribution of perplexities

there are 4 possible words the disfluency could occur before (no disfluencies occur before the first word). Given random chance, we would expect a disfluency at the highest perplexity 25% of the time, but we see it closer to 30%, showing that our results are likely not a result of random chance.

Is there a bias that causes this pattern? 41% of utterances in our dataset have a disfluency at the second word, and disfluencies are known to occur more often near the beginning of the sentence (Shriberg, 1994). 46% of our highest perplexities are also at the second word. To test if we have just identified a sentence-initial bias, we run our calculations excluding examples where the disfluency or maximum perplexity is at the second word. In this filtered dataset, we find that 18% of disfluencies occur before the maximum perplexity, and 41% occur before the highest, second highest, or within one token of the highest perplexity. While these numbers are lower than on the full dataset, they still show the same pattern. This suggests that our results are not just due to a bias, and may suggest that this pattern in perplexity is related to higher planning demands at the beginning of a sentence.

Finally, we measure if disfluencies occur at higher points of statistical uncertainty compared to fluent contexts. To calculate this, we normalize the perplexities of each sentence by dividing by the sum of all perplexities in the sentence. We compare the distribution of perplexities with no disfluency against perplexities with a disfluency. The results are shown in Figures 4 and 5 and Table 3. The histogram in Figure 4 shows that the distribution of disfluent perplexities is flatter at the head and heavier in the tail, which is reflected by a higher median and third quartile in Table 3. The log-log plot in Figure 5 also shows more disfluencies at higher perplexities. After a perplexity of 0.2, disfluent and fluent perplexities diverge into two different lines, showing they follow two different distributions. The linear relationships only hold for one order of magnitude, and so they don't fully result in a power law. To calculate significance, we run both an independent t-test and a two-sided Mann-Whitney rank test, to account for the non-normal distribution. Both of these tests show significance with p-values <0.01. Based on these results, we find that disfluencies occur before words with significantly higher perplexity than fluent contexts.

6 Conclusion

In this paper, we provide new evidence using a large-scale neural language model that disfluencies occur more often before less predictable words. We consider this relationship between perplexity and disfluencies useful for applications in NLP and see the following areas as promising future directions:

- Most NLP tasks optimize to return predictions with low perplexity. However, given that disfluencies occur with higher perplexity, does preferring higher perplexity words following a disfluency give us better performance in speech or entity recognition tasks?

- Spoken language understanding tasks often need to detect disfluencies (e.g. 'a' vs. 'uh'; is a repetition part of the entity). Can we use perplexity as a signal to determine if a token is a disfluency?

- Disfluencies are uncommon, so disfluency training data is often augmented with synthetic disfluencies (Dong et al., 2019; Bach and Huang, 2019). Can we use perplexity to guide synthetic disfluency generation, and would that be more natural or useful than disfluencies inserted at random?

References

Jennifer E Arnold, Carla L Hudson Kam, and Michael K Tanenhaus. 2007. If you say thee uh you are describing something hard: The on-line attribution of disfluency during reference comprehension. *Journal of Experimental Psychology: Learning, Memory, and Cognition*, 33(5):914.

Nguyen Bach and Fei Huang. 2019. Noisy BiLSTM-based models for disfluency detection. In *Proc. Interspeech 2019*, pages 4230–4234.

Dale J Barr. 2001. Trouble in mind: Paralinguistic indices of effort and uncertainty in communication. *Oralité et gestualité: Interactions et comportements multimodaux dans la communication*, pages 597–600.

Geoffrey W Beattie and Brian L Butterworth. 1979. Contextual probability and word frequency as determinants of pauses and errors in spontaneous speech. *Language and Speech*, 22(3):201–211.

Mark Cook. 1969. Transition probabilities and the incidence of filled pauses. *Psychonomic Science*, 16(4):191–192.

Martin Corley and Oliver W Stewart. 2008. Hesitation disfluencies in spontaneous speech: The meaning of um. *Language and Linguistics Compass*, 2(4):589–602.

Nivja H De Jong. 2016. Predicting pauses in L1 and L2 speech: The effects of utterance boundaries and word frequency. *International Review of Applied Linguistics in Language Teaching*, 54(2):113–132.

Qianqian Dong, Feng Wang, Zhen Yang, Wei Chen, Shuang Xu, and Bo Xu. 2019. Adapting translation models for transcript disfluency detection. In *Proceedings of the AAAI Conference on Artificial Intelligence*, volume 33, pages 6351–6358.

John J Godfrey, Edward C Holliman, and Jane McDaniel. 1992. Switchboard: Telephone speech corpus for research and development. In *IEEE International Conference on Acoustics, Speech, and Signal Processing*, volume 1, pages 517–520. IEEE Computer Society.

Frieda Goldman-Eisler. 1958. Speech production and the predictability of words in context. *Quarterly Journal of Experimental Psychology*, 10(2):96–106.

Zara Harmon and Vsevolod Kapatsinski. 2015. Studying the dynamics of lexical access using disfluencies. In *Papers presented at DISS 2015: The 7th Workshop on Disfluency in Spontaneous Speech*, page 41.

Robert J Hartsuiker and Lies Notebaert. 2009. Lexical access problems lead to disfluencies in speech. *Experimental Psychology*.

Stanislav V Kasl and George F Mahl. 1965. Relationship of disturbances and hesitations in spontaneous speech to anxiety. *Journal of Personality and Social Psychology*, 1(5):425.

Floyd G Lounsbury. 1954. Transitional probability, linguistic structure, and systems of habit-family hierarchies. *Psycholinguistics: A survey of theory and research problems*, pages 93–101.

Sandra Merlo and Letícia Lessa Mansur. 2004. Descriptive discourse: Topic familiarity and disfluencies. *Journal of Communication Disorders*, 37(6):489–503.

Sharon Oviatt. 1995. Predicting spoken disfluencies during human-computer interaction. *Computer Speech and Language*, 9(1):19–36.

Alec Radford, Jeffrey Wu, Rewon Child, David Luan, Dario Amodei, and Ilya Sutskever. 2019. Language models are unsupervised multitask learners. *OpenAI Blog*, 1(8):9.

Claude E Shannon. 1951. Prediction and entropy of printed English. *Bell System Technical Journal*, 30(1):50–64.

Elizabeth Shriberg and Andreas Stolcke. 1996. Word predictability after hesitations: A corpus-based study. In *Proceeding of Fourth International Conference on Spoken Language Processing. ICSLP'96*, volume 3, pages 1868–1871. IEEE.

Elizabeth Ellen Shriberg. 1994. *Preliminaries to a theory of speech disfluencies*. Ph.D. thesis, University of California, Berkeley.

Man-hung Siu and Mari Ostendorf. 1996. Modeling disfluencies in conversational speech. In *Proceeding of Fourth International Conference on Spoken Language Processing. ICSLP'96*, volume 1, pages 386–389. IEEE.

Percy H Tannenbaum, Frederick Williams, and Carolyn S Hillier. 1965. Word predictability in the environments of hesitations. *Journal of Verbal Learning and Verbal Behavior*, 4(2):134–140.

Wilson L Taylor. 1953. Cloze procedure: A new tool for measuring readability. *Journalism Bulletin*, 30(4):415–433.

Jean E Fox Tree. 1995. The effects of false starts and repetitions on the processing of subsequent words in spontaneous speech. *Journal of Memory and Language*, 34(6):709–738.

Michiko Watanabe, Keikichi Hirose, Yasuharu Den, and Nobuaki Minematsu. 2008. Filled pauses as cues to the complexity of upcoming phrases for native and non-native listeners. *Speech Communication*, 50(2):81–94.

Thomas Wolf, Lysandre Debut, Victor Sanh, Julien Chaumond, Clement Delangue, Anthony Moi, Pierric Cistac, Tim Rault, R'emi Louf, Morgan Funtowicz, and Jamie Brew. 2019. Huggingface's transformers: State-of-the-art natural language processing. *ArXiv*, abs/1910.03771.

Vicky Zayats, Trang Tran, Richard Wright, Courtney Mansfield, and Mari Ostendorf. 2019. Disfluencies and Human Speech Transcription Errors. In *Proc. Interspeech 2019*, pages 3088–3092.

Bilingual Lexical Access and Cognate Idiom Comprehension

Eve Fleisig
Princeton University
Princeton, NJ
`efleisig@princeton.edu`

Abstract

Language transfer can facilitate learning L2 words whose form and meaning are similar to L1 words, or hinder speakers when the languages differ. L2 idioms introduce another layer of challenge, as language transfer could occur on the literal or figurative level of meaning. Thus, the mechanics of language transfer for idiom processing shed light on how literal and figurative meaning is stored in the bilingual lexicon. Three factors appear to influence how language transfer affects idiom comprehension: bilingual fluency, processing of literal-figurative vs. figurative cognate idioms (idioms with the same wording and meaning in both languages, or the same meaning only), and comprehension of literal vs. figurative meaning of a given idiom. To examine the relationship between these factors, this study investigated English-Spanish bilinguals' reaction time on a lexical decision task examining literal-figurative and figurative cognate idioms. The results suggest that fluency increases processing speed rather than slow it down due to language transfer, and that language transfer from L1 to L2 occurs on the level of figurative meaning in L1-dominant bilinguals.

1 Introduction

Speakers learning a new language may be helped or hindered by similarities with their native language. Language transfer—the influence of a speaker's native language (L1) on the new language (L2)—can facilitate learning L2 words whose form and meaning are similar to L1 words, but can confuse speakers when the languages differ (as with false cognates). Thus, understanding the mechanics of language transfer helps to illuminate potential difficulties for language learners.

L2 idioms introduce another challenge, as idioms have both a literal meaning and a figurative one that cannot be fully decomposed from the meanings of the individual words. Whereas experiments involving non-idiom words have investigated language transfer between the visual forms and the literal meanings of words, idioms introduce a third level on which language transfer may occur: that of figurative meaning.

The effects of language transfer provide key insight into questions of idiom representation in the bilingual lexicon. Although some argue that idioms are stored as unanalyzable, fixed units in the lexicon, other studies have suggested hybrid models of idiom compositionality in which idioms may be interpreted both figuratively and literally to different extents depending on factors such as a speaker's familiarity with the idiom (Fellbaum, 2015). Recent studies have investigated how bilingual fluency affects the degree to which literal and figurative meanings are activated during lexical access. L2 learners generally develop the ability to understand the literal meanings of L2 idioms before they can understand their figurative meanings. Other studies preliminarily suggest that language transfer helps L1-dominant bilinguals with comprehension of L2 cognates but may in fact slow down L2-dominant bilinguals (see Section 2).

Three factors appear to influence how language transfer affects idiom comprehension: bilingual fluency, processing of literal-figurative vs. figurative cognate idioms (idioms with the same wording and meaning in both languages, or with only the same meaning), and comprehension of literal vs. figurative

Proceedings of the Workshop on Cognitive Aspects of the Lexicon, pages 98–106
Barcelona, Spain (Online), December 12, 2020

meaning of a given idiom (Figure 1). Previous work has only examined some relationships between these factors, but none have examined either (1) the relationship between bilingual fluency and the processing of literal-figurative and figurative cognate idioms or (2) comprehension of literal vs. figurative meaning for literal-figurative and figurative cognate idioms. This study examines both of those questions by measuring the relationship between bilingual fluency and the speed of processing literal vs. figurative meaning for literal-figurative and figurative cognate idioms.

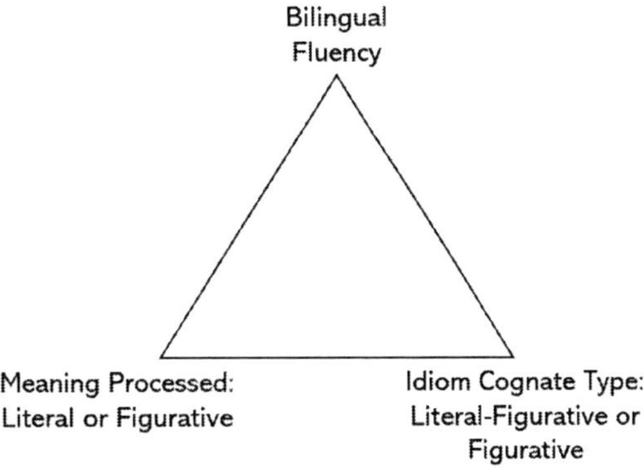

Figure 1: Factors affecting bilingual processing of cognate idioms.

The relationship between processing speed and fluency for different idiom types (literal-figurative cognate or figurative cognate) and target types (literal or figurative processing) shines light on whether increased fluency indeed affects comprehension of literal-figurative cognates compared to figurative cognates, and whether language transfer affects literal or figurative processing more significantly. This study began with the hypothesis that L1-dominant bilinguals would process L2 cognate idioms more quickly than non-cognates, but L2-dominant bilinguals would not, as Heredia et al. (2007) proposed that language transfer slows down processing as fluency increases (see Section 2). It was also hypothesized that processing of literal meaning, as well as processing of figurative meaning, would become faster as fluency increased—i.e., that there is no tradeoff between comprehension of figurative and literal meaning—in keeping with the argument that the literal meanings of idioms, not only figurative ones, may be stored in the bilingual lexicon to some extent. The results suggest that, contrary to Heredia et al.'s hypothesis, fluency sped up processing rather than slow it down because of language transfer. More strikingly, they also suggest that language transfer from L1 to L2 occurs on the level of figurative meaning in L1-dominant bilinguals.

2   Related Work

Language transfer occurs when a speaker's native language influences the acquisition or use of their L2; in particular, it affects the processing of cognate words between the speaker's L2 and L1. Bilinguals process L2 words with L1 cognates more quickly than L2 words without L1 cognates and are more accurate at mapping form to meaning for cognates, but tend to process false friends (L2 words visually or phonetically similar to L1 words but with different meanings) more slowly (Pham et al., 2017; Poort and Rodd, 2017). Thus, language transfer may increase or decrease processing speed depending on whether the forms and meanings of words are aligned between two languages.

Unlike expressions whose meaning can be decomposed from the meanings of individual words, the meaning of idioms is at least partially non-compositional. Thus, idioms may have a literal meaning (*kick the bucket* as in touching a pail with a foot) alongside a figurative one (to die),[1] both of which may be

---

[1] For the purposes of understanding language transfer on the literal and figurative level, this study excludes idioms that might be said to have a figurative meaning alone; rather, it examines idioms with clear literal and figurative meanings, such as *throw in the towel* or *playing with fire*.

	Literal-Figurative Cognate	**Figurative Cognate**
Spanish Idiom	*tirar la toalla* throw the towel	*de tal palo, tal astilla* from such stick, such splinter
English Equivalent	throw in the towel	the apple doesn't fall far from the tree
Figurative Meaning	"give up"	"the child is similar to the parent"

Table 1: Sample figurative and literal-figurative cognate idioms.

affected by language transfer.

L2 learners generally develop the ability to understand the literal meanings of idioms before they can understand their figurative meanings. Cieślicka (2006) argues that, regardless of the context in which a specific idiom is seen, idioms are interpreted according to their overall salience—the meaning (literal or figurative) that is more readily accessible in the lexicon due to factors such as familiarity with the idiom and the context in which the idiom has been seen. Thus, as L2 learners see an idiom in more figurative contexts, the figurative meaning becomes more salient and they are more likely to interpret it figuratively regardless of context. In one study, for example, Spanish-dominant English-Spanish bilinguals were slower to process English target words similar in figurative meaning to an English idiom than those similar in literal meaning to the idiom, compared to English-dominant bilinguals (Cieślicka et al., 2017).

Idioms in two languages may be cognates with respect to their literal and/or figurative meanings (Table 1). For example, the English idiom *the apple doesn't fall far from the tree* and the Spanish *de tal palo, tal astilla* ("from that stick, that splinter") have the same figurative meaning but different literal meanings, whereas the English *throw in the towel* and Spanish *tirar la toalla* have the same literal and figurative meanings. We refer to idioms with the same figurative meaning but different literal meanings as figurative cognates, and idioms with the same literal and figurative meanings as literal-figurative cognates.

Two similar studies suggest that language transfer helps L1-dominant bilinguals with comprehension of L2 cognates but slows down L2-dominant bilinguals. Irujo (1986) found that Spanish-dominant bilinguals were more accurate at comprehending literal-figurative cognate idioms in English than non-cognate English idioms. However, Heredia et al. (2007) found that, surprisingly, English-dominant English-Spanish bilinguals were slower at reading literal-figurative cognate idioms in English than figurative cognate idioms. Heredia et al. suggested that language transfer between literally similar English and Spanish idioms might slow down bilinguals as they become more fluent in their L2 (English): whereas different idioms might be stored as single words, literally similar idioms might activate both L1 and L2 lexicons, slowing down processing. However, because Heredia et al. did not examine Spanish-dominant bilinguals, and Irujo did not examine English-dominant bilinguals, there remains the open question of the extent to which language transfer confers an advantage or disadvantage on the processing of literal-figurative cognate idioms as bilingual fluency increases.

Some studies have investigated the relationship between bilingual fluency and the comprehension of literal and figurative meaning, while others have investigated the differences between bilingual processing of literal-figurative and figurative cognate idioms. The relationship between bilingual fluency and the processing of literal and figurative cognate idioms, as well as the comprehension of literal vs. figurative meaning for literal-figurative and figurative cognate idioms, have remained open questions. To address them, this study examines the relationship between bilingual fluency and processing of literal vs. figurative meaning for literal-figurative and figurative cognate idioms.

3 Methods

3.1 Participants

31 English-Spanish bilinguals between the ages of 18 and 22 who began learning Spanish between ages 0 and 17 were recruited. Participants' Spanish ability was measured using the Bilingual Dominance Scale (Dunn and Tree, 2009), which quantifies bilingual dominance in the range ±30 (where +30 indicates complete Spanish dominance, -30 complete English dominance) using weighted factors including age of acquisition and percent of language use. Participants' bilingual dominance scores ranged from -30 to

Idiom	Literally Congruent Target	Figuratively Congruent Target	Incongruent Target	Nonce Distractor
de tal palo, tal astilla from such stick, such splinter "the apple doesn't fall far from the tree"	*rama* branch	*familia* family	*cielo* sky	*avapa*
tirar la toalla throw the towel "throw in the towel"	*secar* to dry	*vencido* defeated	*pájaro* bird	*frapo*

Table 2: Sample targets for idioms in the CCDMD index.

+24, with a mean score of -11 and median of -14.[2]

3.2 Materials

50 Spanish idiomatic expressions with both a literal and a figurative interpretation were gathered, 25 with literal English cognates and 25 with figurative English cognates.[3] In addition, 25 non-idiomatic control sentences with no close English equivalent were gathered, which acted as fillers. Idioms were gathered from the Quebec Collegial Centre for Educational Materials Development (CCDMD)'s index of trilingual idioms (CCDMD, 2009). Each idiom was then paired with three potential target words: one literally congruent to the idiom (e.g., *rama* "branch" for *de tal palo, tal astilla* "from such a stick, such a splinter"), one figuratively congruent (e.g., *familia* "family" for the same idiom), and one incongruent. The control sentences were paired with a literally congruent target and an incongruent target (Table 2).

Tests were randomly generated by sampling the lists of literal-figurative cognate idioms, figurative cognate idioms, and control sentences. Each test consisted of 12 of each type of idiom, four of which were paired with each type of target (literally congruent, figuratively congruent, or incongruent). For the control sentences, half were paired with (literally) congruent targets and half with incongruent targets. A nonce target (created by randomly generating strings and keeping only those obeying Spanish phonotactic constraints that were not valid Spanish words) was added to each sentence-target pair. The order of the questions and of the nonce and valid target words was randomly shuffled.

3.3 Lexical Decision Task

Oración	Opción 1	Opción 2	Respuesta (1 o 2)
			2
			1
			2
Él guarda una carta en la manga.	naipe	pargen	1

Figure 2: A sample test in progress. The idiom *Él guarda una carta en la manga* ("He has an ace up his sleeve") was paired with the literal target *naipe* ("playing card") and the nonce word *pargen*. The participant then types the number of the correct answer, 1, in the response column.

The experiment was conducted virtually over Google Sheets (Figure 2). Clicking on a cell revealed the priming sentence, after which there was a 3-second delay during which participants were instructed to read the sentence carefully. Then, two answer choices (the valid Spanish target and the random nonce word) appeared for 5 seconds in cells labelled 1 and 2. Participants were instructed to type the number of the valid word as quickly as possible in another cell. All instructions on the test were given in

---

[2]Reaction time was tested on Spanish idioms and the range of abilities tested was limited from -30 (full English dominance) to +24 (significant Spanish dominance) because of the difficulty of recruiting completely Spanish-dominant speakers.

[3]The full cognate list will be made available at `github.com/efleisig/bilingual-cognate-idiom-study`.

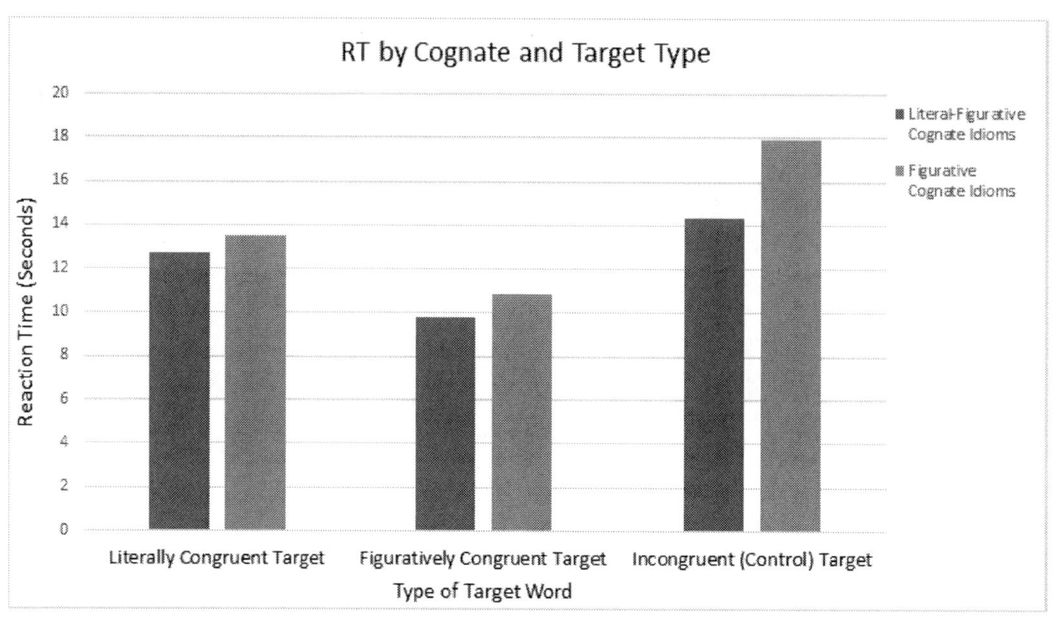

Figure 3: RT by idioms' cognate and target type.

Spanish.[4] To record participants' reaction time (RT), the time when the priming sentence appeared and when participants typed the answer for each idiom after the answer choices appeared was then recorded.

Six results were discarded: one for failing to complete the test, two for not following the directions, and three for participants' Internet lag issues that prevented time from being recorded accurately. Analysis was performed on the remaining 25 participants' responses.

4 Results

4.1 Effect of Cognate and Target Type on Reaction Time

On average, all the bilingual participants processed literal-figurative cognate idioms faster than figurative cognate idioms regardless of the target type (Figure 3). In addition, they processed target words related to both the figurative and the literal meaning of the idiom faster than unrelated target words, and processed target words related to the figurative meaning slightly faster than words related to the literal meaning.

4.2 Effect of Bilingual Dominance on Reaction Time

For each combination of idiom type (literal-figurative cognate, figurative cognate, or control) and target type (literally congruent, figuratively congruent, or incongruent), the relationship between bilingual dominance and RT was measured using Spearman's rank correlation (Table 3).

As Spanish fluency increased (measured by the Bilingual Dominance Scale), reaction time overall decreased (Figure 4), indicating a correlation between fluency and RT ($r_s = -0.56$, $p = .004$). There was also a moderate correlation significant at the 0.05 level between Spanish fluency and RT for figurative cognate idioms, for both literally ($r_s = -.56$, $p = .004$) and figuratively ($r_s = -.47$, $p = .017$) congruent targets (Figures 5 and 6). However, for literal-figurative cognate idioms, there was a significant correlation between Spanish fluency and RT for literally ($r_s = -.48$, $p = .015$), but not figuratively ($r_s = -.16$, $p = .43$) congruent targets (Figures 7 and 8).

---

[4]A separate instructions page, not visible during the test itself, was given in Spanish and English in case some participants were unable to fully understand the Spanish instructions.

Cognate-Target Pair	Spearman's Rank Correlation	p-Value
Literal-Figurative Cognate, Literal Target	**-0.4814**	**0.0148**
Literal-Figurative Cognate, Figurative Target	-0.1647	0.431
Literal-Figurative Cognate, Incongruent Target	-0.1147	0.585
Figurative Cognate, Literal Target	**-0.5555**	**0.00394**
Figurative Cognate, Figurative Target	**-0.4735**	**0.0168**
Figurative Cognate, Incongruent Target	-0.3450	0.0913
Control Sentence, Literal Target	-0.2052	0.325
Control Sentence, Incongruent Target	-0.3842	0.0579
Average for All Types	**-0.5553**	**0.00396**

Table 3: Spearman rank correlation for bilingual dominance and RT, for each idiom and target type. Results significant at the 0.05 level are in bold.

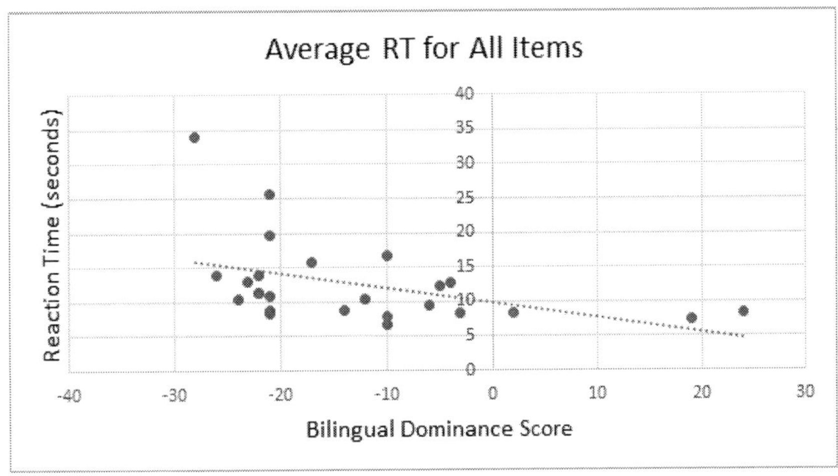

Figure 4: Average RT on all test items by Bilingual Dominance Score.

4.3 Differences between Strongly L1 and L2-Dominant Bilinguals

The differences in performance between the highest and lowest quartiles of Spanish dominance (i.e., the most English-dominant and the most Spanish-dominant bilinguals) were also measured (Figure 9). The Spanish-dominant bilinguals had relatively similar RTs for literal and figurative targets regardless of whether the idioms were literal-figurative or figurative cognates. By contrast, English-dominant bilinguals processed figurative targets faster when the idioms were literal-figurative cognates. This suggests that the fact that bilingual fluency correlates with RT for literal targets for literal-figurative cognate idioms, but not of figurative targets for literal-figurative cognate idioms, is due to effects on English-dominant bilinguals, not Spanish-dominant bilinguals—i.e., English-dominant bilinguals are faster at processing figurative targets than literal targets for literal-figurative cognate idioms.

5 Discussion

5.1 Bilingual Fluency and Processing Speed

In contrast with Heredia et al.'s results, bilinguals processed literal targets for literal-figurative cognate idioms significantly faster as bilingual fluency increased. This finding could suggest that the primary factor affecting bilingual processing of literal targets for literal-figurative cognate idioms is not language transfer that slows down more fluent bilinguals. Rather, increased fluency results in shorter reaction times (RTs) in bilinguals with greater Spanish dominance.

One possibility explaining these results is the languages tested. Both this study and Heredia et al.

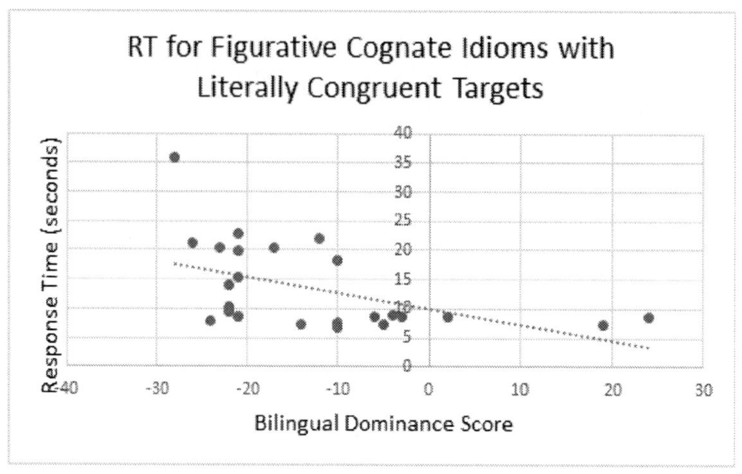

Figure 5: RT for figurative cognate idioms with literally congruent targets.

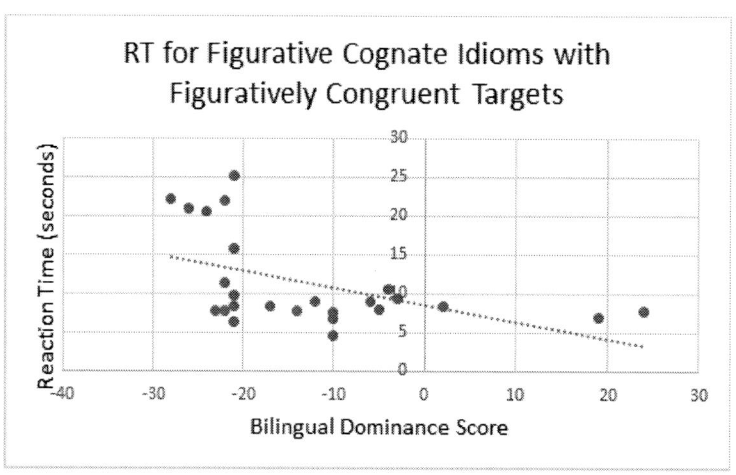

Figure 6: RT for figurative cognate idioms with figuratively congruent targets.

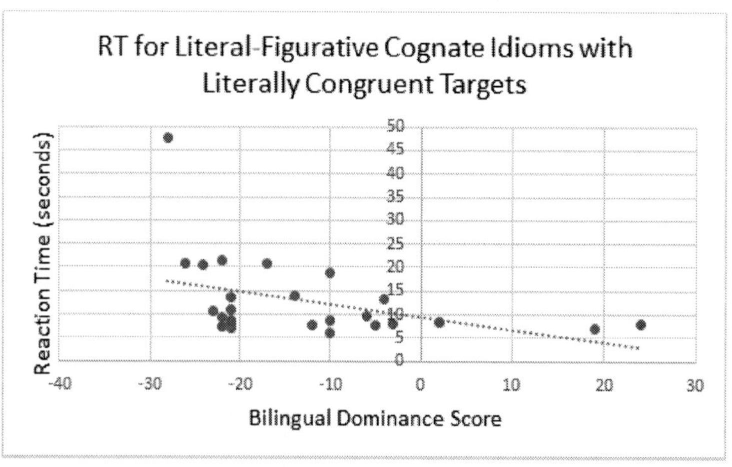

Figure 7: RT for literal-figurative cognate idioms with literally congruent targets.

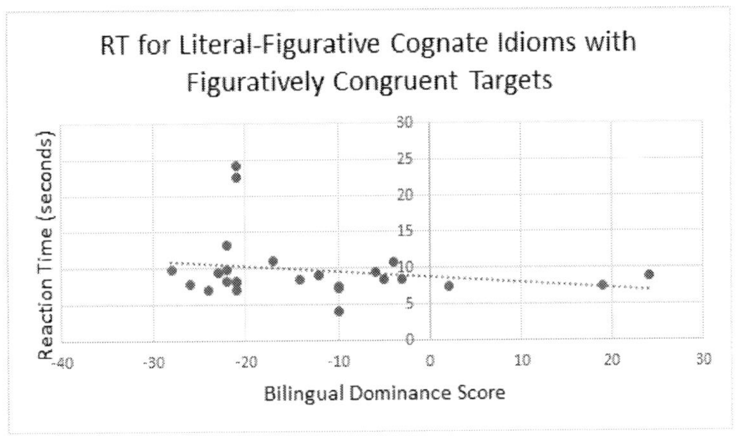

Figure 8: RT for literal-figurative cognate idioms with figuratively congruent targets.

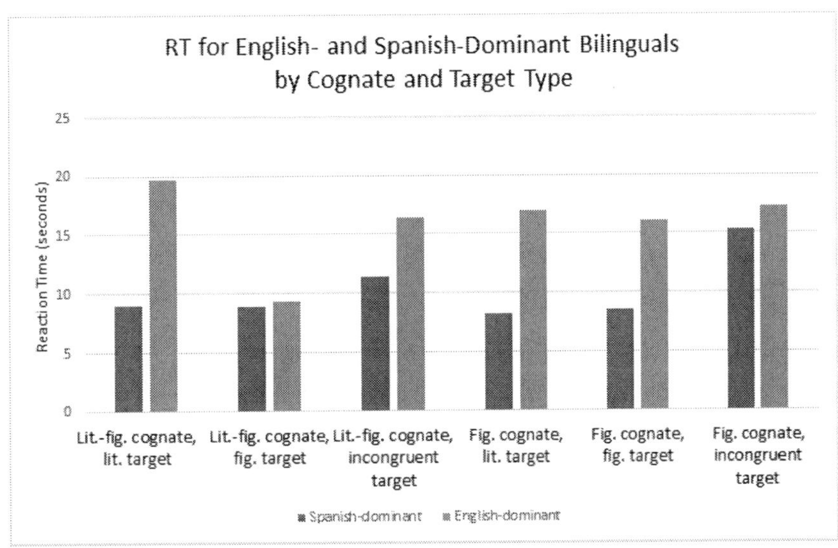

Figure 9: RT by cognate and target type for the most English-dominant and Spanish dominant participants.

tested English-Spanish bilinguals, of whom the most Spanish-dominant bilinguals had learned Spanish earlier in life. However, Heredia et al. tested participants in English, whereas this experiment examined them in Spanish. Thus, in that study, language transfer might result in longer RTs in the tested language, which was learned later on, but in this one, higher fluency resulted in shorter RTs in the tested language, which was learned earlier on. Future work could repeat this study with English idioms to investigate that possibility.

5.2   Transfer of Figurative Meaning

The experiment also found that bilingual fluency results in shorter RTs for both literally and figuratively congruent targets for figurative cognate idioms. This suggests that as bilingual fluency increases, ability to interpret idioms in one language independent of a literal cognate with the other language increases. However, for literal-figurative cognate idioms, there was a significant correlation between Spanish fluency and RT for literally congruent targets, but not figuratively congruent targets. Highly Spanish-dominant bilinguals processed literal and figurative targets for literal-figurative and figurative cognate idioms at similar speeds, but English-dominant bilinguals were much slower at processing literal targets for literal-figurative cognate idioms than figurative ones.

In terms of bilingual representation of cognates in the mental lexicon, one explanation for this trend is that while Spanish-dominant bilinguals gained little advantage from an idiom's status as a literal-figurative cognate, English-dominant bilinguals were quicker at accessing the figurative meaning of idioms that were literal-figurative cognates with a familiar English idiom. That is, Spanish-dominant bilinguals may have processed idioms quickly regardless of whether they had a literal-figurative cognate idiom in English because their processing of idioms in Spanish had little to no reliance on the English lexicon. By contrast, the figurative meaning of the idiom was more readily accessible to the English-dominant bilinguals when processing a literal-figurative cognate because they were accustomed to seeing the idiom used figuratively in English: the idiom's figurative meaning, interpreted non-compositionally, was more salient in the English lexicon. This suggests that language transfer from L1 to L2 does occur on the figurative level in L1-dominant bilinguals.

Future studies testing other languages on a larger scale are needed to examine whether these preliminary results indeed hold cross-linguistically. In addition, conceding the limitations of examining idioms without context, future work could provide insight into how context affects the speed with which literal or figurative meaning is interpreted. These extensions could provide further insight into idiom representation in the bilingual lexicon.

Acknowledgments

Many thanks to Christiane Fellbaum for her advice on this work.

References

Anna Cieślicka, Roberto R. Heredia, and Tanya García. 2017. Task effects in bilingual idiom comprehension. *Poznań Studies in Contemporary Linguistics*, 53.

Anna Cieślicka. 2006. Literal salience in on-line processing of idiomatic expressions by second language learners. *Second Language Research*, 22:115–144.

Alexandra Dunn and Jean Fox Tree. 2009. A quick, gradient bilingual dominance scale. *Bilingualism: Language and Cognition*, 12:273 – 289, 07.

Christiane Fellbaum. 2015. Syntax and grammar of idioms and collocations. *Handbücher Zur Sprach- Und Kommunikationswissenschaft [Handbooks of Linguistics and Communication Science]*, 42.

CCDMD [Quebec Collegial Centre for Educational Materials Development]. 2009. Index of expressions with equivalent meanings.

Roberto R. Heredia, Omar García, and Mary R. Penecale. 2007. The comprehension of idiomatic expressions by spanish-english bilinguals. *PsycEXTRA Dataset*.

Suzanne Irujo. 1986. Don't put your leg in your mouth: Transfer in the acquisition of idioms in a second language. *TESOL Quarterly*, 20.

Eva D. Poort and Jennifer M. Rodd. 2017. The cognate facilitation effect in bilingual lexical decision is influenced by stimulus list composition. *Acta Psychologica*, 180:52–63.

Schwa-deletion in German noun-noun compounds

Tom Juzek
Saarland University
Saarbrücken, Germany
`tom.juzek@`
`posteo.net`

Jana Häussler
Bielefeld University
Bielefeld, Germany
`jana.haeussler@`
`uni-bielefeld.de`

Abstract

We report ongoing research on linking elements in German compounds, with a focus on noun-noun compounds in which the first constituent is ending in schwa. We present a corpus of about 3000 nouns ending in schwa, annotated for various phonological and morpho-syntactic features, and critically, the dominant linking strategy. The corpus analysis is complemented by an unsuccessful attempt to train neural networks and by a pilot experiment asking native speakers to indicate their preferred linking strategy for nonce words. While neither the corpus study nor the experiment offer a clear picture, the results nevertheless provide interesting insights into the intricacies of German compounding. Overall, we find a predominance of the paradigmatic linking element *-n*. At the same time, the results show that *-n* is not a default strategy.

1 Introduction

German compounds and especially noun-noun compounds often include a linking element (*LE*), i.e. segmental material between the two constituents of a compound, such as *-s* in *Liebesbrief* 'love letter' (*liebe-s-brief* [love-LE-letter]) or *-er* in *Kindergarten* 'nursery' (*kind-er-garten* [child-LE-garden]). Though linking elements are a common phenomenon in Germanic languages, German is special because of its rich inventory of linking elements: *-e, -en, -ens, -er, -es, -n, -ns, -s,* and *-i/-o*. Furthermore, deletion and substitution may occur. Whether the number of linking elements can be diminished by assuming variation similar to the allomorphic variation of the homophoneous inflectional affixes (e.g. *-(e)n*) is a disputed topic (cf. Neef, 2015 and Nübling & Szczepaniak, 2013). The rules governing linking element selection are anything but obvious, even native speakers of German are sometimes unsure of the "correct" choice. Linking elements also constitute a major challenge for natural language generation and machine translation (e.g. Matthews et al. 2016)..

Our study investigates a very specific linking strategy, which has received less attention so far: the deletion of a final schwa, in the literature sometimes referred to as *subtractive linking element*. An example for this strategy is *Endpunkt* ('endpoint') which combines *Ende* ('end') and *Punkt* ('point'). Though schwa-deletion in itself does not apply to too many words, it affects some high frequency nouns like *Sache* ('thing', 'matter') and *Farbe* ('colour', 'paint'). To explore the phenomenon systematically, we created a corpus of (almost) all simple nouns ending in schwa and asked two annotators to indicate the preferred linking strategy for each of those nouns. Furthermore, we conducted a forced choice experiment to gain further insights. We report both studies in turn.

2 Linking element selection in German

It is consensus that the choice of linking element is mainly determined by the left constituent in a compound. Evidence comes from tupels like *Tag-e-buch* 'diary', lit. 'day book', *Kind-er-buch* 'children's book', *Jugend-buch* 'book for adolescents', *Liebling-s-buch* 'favorite book', *Schul-buch* (*Schule+Buch*) 'school book' which share the second constituent but differ in the first constituent and the linking element. Further evidence comes from coordinated compounds, such as *Gesundheits- und Sozialwesen*

Proceedings of the Workshop on Cognitive Aspects of the Lexicon, pages 107–111
Barcelona, Spain (Online), December 12, 2020

'health care and welfare system'. Expanding this conclusion, Fuhrhop (1996) proposed that the lexical representations of nouns includes specific stems for compounding. Notably, there a several cases that weaken this proposal as they exhibit variation within a single noun, e.g. *Tag-e-buch* 'diary', *Tagtraum* 'day dream', *Tag-es-satz* 'daily rate' or *Beere-n-schnaps* 'berry liquor' and *Blaubeer-schnaps* 'blue berry liquor'. Arguably, though, some of the variation can be explained with reference to diachrony, e.g. through fossilised forms. However, in the present paper, we focus on the role of the left constituent.

There is less consensus about the function of linking elements (for a critical overview see Neef 2015) and the conditions on LE selection for a given noun as the first constituent in a compound, but see Fuhrhop (1996) and Nübling and Szczepaniak (2013) for comprehensive overviews of morpho-phonological factors. For nouns ending in a schwa, the following descriptive generalisations have been hypothesised. Feminine nouns as well as masculine nouns with weak declension pattern almost obligatorily take *-n* as the linking element, cf. Libben et al. (2002), Köpcke (1993). Schwa-deletion occurs rarely, but for some nouns regularly, cf. Ortner et al. (1991). Schwa is never deleted when it constitutes a suffix, cf. Aronoff and Fuhrhop (2002).

Previous studies examined the distribution of linking elements across the board, i.e. for all kinds of nouns and all kinds of linking elements, by counting the occurrences in compounds in text corpora (e.g. Ortner et al. 1991) or lexical resources like CELEX (e.g. Krott et al. 2007). The present study in contrast focuses on a particular type of left constituent, namely nouns ending in schwa. In this sense the present study is more limited; at the same time, it is more comprehensive since the corpus we present below captures virtually all nouns of this specific type.

3 Corpus study

There is no resource one could use to look up compound strategies of German nouns. We therefore created a new corpus, focusing on items that could in principle make use of schwa-deletion. The entire corpus can be found at: `https://gitlab.com/superpumpie/schwa_deletion`.

3.1 Corpus creation

We web scraped all nouns ending in an <e> from the German Wiktionary (The Wikimedia Foundation, 2017b), using Beautiful Soup (Richardson, 2018). Using the information provided in the corresponding Wiktionary entry, we restricted the extraction to nouns in which the final <e> represents a schwa and which are not compounds themselves. We permitted derived nouns like *Tränke* ('drinking trough') because it has been claimed that schwa-deletion is permitted when schwa represents a suffix, cf. Aronoff and Fuhrhop (2002). We manually corrected the output of the extraction scripts, and we excluded proper names but kept demonyms. In a next step, we web scraped and extracted the following features: number of phonemes, CV structure, the phoneme preceding the schwa, grammatical gender, plural marker, as well as an entry's logged frequency in discussion threads of the German Wikipedia (The Wikimedia Foundation, 2017a), an entry's most common preceding word, and most common succeeding word. Further, a native speaker tagged whether an entry is or could be derived by means of schwa-suffixing.

3.2 Corpus annotation for linking strategies

Two annotators, native speakers of German and professional linguists, tagged their preferred linking strategy for each of the items as the first constituent in a noun-noun compound. Whenever the two annotators disagreed (prevalence: 26.6% of all items), a third linguist's judgements were used as a tiebreaker. If all three judgements diverged, we noted down a disagreement (prevalence: about 5%).

3.3 Corpus analysis

3.3.1 Probabilistic analysis

The corpus consists of 2994 critical items, 9 features as independent variables, and preferred linking strategy as our dependent variable. Table 1 gives the distribution of linking elements broken down by gender, excl. items for which the gender was not specified. Overall, we see a dominance of *n*-insertion as the linking strategy in compounds, which is most pronounced in masculine nouns. Since *-(e)n* is the

	schwa-deletion	null	*n*-insertion	other	disagreement
feminine (N=2437)	6.2% (152)	18.9% (460)	69.8% (1700)	0.01% (2)	5.0% (123)
masculine (N=425)	0.0% (0)	8.5% (36)	85.6% (364)	1.2% (5)	4.7% (20)
neuter (N=132)	11.4% (15)	60.6% (80)	17.4% (23)	1.5% (2)	9.1% (12)
all (N=2994)	5.6% (167)	19.2% (576)	69.7% (2087)	0.3% (9)	5.2% (155)

Table 1: Distribution of linking strategies for nouns ending in schwa as tagged by the annotators.

plural marker for feminine nouns and marks both case (incl. genitive) and plural in masculine nouns in the weak declension, which prototypically end in a schwa (Köpcke, 1995), the dominance of *n*-insertion can be interpreted as a preference for paradigmatic linking elements.

Neuter nouns in contrast rarely form the plural and never the genitive with -*n*. Notably, only five of the 23 neuter nouns for which our annotators marked *n*-insertion as the preferred linking strategy form the plural with -*n*. And although *n*-insertion is predominant in our corpus, it is by no means the only linking strategy for feminine nouns ending in schwa – nor for masculine and neuter nouns.

The second most frequent compounding strategy is concatenation without a linking element (labelled "null" in Table 1). Previous studies counting the frequency of linking elements for all types of nouns, i.e. not just ending in a schwa, report that the majority of compounds lack an overt linking element: up to 73% in Ortner et al. (1991), 65% in Krott et al. (2007). Finding only 19% in our sample underscores the assumption that linking elements are determined by the left constituent. For the few neuter nouns in our corpus, *null* is the preferred linking strategy. Finally, as expected, schwa-deletion was rare, occurring in less than 6% of all schwa-nouns. As before, there is a considerable gender effect.

A spot check of the corpus annotations seem to confirm the claim made in Aronoff and Fuhrhop (2002) that suffix-schwa is never deleted. For all of the 19 apparent counterexamples, it seems that corresponding compounds do involve the noun ending schwa but rather an alternative or older form without the schwa (e.g. *Geschrei(e)* 'yelling', *Piss(e)* 'piss') or the base form from which the noun is derived (e.g. the adjective *süß* 'sweet' versus *Süße* 'sweetness' in *Süßholz* or the verb stem *schimpf* 'rant' rather than the noun *Schimpfe* 'ranting' in *Schimpfkanonade* 'long rant').

3.3.2 Linear mixed effects models

To gain further insights, we analysed our corpus with several multi-factorial linear models, using R (R Core Team, 2018) and the *lme4* package (Bates et al., 2015), with the linking strategy as our dependent variable and the other factors listed above, i.e. logged frequency, etc., as predictors. We vary the predictors across models to be able to estimate their importance in explaining the observed variance. Crucially, there is not a single good predictor and a great deal of the variance remains unexplained: The residual SEs are around 0.22. The full output is too lengthy to be added here and a partial output would lack context, and is thus omitted. In case of interest, it can be accessed on our GitLab (see above).

3.3.3 Machine learning models

We have also tried to train various machine learning models, incl. MLPs, CNNs, and LSTMs, using various parameter settings. The difficulty is that we are facing a scarce data problem and that our attempts result in F1-scores below 0.2. Since the results are poor and not very informative, we omit them for the sake of brevity. However, in case of interest, they can be accessed at on our Gitlab. It is an open question whether the results are due to the nature of the phenomenon or due to limitations of our set of features.

4 Production experiment

The lack of effective predictors and the dominance of -*n* suggest that *n*-insertion could be a form of default strategy for nouns ending in schwa. Under this view, -*n* should also predominate in the absence of lexical information, and schwa-deletion would be an exception that is lexically encoded. If so, compounding of nonce words ending in schwa should apply *n*-insertion as the linking strategy.

To test this prediction, we conducted a forced choice experiment with nonce words. In contrast to Dressler et al. (2000), who used existing words as the first constituent and nonce words as the second

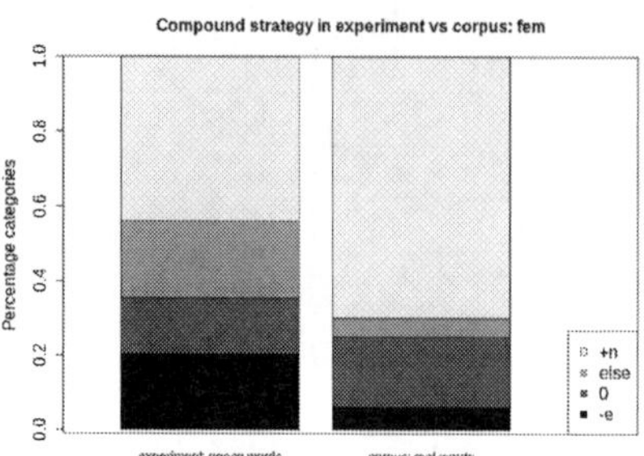

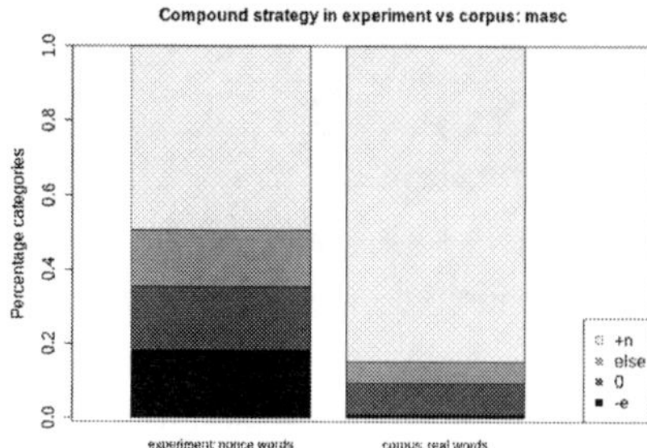

Figure 1: Results for nonce words in the experiment compared to the strategies observed in our corpus (left: feminine nouns, right: masculine nouns). For corpus data, "else" includes "disagreement".

constituent (e.g. *Suppe* 'soup' + *Fend*), we use nonce words as the first constituent and combine them with an existing word. Items were created with a script using Python (Python Software Foundation, 2018), all having the following syllable structure: one or more consonants, followed by a vowel or diphthong, followed by one or more consonants, plus a final schwa. Examples include *Trulve* and *Knüpse*. We manually checked the list for phonological and graphematic well-formedness and excluded items that were phonologically or orthographically too close to existing words. From the remaining set, we randomly sampled 16 items and varied their gender in a within-items design. We created two lists such that each list contained each item in one of its two versions (fem. or masc.) and an equal number of fem. and masc. critical items. In addition, each list contained 8 real nouns ending in schwa (4 fem., 4 masc., all the same in both lists), as well as 24 fillers, both nonce and real nouns not ending in a schwa.

Using Prolific (https://www.prolific.co), we recruited 24 native speakers of German. Participants were requested to choose a linking element for compounding our experimental items with *Beschreibung* ('description'). The words were presented with the corresponding article to indicate the gender (e.g. *der Knüpse + die Beschreibung*). Participants could choose between 7 response categories: *null* (concatenation without an LE), *+e*, *+er*, *+n*, *+s*, *schwa-deletion*, and "others". In total, we collected 304 data points for the critical nonce items. The data reveal a striking discrepancy between the distribution in the corpus of existing nouns ending in a schwa and the nonce words we tested in the experiment (Figure 1). *n*-insertion as a default strategy would have predicted that almost all nonce words select that strategy. However, this is not the case. Compared to the corpus data, the *-n* strategy is less prevalent in nonce compounding.

These surprising findings challenge the idea of *-n* as a default strategy for nouns ending in schwa. Assuming that linking strategies are encoded lexically, e.g. in form of specific compositional stems as part of the lexical representations of the nouns (cf. Fuhrhop 1996), could explain both the lack of a consistent default strategy observed with the nonce words and the failure of the LME model on the corpus data to explain a great deal of the variance.

5   Concluding remarks

While many linking elements in German are well-researched, the phenomenon of schwa-deletion is still an open question. The present paper explores the phenomenon in greater detail, by approaching it in various ways. However, the results of all our approaches paint a picture that is complex. A first analysis provides some probabilistic tendencies – pointing towards a predominance of paradigmatic linking elements. A linear mixed effects model could not identify a set of critical factors, though. The machine learning models that we trained also return poor results. And the results of the production experiment were also complex, hinting at the possibility that there is no default strategy. A plausible interpretation of all our approaches is that the choice of strategy is often encoded lexically. We hope that the results and the provided resources will be a starting point for further research and insights.[1]

---

[1]Both authors contributed equally. We thank the CogALex reviewers for their valuable feedback.

References

Mark Aronoff and Nanna Fuhrhop. 2002. Restricting suffix combinations in German and English: closing suffixes and the Monosuffix Constraint. *Natural Language & Linguistic Theory*, 20(3):451–490.

Douglas Bates, Martin Mächler, Ben Bolker, and Steve Walker. 2015. Fitting linear mixed-effects models using lme4. *Journal of Statistical Software*, 67(1):1–48.

Wolfgang U. Dressler, Gray Libben, Jacqueline Stark, Christiane Pons, and Gonia Jarema. 2000. The processing of interfixed German compounds. *Yearbook of Morphology, 1999*, pages 185–220.

Nanna Fuhrhop. 1996. Fugenelemente. In Ewald Lang and & Gisela Zifonun, editors, *Deutsch – typologisch*, pages 525–549. De Gruyter, Berlin.

Klaus-Michael Köpcke. 1993. *Schemata bei der Pluralbildung im Deutschen. Versuch einer kognitiven Morphologie*. Niemeyer, Tübingen.

Klaus-Michael Köpcke. 1995. Die Klassifikation der schwachen Maskulina in der deutschen Gegenwartssprache. *Zeitschrift für Sprachwissenschaft*, 14(2):159–180.

Andrea Krott, Robert Schreuder, Harald R. Baayen, and Wolfgang U. Dressler. 2007. Analogical effects on linking elements in German compound words. *Language and Cognitive Processes*, 22:25–57.

Gary Libben, Gonia Jarema, Wolfgang Dressler, Jacqueline Stark, and Christiane Pons. 2002. Triangulating the effects of interfixation in the processing of German compounds. *Folia Linguistica*, 36:23–44.

Austin Matthews, Eva Schlinger, Alon Lavie, and Chris Dyer. 2016. Synthesizing compound words for machine translation. In *Proceedings of the 54th Annual Meeting of the Association for Computational (Volume 1: Long Papers)*, pages 1085–1094, Berlin, Germany.

Martin Neef. 2015. The status of so-called linking elements in German: Arguments in favor of a non-functional analysis. *Word Structure*, 8:29–52, 04.

Damaris Nübling and Renata Szczepaniak. 2013. Linking elements in German: Origin, change, functionalization. *Morphology*, 23:67–89.

Lorelies Ortner, Elgin Müller-Bollhagen, Hanspeter Ortner, Hans Wellmann, Maria Pümpel-Mader, and Hildegard Gärtner. 1991. *Deutsche Wortbildung. Typen und Tendenzen in der Gegenwartssprache, vol. 4*. de Gruyter, Berlin & New York.

Python Software Foundation, 2018. *Python: A dynamic, open source programming language.*

R Core Team, 2018. *R: A Language and Environment for Statistical Computing.* R Foundation for Statistical Computing, Vienna, Austria.

Leonard Richardson. 2018. Beautiful soup documentation. `https://www.crummy.com/software/BeautifulSoup/bs4/doc/`.

The Wikimedia Foundation. 2017a. Wikipedia, the free encyclopedia. `https://www.wikipedia.de/`.

The Wikimedia Foundation. 2017b. Wiktionary, the free dictionary. `https://de.wiktionary.org/`.

Translating Collocations: The Need for Task-driven Word Associations

Oi Yee Kwong
Department of Translation
The Chinese University of Hong Kong
oykwong@cuhk.edu.hk

Abstract

Existing dictionaries may help collocation translation by suggesting associated words in the form of collocations, thesaurus, and example sentences. We propose to enhance them with task-driven word associations, illustrating the need by a few scenarios and outlining a possible approach based on word embedding. An example is given, using pre-trained word embedding, while more extensive investigation with more refined methods and resources is underway.

1   Introduction

In practical bilingual lexicography, there is an important distinction between context-free and context-sensitive translation. Context-free translation refers to the general equivalents in a target language given for a particular headword in a source language; and context-sensitive translation refers to the rendition of a headword appropriately according to its occurrence in a given sentence or context. What lexicographers often do is to first produce many translations of a headword in context, and then distill from them a safest equivalent to be the "direct translation" of the headword in the entry, which could be suitably used in most contexts (Atkins and Rundell, 2008). This is in response to the habit of many users of bilingual dictionaries who will take the first equivalent found in the entry and use it without paying much attention to the actual context (Atkins and Varantola, 1997).

In actual translation, however, plugging in the first equivalent found in a dictionary regardless of the context in front of the translator is exactly what is most discouraged. Hence for a bilingual dictionary to be helpful to translators, adequate example sentences should be provided to enlighten users of different rendition possibilities and their appropriateness in a variety of contexts. On the other hand, for a translator to use a bilingual dictionary properly and smartly, one has to possess the skills to access the diverse contexts embedding a certain word and thus a whole range of context-sensitive equivalents in addition to the neutral but probably duller word choices.

In this study, we focus on the translation of ADJ-N collocations from English to Chinese, and consider the lexical information demand on the translator's part. In addition to the access means in existing dictionaries, in the form of collocations, thesaurus, and examples, we propose to enhance them with task-driven word associations filtered from pre-trained word embedding. This is expected to achieve three purposes: to extend the coverage of less common collocations, to assist translators in more precise word choices, and to encourage the use of different translation strategies appropriate in specific contexts.

2   Collocations and Translation Strategies

The translation of collocations has long been an issue (e.g. Chukwu, 1997; Shraideh and Mahadin, 2015), and different languages may not have the same collocations (McKeown and Radev, 2000). In the current discussion, we focus on the translation of English ADJ-N collocations to Chinese, which may seem straightforward at times but could always be challenging when considered from the context-sensitive side. Take a simple example like *good friend*. It can be directly and compositionally rendered as 好朋友 (*good*=好 + *friend*=朋友). While in most cases this would be perfectly fine and most acceptable, in

Proceedings of the Workshop on Cognitive Aspects of the Lexicon, pages 112–116
Barcelona, Spain (Online), December 12, 2020

translation teaching we are nevertheless told that there are always other alternatives which may fit the contexts even better, and there are different strategies to achieve equivalence at various levels (e.g. Baker, 2011). This is especially salient for literary translation. Hence, if the *good friend* in the source text refers to more or less a *confidant*, we may use another Chinese word 知己; or if the original emphasises the length and intensity of the friendship, phrases like 相知多年 (literally meaning "mutually know well for many years") and 友情深厚 (literally meaning "friendship is deep and thick") may be used, amongst many other possible renditions.

The above example shows that even for a simple ADJ+N collocation, a translator may need access to thesaural information, or near-synonyms, in both the source and target languages, to make appropriate lexical choices. In addition to paradigmatic associations, syntagmatic associations are also necessary, to find out what words can naturally describe good and long friendship in the target language. Moreover, even broader word associations are required to enable other translation strategies like transposition, modulation, and paraphrase, which involve the shift in word class and probably an extension into more culturally specific vocabulary items. These three scenarios are further illustrated below, with reference to the Macmillan Dictionary[1] and the Cambridge English-Chinese Dictionary[2].

2.1 Less Common Collocations

The thesaural and collocational information available in a dictionary often only covers the most typical cases. For instance, in the citations for honorary degrees or honorary fellowships in some universities in Hong Kong, the recipients are often praised for their *remarkable contributions*. Looking up both words in the Macmillan Dictionary, the combination is not found in the entries, and also not under Collocations and examples. The adjectives frequently used with *contribution* are: *great, huge, important, major, outstanding, positive, significant, useful,* and *valuable*. Nouns frequently used with *remarkable* are given in several groups, like something done or achieved: *achievement, career, feat, progress, recovery, success*; being similar: *resemblance, similarity*; person or people: *man, people, woman*; etc. Meanwhile, from the bilingual Cambridge Dictionary, the combination is not demonstrated in any of the examples, and the context-free equivalents for *remarkable* (非凡的; 奇異的; 引人注目的 – all leaning toward the sense of extraordinary and unusual) cannot naturally collocate with *contribution* (貢獻 – something you do to help achieve something, disambiguated from money you give and article you write).

2.2 Very Common Collocations

While one has to find ways to think of the appropriate renditions for less common collocations, very common collocations may also demand some creativity on the translator's side to go beyond the context-free combinations. For instance, when a high-level or general adjective (like *good, great*, or *nice*) is used to modify a noun, there could be a better and more specific adjective in the target language to go with the noun. In practice, anything can be good and the most general equivalent of *good* is 好. But to render *good idea* as 好主意 may not always be a good idea, depending on the actual context and style of the source text. Under the *idea* entry in the Cambridge Dictionary, two of the example sentences show the use of *good idea* but both are rendered as 好主意. There is another example with *bright (=good) idea*, translated as 好點子 (slightly informal). The problem is how we may inspire translators with the other alternatives.

2.3 Beyond Literal Translation

There are times when literal translation is not all acceptable from the target language side, and a translator must resort to other strategies that inevitably involve a shift in word class, or when there is a much more idiomatic expression, sometimes cultural specific, for the rendition. An example is *vivid memories*, as in "I still have vivid memories of my childhood". The bilingual Cambridge dictionary gives 栩栩如生的; 鮮活的; 生動的 (which are more like "seeing something brought to life") for *vivid* which are not likely to collocate with the equivalent of *memory* (記憶). So the best translation is not necessarily in the

---

[1] https://www.macmillandictionary.com/
[2] https://dictionary.cambridge.org/

form of ADJ+N, but rather done with a shift in word class, like 清楚記得 (clearly remember), 印象難忘 (impressive, unforgettable), as well as other four-character Chinese idioms like 記憶猶新 and 歷歷在目 which all suggest how clearly one remembers something.

3 Task-driven Word Associations

The issue here is therefore to expand lexical access routes in dictionaries, on top of the thesaural and collocational information as well as example sentences already found therein, to facilitate translators' work and to inspire them of the possibilities for rendition. Lexical access is largely concerned with word associations which form the basis of modelling the mental lexicon as a vast network (e.g. Aitchison, 2003). The interconnection of words in such a network can be used to account for and model various phenomena of the semantic memory like tip-of-the-tongue problem (e.g. Zock and Biemann, 2016). Free word associations include associative relations of different types and strengths. Their statistical modelling from large corpora (e.g. Church and Hanks, 1990; Wettler and Rapp, 1993) has contributed to lexicography for finding collocations and thesaural groups. There is a class of models and methods under distributional semantics (Harris, 1954; Baroni and Lenci, 2010; Clark, 2012), where word senses are represented by means of word co-occurrence vectors. The main assumption is that similar words appear in similar contexts, and by comparing the similarity of the vector spaces, it makes a popular approach for extracting paradigmatically related words (e.g. Agirre et al., 2001; Biemann et al., 2004; Hill et al., 2015; Santus et al., 2016). Word embedding (Mikolov et al., 2013) is a vector model among the latest trends.

3.1 Associations for Different Purposes

Kwong (2016) has shown from a comparison of English and Chinese free association norms that the association patterns are quite different. Free associations tend to be paradigmatic relations in English (e.g. *correct – right*), but syntagmatic or collocational relations in Chinese (e.g. 正確 *correct –* 答案 *answer*). Collocations and thesaural groups obtained from large corpora, like those computed by the Sketch Engine (Kilgarriff et al., 2004), may not always agree with the word association norms. Sometimes apparently strong associations may not rank high. The main problem, however, is that the associations are not task-specific.

As discussed in Section 2, when translating collocations, we need both paradigmatic and syntagmatic associations, and even broader relations. At the same time, the associations should not be free, because they should be relevant to the collocation being translated. Hence, while it is interesting to know what words are synonymous to *remarkable*, not all of them are relevant if they do not usually modify *contributions*. Similarly, it is useful to know what *remarkable* often modifies, but for this task they would not be informative if they are not also closely associated with *contributions*. Hence, we need to be able to refer to the associations relevant for a particular purpose. In other words, free associations should be re-prioritised for specific language tasks.

3.2 An Example

In this example, we try to address the kind of situations discussed in Section 2.1. Cosine similarities between words are computed with the pre-trained GloVe (6B tokens, 50d) word vectors (Pennington et al., 2014). As the models learn the word representations from their usual contexts, word embeddings are known for their good job on computing word similarity and analogies, which are surprisingly intuitive and interesting. But in contrast to what is usually highlighted, words with high similarities are not restricted to paradigmatically related words. As shown in Figure 1, although *remarkable* and *outstanding* are expected to be similar to each other, the similarity scores may actually be even higher between the adjectives and the nouns they modify. For instance, the similarities for *remarkable – achievements*, *outstanding – achievements*, and *outstanding – contributions* are higher than those for *remarkable – outstanding* and *contributions – achievements*, which are paradigmatically related. This observation implies two things: First, the words found similar to a given word may be considered free associations. Such associations may cover different kinds of relations. Second, ADJ+N may share high similarity if they often co-occur in the same context. In this case, it is quite obvious that *remarkable contributions* may be a less seen combination compared with the others. Thus this is another piece of information revealed from the similarity scores with respect to the closeness of the syntagmatically related words. Also, the similarity scores should be considered in a relative sense. So depending on the task at hand, we should re-order the so-called similar words based on their parts of speech and relative scores to filter the useful information.

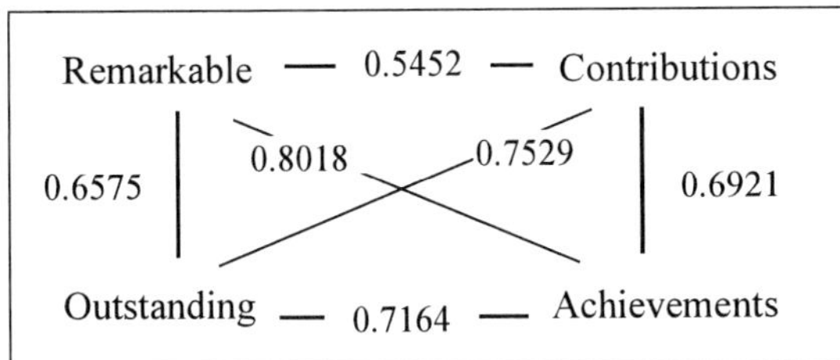

Figure 1: Similarity scores compared

Remarkable		Contribution	
astonishing		contributions	
accomplishment	✓	exceptional	✓
impressive		substantial	
incredible		outstanding	✓
amazing		achievement	✓
surprising		extraordinary	✓

Table 1: Some top associations

3.3 Proposed Steps

Hence, we should have a further interpretation of word embedding, and the information it may provide for our task. What we do here is not only to look for similar words for one word, but check out similar adjectives and nouns back and forth to gather similar collocations for reference, to supplement the less seen combinations not covered in dictionaries. Table 1 shows the top associations for *remarkable* and *contribution* based on similarity scores.

First, screen the adjectives similar to *remarkable* and select those which have higher similarity with *contribution* than *remarkable – contribution*. This gives us *outstanding, extraordinary* and *exceptional*. They are not shown in Table 1 because they were lower in the list, while it illustrates how we discard words highly similar to *remarkable*, like *astonishing* and *amazing*, for they are really less relevant with *contribution*.

Second, are there any nouns associated with *remarkable* that are also similar to *contribution*? In other words, find the words closely related to *contribution* that may be more commonly modified by *remarkable*. This gives us *accomplishment(s), achievement(s)* and *success(es)*. Words like *milestone, inspiration* and *impression* are close to *remarkable*, but not to *contribution*, and they are pushed further down.

Seeded by the selected associations, the links to them in bilingual dictionaries can offer more navigation routes for users, not only to the context-free equivalents, but the corresponding example sentences which may showcase more context-sensitive translations. In this case, 卓越 (more used for *outstanding*) may be a better choice to go with 貢獻 (*contribution*), and of course, the latter may also have other synonymous alternatives in Chinese.

4 Ongoing Work

We have only outlined the steps to be tried, in their primitive and crude forms. But while the means are still under investigation, the ends are clear. The word associations modelled from large corpora may give nice results in certain cases, but in practice the associated words can often be so broadly related that they will simply not be equally activated when a person is performing a particular language task. Hence, we need task-driven associations to focus on the most relevant associated words in a given context. In this study, we have used collocation translation as a task and proposed to filter the associations by means of similarity or closeness obtained from word embedding. By doing so, we expect to enhance the lexical access means in dictionaries to assist translators in producing both faithful and fluent renditions.

In the present discussion, we only used a pre-trained embedding for some preliminary exploration for one scenario. More extensive work is underway, including the refinement of the method to handle different scenarios, the development of a systematic collocation set for testing, and the use of both English and Chinese word embedding in the process.

Acknowledgements

The work described in this paper was fully supported by a grant from the Research Grants Council of the Hong Kong Special Administrative Region, China (Project No. CUHK 14616317).

References

Agirre, E., Ansa, O., Martinez, D. and Hovy, E. 2001. Enriching WordNet concepts with topic signatures. In *Proceedings of the NAACL 2001 Workshop on WordNet and Other Lexical Resources: Applications, Extensions and Customizations*, Pittsburgh, pp.23-28.

Aitchison, J. 2003. *Words in the Mind: An Introduction to the Mental Lexicon*. Blackwell Publishers.

Atkins, B. and K. Varantola. 1997. Monitoring Dictionary Use. *International Journal of Lexicography, 10*: 1-45.

Atkins, B.T.S. and Michael Rundell. 2008. *The Oxford Guide to Practical Lexicography*. New York: Oxford University Press.

Baker, Mona. 2011. *In Other Words: A Coursebook on Translation*. New York: Routledge.

Baroni, M. and A. Lenci. 2010. Distribution memory: A general framework for corpus-based semantics. *Computational Linguistics, 36(4)*: 673-721.

Biemann, C., Bordag, S. and Quasthoff, U. 2004. Automatic Acquisition of Paradigmatic Relations using Iterated Co-occurrences. In *Proceedings of 4th International Conference on Language Resources and Evaluation (LREC 2004)*, Lisbon, Portugal, pp.967-970.

Chukwu, Uzoma. 1997. Collocations in translation: Personal textbases to the rescue of dictionaries. *ASp, 15-18*: 105-115.

Church, K.W. and P. Hanks. 1990. Word Association Norms, Mutual Information, and Lexicography. *Computational Linguistics, 16(1)*:22-29.

Clark, S. 2012. Vector Space Models of Lexical Meaning. In S. Lappin and C. Fox (Eds.), *The Handbook of Contemporary Semantic Theory* (pp.493-522). Hoboken: John Wiley & Sons.

Harris, Z. 1954. Distributional structure. *Word, 10(2-3)*: 146-162.

Hill, F., Reichart, R. and Korhonen, A. 2015. SimLex-999: Evaluating Semantic Models with (Genuine) Similarity Estimation. *Computational Linguistics, 41(4)*: 665-695.

Kilgarriff, A., Rychly, P., Smrz, P. and Tugwell, D. 2004. The Sketch Engine. In *Proceedings of EURALEX 2004*, Lorient, France.

Kwong, O.Y. 2016. Strong Associations Can Be Weak: Some Thoughts on Cross-lingual Word Webs for Translation. To appear in *Proceedings of the 30th Pacific Asia Conference on Language, Information and Computation (PACLIC 30)*, Seoul, Korea.

McKeown, K.R. and D.R. Radev. 2000. Collocations. In R. Dale, H. Moisl and H. Somers (Eds.), *A Handbook of Natural Language Processing*. Marcel Dekker.

Mikolov, T., Chen, K., Corrado, G. and Dean, J. 2013. Efficient estimation of word representations in vector space. *CoRR*, abs/1301.3781.

Pennington, Jeffrey, Richard Socher, and Christopher D. Manning. 2014. GloVe: Global Vectors for Word Representation.

Santus, E. Lenci, A., Chiu, T-S., Lu, Q. and Huang, C-R. 2016. Nine Features in a Random Forest to Learn Taxonomical Semantic Relations. In Proceedings of the Tenth International Conference on Language Resources and Evaluation (LREC 2016), Portorož, Slovenia, pp.4557-4564.

Shraideh, Khetam W. and Radwan S. Mahadin. 2015. Difficulties and Strategies in Translating Collocations in BBC Political Texts. *Arab World English Journal, 6(3)*: 320-356.

Wettler, M. and R. Rapp. 1993. Computation of word associations based on the co-occurrences of words in large corpora. In *Proceedings of the 1st Workshop on Very Large Corpora: Academic and Industrial Perspectives*, Columbus, Ohio, pp.84-93.

Zock, Michael and Chris Biemann. 2016. Towards a resource based on users' knowledge to overcome the Tip-of-the-Tongue problem. In *Proceedings of the Workshop on Cognitive Aspects of the Lexicon*, Osaka, Japan, pp.57-68.

Characterizing Dynamic Word Meaning Representations in the Brain

Nora Aguirre-Celis[1,2] and Risto Miikkulainen[2]

[1] ITESM, E. Garza Sada 2501, Monterrey, NL, 64840, Mexico
[2] The University of Texas in Austin, 2317 Speedway, Austin, TX, 78712 USA
{naguirre,risto}@cs.utexas.edu

Abstract

During sentence comprehension, humans adjust word meanings according to the combination of the concepts that occur in the sentence. This paper presents a neural network model called CEREBRA (Context-dEpendent meaning REpresentation in the BRAin) that demonstrates this process based on fMRI sentence patterns and the Concept Attribute Representation (CAR) theory. In several experiments, CEREBRA is used to quantify conceptual combination effect and demonstrate that it matters to humans. Such context-based representations could be used in future natural language processing systems allowing them to mirror human performance more accurately.

1 Introduction

A word meaning is more than an entry in a dictionary. It involves a vast amount of knowledge relating the scenes and experiences people encounter (i.e., a rich encyclopedic knowledge), a set of referents to which the word properly applies (i.e., *the boy was angry* vs. *the chair was angry*), combination of other words, and grammatical constructions in which the word occurs. The meaning of the word varies from situation to situation and across contexts of use. For example, the word *small* means something different when used to describe a mosquito, a whale, or a planet. The properties associated with *small* vary in context-dependent ways: It is necessary to know what the word means, but also the context in which is used, and how the words combine in order to construct the word meaning (Medin & Shoben, 1988).

While humans have a remarkable ability to form new word meanings by combining existing concepts, modeling this process is challenging (Hampton, 1997; Janetzko 2001; Middleton et al, 2011; Murphy, 1988; Sag et al., 2002). The same concept can be combined to produce different meanings: *corn oil* means oil made of corn, *baby oil* means oil rubbed on babies, and *lamp oil* means oil for lighting lamps (Wisniewski, 1997, 1998). Since *lamp* is an object, oil is likely to be a member of the inanimate category. However, *corn* and *baby* are living things, which suggest otherwise. How do language users determine the membership structure of such combinations of concepts, and how do they deduce the interpretation? As this example illustrates, there is no simple rule on how to combine concepts (Cohen et al., 1984).

Computational models of such phenomena could potentially shed light into human cognition and advance AI applications that interact with humans via natural language. Such applications need to be able to understand and to form by themselves novel combinations of concepts. Consider for example virtual assistants such as Siri, OK Google, or Alexa. These applications are built to answer questions posed by humans in natural language. All of them have natural language processing software to recognize speech and to give a response. However, whereas humans process language at many levels, machines process linguistic data with no inherent meaning. Given the ambiguity and flexibility of human language, modeling human conceptual representations is essential in building AI systems that interact effectively with humans.

Today's experimental methods allow studying neural mechanisms underlying the semantic memory system. Neuroimaging (fMRI) technology, for instance, provides a way to measure brain activity during

Proceedings of the Workshop on Cognitive Aspects of the Lexicon, pages 117–128
Barcelona, Spain (Online), December 12, 2020

">

word and sentence comprehension. When humans listen or read sentences they use different brain systems to simulate seeing the scenes and performing the actions that are described. As a result, parts of the brain that control these actions light up in the fMRI. Hence, semantic models have become a popular tool for prediction and interpretation of brain activity.

Recently, Machine Learning systems in vision and language processing have been proposed based on single-word vector spaces (Mikolov et al., 2013; Vinyals et al., 2015). They are able to extract low-level features in order to recognize concepts (e.g. cat), but such representations are shallow and fall short from symbol grounding (meaning). In general, these models build semantic representations from text corpora, where words that appear in the same context are likely to have similar meanings (Baroni et. al., 2010; Burgess, 1998; Devlin et al., 2018; Harris, 1970; Landauer & Dumais, 1997; Mikolov et al., 2013 Peters et al., 2018;). This problem has driven researchers to develop new componential approaches where concepts are represented by a set of basic features, integrating different modalities like textual and visual inputs. (Anderson et al., 2019; Bruni et al., 2012; Silberer & Lapata, 2014, Vinyals et. al., 2015). However, even with these multimodal embedding spaces, such vector representations lack intrinsic meaning, and therefore sometimes different concepts may appear similar.

A truly multimodal representations should account for the full array of human senses (Bruni et al., 2014). Embodiment theories of concept representation provide such an array (Barsalou, 1987; Binder et al., 2009; Landau et al., 1998; Regier, 1996). They allow for a direct analysis in terms of sensory, motor, spatial, temporal, affective, and social experience. Further, these theories can be mapped to brain systems. Recent fMRI studies helped identify a distributed large-scale brain network of multimodal sensory systems linked to the storage and retrieval of conceptual knowledge (Binder et al., 2009). This network was then used as a basis for Concept Attribute Representation (CAR) theory (a.k.a. the experiential attribute representation model). This theory is a semantic approach that represents concepts as a set of features that are the basic components of meaning, and grounds them in brain systems (Binder et al., 2009, 2011, 2016a, 2016b).

An intriguing challenge to semantic modeling is that concepts are dynamic, i.e. word meaning depends on context and recent experiences (Barsalou et al., 1993; Pecher et al., 2004; Yee et al., 2016). For example, a pianist would invoke different aspects of the word *piano* depending on whether he will be playing in a concert or moving the *piano*. When thinking about a coming performance, the emphasis will be on the piano's function, including sound and fine hand movements. When moving the piano, the emphasis will be on shape, size, weight and other larger limb movements (Barclay et al., 1974).

This paper addresses the challenge of dynamic representations based on CAR theory. The assumption is that words in different sentences have different representations. Therefore, different features in CARs should be weighted differently depending on context, that is, according to the combination of concepts that occur in the sentence. A neural network model is used to map brain-based semantic representations of words (CARs) into fMRI data of subjects reading everyday sentences. The goal is to identify how the weightings of the attributes in the CARs change to account for context (Aguirre-Celis & Miikkulainen, 2017, 2018, 2019, 2020). In this paper, the CAR theory is first reviewed, and the sentence collection, fMRI data, and word representation data described. Then, the computational model is presented followed by three evaluation studies: an individual example on the conceptual combination effect on word meanings, an aggregate study across the entire corpus of sentences, and a behavioral analysis to evaluate the neural network model.

2   Modeling Framework

To understand how word meanings change under the context of a sentence, three issues are addressed: (1) How are concepts represented? Componential theories of lexical semantics assume that concepts consist of a set of features that constitute the basic components of meaning. CAR theory represents such features in terms of known brain systems, relating semantic content to systematic modulation in neuroimaging activity. (2) How do word meanings change in the context of a sentence? A word is broken into various features that can become active at different rates in different situations. According to CAR theory, the weights given to different feature dimensions are modulated by context. (3) What tools and approaches can be used to quantify such changes? CAR theory assumes that context modifies the baseline meaning of a concept. A computational model can test this assumption by using sentence fMRI patterns and the CAR semantic feature model to characterize how word meanings are modulated within the context of a sentence. The first two issues are addressed by the CAR theory. The third issue is addressed by CEREBRA, or Context-dependent mEaning REpresentation in the BRAin, a neural network model based on CAR theory.

2.1 Concept Attribute Representation (CAR) Theory

CAR theory is a semantic approach that represents concepts as a set of features that are the basic components of meaning (Anderson et al 2016, Binder, 2016a; Smith et al, 1974). They are composed of a list of well-known modalities that correspond to specialized sensory, motor and affective brain processes, systems processing spatial, temporal, and casual information, and areas involved in social cognition. The features directly relate semantic content to systematic modulation of neuroimaging activity. This theory has been mostly applied to the task of prediction of neural activity patterns for individual concepts and entire sentences (Anderson et al., 2016, 2017, 2018, 2019; Binder et al., 2009, 2011, 2016a, 2016b, Fernandino et al., 2015).

Each word is modeled as a collection of 66 features that captures the strength of association between each neural attribute and word meaning. Furthermore, the degree of activation of each attribute associated with the concept can be modified depending on the linguistic context, or combination of words in which the concept occurs. Thus, people weigh concept features differently to construct a representation specific to the combination of concepts in the sentence.

Figure 1 shows the weighted CARs for the generic representation of the concept *bicycle*. The weight values represent average human ratings for each feature. For a more detailed account of this theory see Binder et al. (2009, 2011, 2016a, and 2016b).

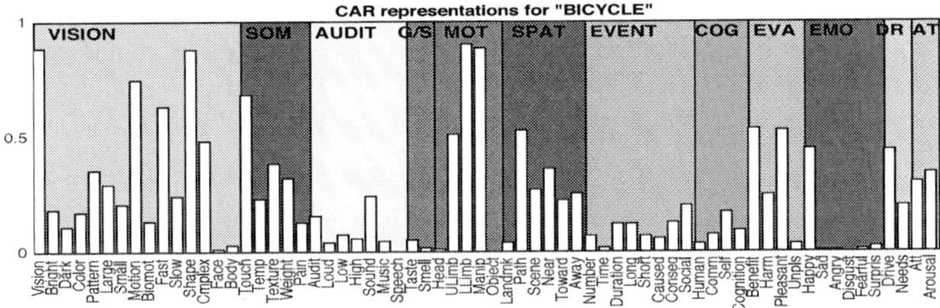

Figure 1: Bar plot of the 66 semantic features for the word *bicycle* (Binder et al., 2009, 2011, 2016a,2016b). It has low weightings on animate attributes such as Face, Body, and Speech, and emotions including Sad, and Fear and high weighting on attributes like Vision, Shape, Touch, and Manipulation. Similarly, it includes high weightings in Motion, Fast, Lower Limb and Path, since *bicycle* is considered a vehicle. CARs for *bicycle*.

2.2 Data Collection and Processing

The CEREBRA model is based on the following sets of data: A sentence collection prepared by Glasgow et al. (2016), the semantic vectors (CAR ratings) for the words obtained via Mechanical Turk, and the fMRI images for the sentences, the last two were collected by the Medical College of Wisconsin (Anderson et al., 2016; Binder et al., 2016a, 2016b). Additionally, fMRI representations for individual words (called SynthWord) were synthesized by averaging the sentence fMRI.

Sentence Collection: A total of 240 sentences were composed of two to five content words from a set of 242 words (141 nouns, 39 adjectives and 62 verbs). The words were selected toward imaginable and concrete objects, actions, settings, roles, state and emotions, and events. Examples of words include *doctor, boy, hospital, desk, red, flood, damaged, drank, agreement, happy, hurricane, summer, chicken,* and *family*. An example of a sentence containing some of those words is *The flood damaged the hospital*.

Semantic Word Vectors: The 242 words (CAR) ratings were collected through Amazon Mechanical Turk (Anderson et al., 2016; Binder et al., 2016a). In a scale of 0-6, the participants were asked to assign the degree to which a given concept is associated with a specific type of neural component of experience (e.g. "To what degree do you think of a *bicycle* as having a fixed location, as on a map?"). Approximately 30 ratings were collected for each word. After averaging all ratings and removing outliers, the final attributes were transformed to unit length yielding a 66-dimensional feature vector (Figure 1). In this manner, the representations map the conceptual content of a word to the corresponding neural representations, unlike other systems where the features are extracted from text corpora and the meaning is determined by associations between words and between words and contexts (Burgess, 1998; Landauer & Dumais, 1997; Mikolov et al., 2013).

Neural fMRI Sentence Representations: To obtain the neural correlates of the 240 sentences, subjects viewed each sentence on a computer screen while in the fMRI scanner. The sentences were presented word-by-word using a rapid serial visual presentation paradigm, with each content word exposed for 400ms followed by a 200ms inter-stimulus interval. Participants were instructed to read the sentences and think about their overall meaning.

Eleven subjects took part in this experiment producing 12 repetitions each. The fMRI data were pre-processed using standard methods. The transformed brain activation patterns were converted into a single-sentence fMRI representation per participant by taking the voxel-wise mean of all repetitions (Anderson et al., 2016; Binder et al., 2016a, 2016b). Due to noise inherent in the neural data, only eight subject fMRI patterns were used for this study. To form the target for the neural network, the most significant 396 voxels per sentence were then chosen (to match six case-role slots of the content words consisting of 66 attributes each) and scaled to [0.2..0.8].

Synthetic fMRI Word Representations: The neural data set did not include fMRI images for words in isolation. Therefore a technique developed by Anderson et al. (2016) was adopted to approximate them. The voxel values for a word were obtained by averaging all fMRI images for the sentences where the word occurs. These vectors, called SynthWords, encode a combination of examples of that word along with other words that appear in the same sentence. Thus, the SynthWord representation for *mouse* obtained from sentence 56:*The mouse ran into the forest* and sentence 60:*The man saw the dead mouse* includes aspects of running, forest, man, seeing, and dead, altogether. Due to the limited number of sentences, some of SynthWords became identical and were excluded from the dataset. The final collection includes 237 sentences and 236 words (138 nouns, 38 adjectives and 60 verbs).

3   Computational Model

CEREBRA model was developed to investigate how words change under the context of a sentence using imaging data (Figure 2). It is based on the CAR semantic feature model and the FGREP neural network architecture (Forming Global Representations with Extended Backpropagation; Miikkulainen & Dyer, 1991). The model is trained to predict fMRI patterns of subjects reading everyday sentences. The FGREP mechanism is used to determine how the CARs would have to change to predict the fMRI patterns more accurately. These changes represent the effect of context; it is thus possible to track the brain dynamic meanings of words by tracking how the CARs feature-weightings change across contexts.

More specifically, the model is first trained to map CARWords (word attribute ratings) to SynthWords (fMRI synthetic words). Once it has learned this task, it is used to modify CAR words in context. SynthWords are combined to form SynthSent for the predicted sentence by averaging all words in the sentence. The SynthSent is then compared to the actual fMRISent (original fMRI data), to form a new error signal. That is, for each sentence, the CARWords are propagated and the error is formed as before, but during backpropagation, the network is no longer changed. Instead, the error is used to change the CARWords themselves (which is the FGREP method; Miikkulainen & Dyer 1991). This modification can be carried out until the error goes to zero, or no additional change is possible (because the CAR attributes are already at their max or min limits). Eventually, the revised CARWord represents the word meaning in the current sentence.

The CEREBRA model was trained 20 times for each of the eight fMRI subjects with different random seeds. A total of 20 different sets of 786 context word representations (one word representation for each sentence where the word appears) were thus produced for each subject. Afterwards, the mean of the 20 representations was used as the final representation for each word (per subject). It is important to emphasize that the goal of the CEREBRA model is not to predict the fMRI patterns as accurately and generally as possible, instead, it is used as a framework to identify and measure context-dependent changes in the CAR words (Aguirre-Celis & Miikkulainen, 2017, 2018, 2019, 2020).

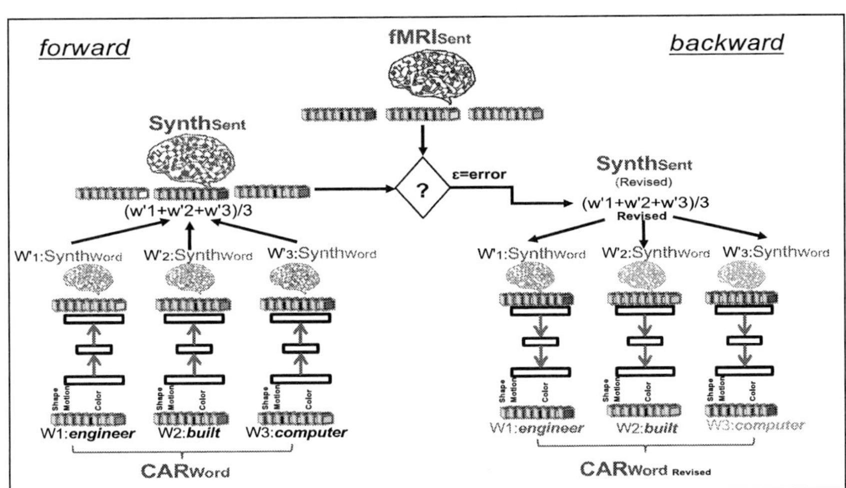

Figure 2: The CEREBRA model to account for context effects. After the model has been trained to map CARWords to SynthWords, it is used to determine how CAR words change in context. (1) Propagate CARWords to SynthWords. (2) Construct SynthSent by averaging the SynthWords into a prediction of the sentence. (3) Compare SynthSent with the observed sentence fMRI. (4) Backpropagate the error with FGREP for each sentence, freezing network weights and changing only CARWords. (5) Repeat until error reaches zero or CAR components reach their upper or lower limits. Thus, the CEREBRA model captures context effects by mapping brain-based semantic representations to fMRI sentence images.

4 Experiments and Results

To evaluate the performance of CEREBRA as well as the context-based representations, two computational experiments and a behavioral analysis were conducted. The first two experiments measure how the CAR representation of a word changes in different sentences, and correlates these changes to the CAR representations of the other words in the sentence (OWS). The behavioral study evaluates the CEREBRA context-based representations against human judgements. Next, an individual example of the conceptual combination effect is first presented, followed by the aggregate analysis and the behavioral study.

4.1 Analysis of an Individual Example

In the CAR theory, concepts' interaction arises within multiple brain networks, activating similar brain zones for both concepts. These interactions determine the meaning of the concept combination (Binder, 2016a, 2016b). As an example, consider the noun-verb interactions in Sentence 200: *The yellow bird flew over the field*, and Sentence 207: *The red plane flew through the cloud*. Since *bird* is a living thing, animate dimensions related to agency such as sensory, gustative, motor, affective, and cognitive experiences are expected to be activated, including attributes like Speech, Taste, and Smell. In contrast, *plane flew* is expected to activate inanimate dimensions related to perceiving an object, as well as Emotion, Cognition, and Attention.

Figure 3 shows the CARs for the word *flew* in the two sentences after they were modified by CERE-BRA as described in Figure 2 and averaged across all eight subjects. In Sentence 200 there were indeed high activations on animate attributes like Biomotion, Smell and Taste, Music, Speech, as well as Communication and Cognition. In contrast, Sentence 207 emphasizes perceptual features like Color, Size, and Shape, Weight, Audition, Loud, Duration, Social, Benefit, and Attention.

The effect of conceptual combination on word meaning is clearly seen in this example. As the context varies, the overlap on neural representations create a mutual enhancement, producing a difference between animate and inanimate contexts. The CEREBRA model encodes this effect into the CAR representations where it can be measured. In other experiments, a similar effect was observed for other noun-verb pairs, as well as several adjective-noun pairs. Next, this effect is quantified statistically across the entire corpus of sentences.

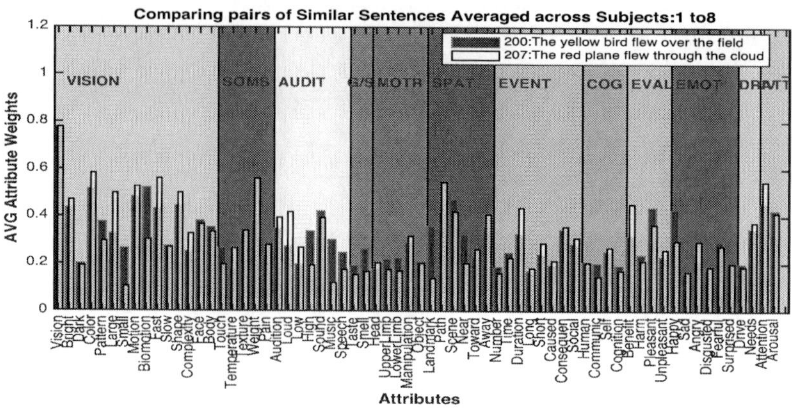

Figure 3: Contrasting the conceptual combination effect in two different sentences. In Sentence 200 (blue bars), the CAR representation modified by CEREBRA for the word *flew* has salient activations on animate features, likely denoting *bird* properties like Biomotion, Smell and Taste, and Communication. In Sentence 207 (white bars), it has high activations on inanimate object features, describing a Loud, Large, and Heavy object such as a *plane*. Thus, there is a clear difference between animate and inanimate features found in each sentence.

4.2 Aggregation Analysis

The aggregation study hypothesis is based on the idea that similar sentences have a similar effect, and this effect is consistent across all words in the sentence. This effect was verified in the following process:

1. For each subject, modified CARs for each word in each sentence were formed through CEREBRA as described in Figure 2.
2. A representation for each sentence, SynthSent, was assembled by averaging the modified CARs.
3. Agglomerative hierarchical clusters of sentences were formed using the set of SynthSents. The Ward method and Euclidean metric were used to measure the distance between clusters and observations respectively. The process was stopped at 30 clusters, i.e., at the point where the granularity appeared most meaningful (e.g., sentences describing open locations vs. closed locations).
4. Each cluster of sentences is expected to reveal similar changes in some of the dimensions. To recognize such common patterns of changes, the next step is to calculate the average of the changes for words with similar roles, e.g., *hospital*, *hotel*, and *embassy* (within the same cluster of sentences). To that end, the differences between the modified and original CAR representations are measured separately for each CAR dimension in each word role, and their significance estimated using Student's *t*-test.
5. The modified CARs of the OWS were averaged.
6. Pearson's correlations were then calculated between the modified CARs and the average CARs of the OWS across all the dimensions.
7. Similarly, correlations were calculated for the original CARs.
8. These two correlations were then compared. If the modified CARs correlate with the CARs of the OWS better than the original CARs, context effect based on conceptual combination is supported.

In other words, this process aims to demonstrate that changes in a target word CAR originate from the OWS. For example, if the OWS have high values in the CAR dimension for Music, then that dimension in the modified CAR should be higher than in the original CAR for such target word. The correlation analysis measures this effect across the entire CAR representations. It measures whether the word meaning changes towards the context meaning. For more detail see (Aguirre-Celis & Miikkulainen, 2019).

The results are shown in Figure 4. The correlations are significantly higher for new CARs than for the original CARs across all subjects and all roles. Furthermore, the AGENT role represents a large part of the context in both analyses (i.e., modified and original CARs). Thus, the results confirm that the conceptual combination effect occurs reliably across subjects and sentences, and it is possible to quantify it by analyzing the fMRI images using the CEREBRA model on CARs. As a summary, the average correlation was 0.3201 (STDEV 0.020) for original CAR representations and 0.3918 (STDEV 0.034) for new CAR representations.

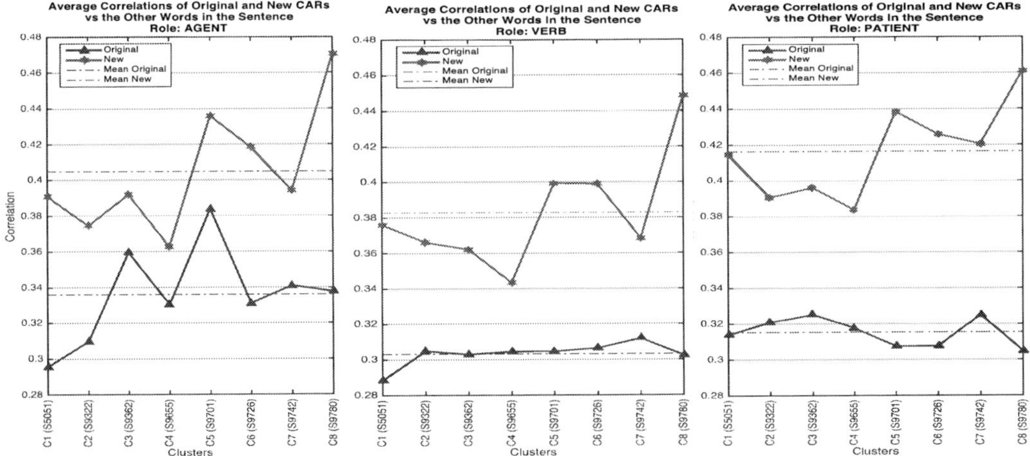

Figure 4: Correlation results. Average correlations analyzed by word class for eight subjects comparing original and new CARs vs. the average of the OWS respectively. A moderate to strong positive correlation was found between new CARs and the OWS, suggesting that features of one word are transferred to OWS during conceptual combination. Interestingly, the original and new patterns are most similar in the AGENT panel, suggesting that this role encodes much of the context.

4.3 Mapping Brain to Behavior

A behavioral analysis was designed to evaluate the CEREBRA's context-based representations via human judgements. That is, Sections 4.1 and 4.2 showed that differences in the fMRI patterns in sentence reading can be explained by context-dependent changes in the semantic feature representations of the words. The goal of this section is to show that these changes are meaningful to humans. Therefore, human judgements are compared to changes predicted by the CEREBRA model.

Measuring Human Judgements: A survey was designed to characterize context-dependent changes by asking the subject directly: In this context, how does this attribute change? Human judgements were crowdsourced using Google Forms in accordance with the University of Texas at Austin Institutional Review Board (2018-08-0114).

The complete survey is an array of 24 questionnaires that include 15 sentences each. For each sentence, the survey measures 10 attribute changes for each target word. Only the top 10 statistically most significant attribute changes for each target words (roles) were used. Overall, each questionnaire thus contains 150 evaluations. For example, a questionnaire might measure changes on 10 specific attributes such as 'is visible', 'living thing that moves', 'is identified by sound', 'has a distinctive taste', for a specific word class such as *politician*, for 15 sentences such as *The politician celebrated at the hotel*. A particular example sentence questionnaire is shown in Figure 5.

Human responses were first characterized through data distribution analysis. Table 1(a) shows the number of answers "less" (-1), "neutral" (0), and "more" (1) for each participant. Columns labeled P1, P2, P3, and P4 show the answers of the participants. The top part of the table shows the distribution of the raters' responses and the bottom part shows the level of agreement among them. As can be seen from the table, the participants agreed only 47% of the time. Since the inter-rater reliability is too low, only questions that were the most reliable were included, i.e., where three out of four participants agreed. There were 1966 such questions, or 55% of the total set of questions.

Measuring Model Predictions: The survey directly asks for the direction of change of a specific word attribute in a particular sentence, compared to the word's generic meaning. Since the changes in the CEREBRA model range within (-1,1), in principle that is exactly what the model produces. However, during the experiments it was found that some word attributes always increase, and do so more in some contexts than others. This effect is related to conceptual combination (Hampton, 1997; Wisniewsky, 1998), contextual modulation (Barclay, 1974), and attribute centrality (Medin & Shoben, 1988): the same property is true for two different concepts but more central to one than to the other (e.g., it is more important for boomerangs to be curved than for bananas).

Figure 5: An example sentence in the survey. The sentence is *The politician celebrated at the hotel*, the target word is *politician* in the role of Agent. Ten different attribute changes are measured by selecting whether the attribute increased ("more"), decreased ("less") or remained "neutral". These human judgements were then matched with those predicted by CEREBRA.

HUMAN RESPONSES DISTRIBUTION						
Resp/Part	P1	P2	P3	P4	AVG	%
-1	2065	995	645	1185	1223	34.0%
0	149	1120	1895	1270	1109	30.8%
1	1386	1485	1060	1145	1269	35.3%
TOT	3600	3600	3600	3600	3600	100%

PARTICIPANT AGREEMENT ANALYSIS						
	P1	P2	P3	P4	AVERAGE	%
P1	0	1726	1308	1650	1561	43%
P2	1726	0	1944	1758	1809	50%
P3	1308	1944	0	1741	1664	46%
P4	1650	1758	1741	0	1716	48%
				TOTAL	6751	
				AVG xPAR	1688	
		AVERAGE	Particip match each other			47%

(a) Human Responses

PARTICIPANTS AVERAGE AGREEMENT			
RATINGS	HUMAN	CEREBRA	CHANCE
-1/0	1074	466	8
1	892	587	886
TOTAL	1966	1052	894
Match each other		54%	45%

(b)Matching Predictions

SUBJECTS	CEREBRA		CHANCE		p-value
	MEAN	VAR	MEAN	VAR	
S5051	1033	707.25	894	6.01	3.92E-24
S9322	1035	233.91	894	7.21	6.10E-33
S9362	1063	224.41	894	11.52	5.22E-36
S9655	1077	94.79	894	7.21	3.89E-44
S9701	1048	252.79	895	12.03	1.83E-33
S9726	1048	205.82	894	4.62	1.73E-35
S9742	1075	216.77	895	7.21	1.65E-37
S9780	1039	366.06	894	2.52	6.10E-30

(c) Statistical Significance

Table 1: Comparing CEREBRA predictions with human judgements. (a) Distribution analysis and inter-rater agreement. The top table shows human judgement distribution for the three responses "less" (-1), "neutral" (0), and "more" (1). The bottom table shows percentage agreement for the four participants. Humans agree 47% of the time. (b) Matching CEREBRA predictions with human data, compared to chance baseline. The table shows the average agreement of the 20 repetitions across all subjects. CEREBRA agrees with human responses 54% while baseline is 45% - which is equivalent to always guessing "more", i.e., the largest category of human responses. (c) Statistical analysis for CEREBRA and baseline. The table shows the means and variances of CEREBRA and chance models for each subject and the p-values of the t-test, showing that the differences are highly significant. Thus, the context-dependent changes are actionable knowledge that can be used to predict human judgements.

The direction of change is therefore not a good predictor of human responses. Instead these changes need to be measured relative to changes in the OWS. Three approaches were thus used to evaluate the changes: (1) What is the effect of the rest of the sentence in the target word? This effect was measured by computing the average of the CEREBRA changes (i.e., new-original) of the OWS, and subtracting that average change from the change of the target word. (2) What is the effect of the entire sentence in the target word? This effect was measured by computing the average of the CEREBRA changes (i.e., new-original) of all the words in the sentence including the target word, and subtracting that average change from the change of the target word. (3) What is the effect of CARs used in context as opposed to CARs used in isolation? This effect was measured by computing the average of the CEREBRA changes (i.e., new-original) of the different representations of the same word in several contexts, and subtracting that average change from the change of the target word .

Matching Model Predictions with Human Judgements: In order to demonstrate that the CEREBRA model has captured human performance, the agreements of the CEREBRA changes and human surveys need to be at least above chance. Therefore a baseline model that generated random responses from the distribution of human responses was created. The three CEREBRA approaches produced very similar results, therefore only those of the third approach are reported in Table 1(b), and the statistical significance of the comparisons in Table 1(c).

The CEREBRA model matches human responses in 54% of the questions when the baseline is 45% - which is equivalent to always guessing "more", i.e., the largest category of human responses. The differences shown in Table 1(c) are statistically strongly significant for all of the eight subjects. These results show that the changes in word meanings (i.e., due to sentence context observed in the fMRI and interpreted by CEREBRA) are real and meaningful to humans (Aguirre-Celis & Miikkulainen, 2020).

5 Discussion and Future Work

An interesting future work direction would be to replicate the study on a more extensive data set with a fully balanced stimuli and with fMRI images of individual words. The differences should be even stronger and it should be possible to uncover more refined effects. Such data should also improve the survey, since it would be possible to identify questions where the effects can be expected to be more reliable.

Compared to other approaches, such as distributional semantic models (DSMs), CAR theory enables a mapping between conceptual content and neural representations. In CARs conceptual knowledge is distributed across a small set of modality-specific neural systems that are engaged when instances of the concept are experienced. In contrast, DSMs reflect conceptual knowledge acquired through a lifetime of linguistic experience, and they are not grounded on perception and action. Experiential data specify the perceived physical attributes or properties associated with the referents of words (e.g., a carrot refers to an object whose attributes describes it as orange, conical/cylindrical, juicy, crispy, sweet). In contrast, linguistic data specify how a given word is statistically distributed across different texts (e.g., a carrot is a root vegetable, usually orange, Dutch invented the orange carrots, it contains high carotene, human body turns carotene into vitamin A). A lot of experiential data is usually unstated in such texts. Thus, experiential data provide a foundation that support both perceptual data (e.g., answering "orange" to "What color are carrots?), as well as associative/encyclopedic data (e.g., answering "rabbit" to "What animal likes to eat carrots?"; Anderson et al., 2019; Andrews et al., 2009; Martin, 2007).

In the future, multimodal CEREBRA representations could be used to make natural language processing systems more robust. For instance, it may be possible to train a neural network to represent context simultaneously from both DSMs and CEREBRA representations as part of a natural language understanding system for service robot applications. For instance, service robots with such representations would have the capability to understand natural language commands (e.g., watering plants), to have encyclopedic knowledge (i.e., to make decisions), to ground language by adapting to the environment (i.e., object recognition, location) and by understanding novel concepts (i.e., "rain water"). Thus, the CEREBRA representations provide the experiential-based data (i.e., concrete words) and the DSMs provide the association-based data (i.e., abstract words), leading to a more robust performance.

6 Conclusion

The CEREBRA model was constructed to test the hypothesis that word meanings change dynamically based on context. The results suggest three significant findings: (1) context-dependent meaning representations are embedded in the fMRI sentences, (2) they can be characterized using brain-based semantic representations (CARs) together with the CEREBRA model, and (3) the attribute weighting changes are real and meaningful to the subjects. CEREBRA thus takes a step towards understanding how the brain constructs sentence-level meanings dynamically from word-level features.

Acknowledgements

We would like to thank J. Binder (Wisconsin), R. Raizada and A. Anderson (Rochester), M. Aguilar and P. Connolly (Teledyne) for providing this data and for their valuable help regarding this research. This work was supported in part by IARPA-FA8650-14-C-7357 and by NIH 1U01DC014922 grants.

References

Nora Aguirre-Celis & Risto Miikkulainen. (2017). From Words to Sentences & Back: Characterizing Context-dependent Meaning Representations in the Brain. *Proceedings of the 39th Annual Meeting of the Cognitive Science Society*, London, UK, pp. 1513-1518.

Nora Aguirre-Celis & Risto Miikkulainen. (2018) Combining fMRI Data and Neural Networks to Quantify Contextual Effects in the Brain. In: Wang S. et al. (Eds.). *Brain Informatics*. BI 2018. Lecture Notes in Computer Science. 11309, pp. 129-140. Springer, Cham.

Nora Aguirre-Celis & Risto Miikkulainen. (2019). Quantifying the Conceptual Combination Effect on Words Meanings. *Proceedings of the 41th Annual Conference of the Cognitive Science Society*, Montreal, CA. 1324-1331.

Nora Aguirre-Celis & Risto Miikkulainen. (2020). Characterizing the Effect of Sentence Context on Word Meanings: Mapping Brain to Behavior. *Computation and Language*. arXiv:2007.13840.

Andrew J. Anderson, Elia Bruni, Ulisse Bordignon, Massimo Poesio, and Marco Baroni. 2013. Of words, eyes and brains: Correlating image-based distributional semantic models with neural representations of concepts. *Proceedings of the Conference on Empirical Methods in Natural Language Processing* (EMNLP 2013); Seattle, WA: Association for Computational Linguistics. pp. 1960–1970.

Andrew J. Anderson, Jeffrey R. Binder, Leonardo Fernandino, Colin J. Humphries, Lisa L. Conant, Mario Aguilar, Xixi Wang, Donias Doko, Rajeev D S Raizada. 2016. Perdicting Neural activity patterns associated with sentences using neurobiologically motivated model of semantic representation. *Cerebral Cortex*, pp. 1-17. DOI:10.1093/cercor/bhw240

Andrew J. Anderson, Douwe Kiela, Stephen Clark, and Massimo Poesio. 2017. Visually Grounded and Textual Semantic Models Differentially Decode Brain Activity Associated with Concrete and Abstract Nouns. *Transaction of the Association for Computational Linguistics* 5: 17-30.

Andrew J. Anderson, Edmund C. Lalor, Feng Lin, Jeffrey R. Binder, Leonardo Fernandino, Colin J. Humphries, Lisa L. Conant, Rajeev D.S. Raizada, Scott Grimm, and Xixi Wang. 2018. Multiple Regions of a Cortical Network Commonly Encode the Meaning of Words in Multiple Grammatical Positions of Read Sentences. *Cerebral Cortex*, pp. 1-16. DOI:10.1093/cercor/bhy110.

Andrew J. Anderson, Jeffrey R. Binder, Leonardo Fernandino, Colin J. Humphries, Lisa L. Conant, Rajeev D.S. Raizada, Feng Lin, and Edmund C. Lalor. 2019. An integrated neural decoder of linguistic and experiential meaning. *The Journal of neuroscience: the official journal of the Society for Neuroscience*.

Mark Andrews, Gabriella Vigliocco, and David Vinson. 2009. Integrating experiential and distributional data to learn semantic representations. *Psychological Review*, 116(3):463–498.

Richard Barclay, John D. Bransford, Jeffery J. Franks, Nancy S. McCarrell, & Kathy Nitsch. 1974. Comprehension and semantic flexibility. *Journal of Verbal Learning and Verbal Behavior, 13*:471–481.

Marco Baroni, Brian Murphy, Eduard Barbu, and Massimo Poesio. 2010. Strudel: A Corpus-Based Semantic Model Based on Properties and Types. *Cognitive Science, 34*(2):222-254.

Lawrence W. Barsalou. 1987. The instability of graded structure: Implications for the nature of concepts. In U. Neisser (Ed.), *Concepts and conceptual development: Ecological and intellectual factors in categorization*. Cambridge, England: Cambridge University Press.

Lawrence W. Barsalou, Wenchi Yeh, Barbara J. Luka, Karen L. Olseth, Kelly S. Mix, Ling-Ling Wu. 1993. Concepts and Meaning. *Chicago Linguistic Society 29: Papers From the Parasession on Conceptual Representations*, 23-61. University of Chicago.

Jeffrey R. Binder and Rutvik H. Desai, William W. Graves, Lisa L. Conant. 2009. Where is the semantic system? A critical review of 120 neuroimaging studies. *Cerebral Cortex*, 19:2767-2769.

Jeffrey R. Binder and Rutvik H. Desai. 2011. The neurobiology of semantic memory. *Trends Cognitive Sciences*, 15(11):527-536.

Jeffrey R. Binder. 2016a. In defense of abstract conceptual representations. *Psychonomic Bulletin & Review*, 23. doi:10.3758/s13423-015-0909-1

Jeffrey R. Binder, Lisa L. Conant, Colin J. Humpries, Leonardo Fernandino, Stephen B. Simons, Mario Aguilar, Rutvik H. Desai. 2016b. Toward a brain-based Componential Semantic Representation. *Cognitive Neuropsychology*, 33(3-4):130-174.

Elia Bruni, Nam Khanh Tran, Marco Baroni. 2014. Multimodal distributional semantics. *Journal of Artificial Intelligence Research (JAIR)*, 49:1-47.

Curt Burgess. 1998. From simple associations to the building blocks of language: Modeling meaning with HAL. *Behavior Research Methods, Instruments, & Computers*, 30:188–198.

Benjamin Cohen & Gregory Murphy. (1984). Models of Concepts. *Cognitive Science 8:25-78.*

Jacob Devlin, Ming-Wei Chang, Kenton Lee, Kristina Toutanova. 2018. BERT: Pre-training of Deep Bidirectional Transformers for Language Understanding. *Computation and Language.* arXiv:1810.04805

Leonardo Fernandino, Colin J Humphries, Mark S Seidenberg, William L Gross, Lisa L Conant, and Jeffrey R Binder. 2015. Predicting brain activation patterns associated with individual lexical concepts based on five sensory-motor attributes. *Neuropsychologia* 76:17–26.

Kimberly Glasgow, Matthew Roos, Amy J. Haufler, Mark Chevillet, Michael Wolmetz. 2016. Evaluating semantic models with word-sentence relatedness. *Computing Research Repository*, arXiv:1603.07253.

James Hampton. 1997. Conceptual combination. In K. Lamberts & D. R. Shanks (Eds.), *Studies in cognition. Knowledge, concepts and categories*, 133–159. MIT Press.

Zellig Harris. 1970. Distributional Structure. *In Papers in Structure and Transformational Linguistics, 775-794.*

Dietmar Janetzko. 2001. Conceptual Combination as Theory Formation. *Proceedings of the Annual Meeting of the Cognitive Science Society*, 23.

Marcel A. Just, Jing Wang, Vladimir L. Cherkassky. 2017. Neural representations of the concepts in simple sentences: concept activation prediction and context effect. Neuroimage, 157:511–520.

Barbara Landau, Linda Smith, and Susan Jones. 1998. Object Perception and Object Naming in Early Development. Trends in Cognitive Science, 27: 19-24.

Thomas K. Landauer and Susan T. Dumais. 1997. A solution to Plato's problem: The latent semantic analysis theory. *Psychological Review*, 104:211-240.

Alex Martin. 2007. The representation of object concepts in the brain. *Annual Review of Psychology*, 58:25–45.

Douglas L. Medin and Edward J. Shoben. 1988. Context and structure in conceptual combination. *Cognitive Psychology*, 20:158-190.

Erica L. Middleton, Katherine A. Rawson, and Edward J. Wisniewski. 2011. "How do we process novel conceptual combinations in context?". *Quarterly Journal of Experimental Psychology.* **64** (4): 807–822.

Risto Miikkulainen and Michael Dyer. 1991. Natural Language Processing with Modular PDP Networks and Distributed Lexicon. Cognitive Science, 15: 343-399.

Thomas Mikolov, Ilya Sutskever, Kai Chen, Greg Corrado, and Jeffrey Dean. 2013. Distributed representations of words and phrases and their compositionality. *Advances in neural information processing systems*, 3111–3119.

Jeff Mitchell and Mirella Lapata. 2010. Composition in distributional models of semantics. *Cognitive Science*, 38(8):1388–1439. DOI: 10.1111/j.1551-6709.2010.01106.x

Gregory Murphy. 1988. Comprehending complex concepts. *Cognitive Science*, 12: 529-562.

Diane Pecher, Rene Zeelenberg, and Lawrence Barsalou. 2004. Sensorimotor simulations underlie conceptual representations Modality-specific effects of prior activation. *Psychonomic Bulletin & Review*, 11: 164-167.

Matthew E. Peters, Mark Neumann, Mohit Iyyer, Matt Gardner, Christopher Clark, Kenton Lee, Luke Zettlemoyer. 2018. Deep contextualized word representations. *Computation and Language.* arXiv:1802.05365.
Terry Regier. 1996. The Human Semantic potential. *MIT Press*, Cambridge, MA.

Ivan A. Sag, Timothy Baldwin, Francis Bond, Ann Copestake, Dan Flickinger. 2001. Multiword expressions: A pain in the neck for NLP. *In International conference on intelligent text processing and computational linguistics*, 1-15. Springer, Berlin, Heidelberg.

Carina Silberer and Mirella Lapata. 2014. Learning Grounded Meaning Representations with Autoencoders. *Proceedings of the 52nd Annual Meeting of the Association for Computational Linguistics*, 721-732.

Edward E. Smith, Edward J. Shoben, and Lance J. Rips. 1974 Structure and process in semantic memory: A featural model for semantic decisions. *Psychological review* 81:214.

Oriol Vinyals, Alexander Toshev, Samy Bengio, and Dumitru Erhan. 2015. Show and Tell: A New Image Caption Generator. *Computing Research Repository*, arXiv:1506.03134v2

Edward J. Wisniewski. 1997. When concepts combine. Psychonomic Bulletin & Review, 4, 167–183.

Edward J. Wisniewski. 1998. Property Instantiation in Conceptual Combination. *Memory & Cognition*, 26, 1330-1347.

Eiling Yee, & Sharon L. Thompson-Schil. 2016. Putting concepts into context. *Psychonomic Bulletin & Review*, 23, 1015–1027.

Contextualized Word Embeddings Encode Aspects of Human-Like Word Sense Knowledge

Sathvik Nair, Mahesh Srinivasan
Cognitive Science Program,
Department of Psychology,
University of California, Berkeley
Berkeley, CA, United States
sathviknair, srinivasan@berkeley.edu

Stephan Meylan
Department of Brain and Cognitive Sciences,
Massachusetts Institute of Technology
Cambridge, MA, United States
smeylan@mit.edu

Abstract

Understanding context-dependent variation in word meanings is a key aspect of human language comprehension supported by the lexicon. Lexicographic resources (e.g., WordNet) capture only some of this context-dependent variation; for example, they often do not encode how closely senses, or discretized word meanings, are related to one another. Our work investigates whether recent advances in NLP, specifically contextualized word embeddings, capture human-like distinctions between English word senses, such as polysemy and homonymy. We collect data from a behavioral, web-based experiment, in which participants provide judgments of the relatedness of multiple WordNet senses of a word in a two-dimensional spatial arrangement task. We find that participants' judgments of the relatedness between senses are correlated with distances between senses in the BERT embedding space. Homonymous senses (e.g., bat as mammal vs. bat as sports equipment) are reliably more distant from one another in the embedding space than polysemous ones (e.g., chicken as animal vs. chicken as meat). Our findings point towards the potential utility of continuous-space representations of sense meanings.

1 Introduction

A key challenge in natural language understanding is grasping the range of meanings that a word can take as a function of linguistic and non-linguistic context. Successful linguistic comprehension involves constantly resolving lexical ambiguity of this nature (Frazier and Rayner, 1990; Klepousniotou, 2002). This re-use of word forms by speakers — relying on listeners to choose the appropriate meaning depending on context — confers language with higher communicative efficiency than it would otherwise have, and may pose a solution to the problem of limited memory (Piantadosi et al., 2012). The re-use of word forms also allows speakers to extend the lexicon to new communicative situations, for example to refer to new objects, entities or processes using existing words in the language (Ramiro et al., 2018; Xu et al., 2020; Srinivasan et al., 2019). How these context-specific meanings are understood and represented pose critical open questions regarding the lexicon.

Following the conventions of lexicographic resources like natural language dictionaries, variation in word meaning is often treated in a categorical fashion: lexical types contain clusters of related meanings, or *word senses*. Under this treatment, word tokens (instances of a word type that are used in context) can be categorized into these word senses. Different sub-types of lexical ambiguity are thus reflected in different relations between word senses: pairs of word senses are *polysemous* if they are semantically related (Pustejovsky, 1998), or *homonymous* if this is not the case (Apresjan, 1974; Tuggy, 1993; Lyons, 1995). For example, using "bottle" to refer to a container as well as to the liquid it contains is an example of polysemy. By contrast, using "bank" to refer to a riverside or a financial institution — two semantically unrelated meanings — constitutes homonymy. Polysemous relations are often *regular* (Apresjan, 1974), such that many word types exhibit the same alternation (e.g., the container-for-contents relation is also exemplified by "box" and "glass"); such patterns can also be generalized to new words (Srinivasan et al., 2019).

Proceedings of the Workshop on Cognitive Aspects of the Lexicon, pages 129–141
Barcelona, Spain (Online), December 12, 2020

Because of variation in the perceived relationship between senses across language users, theories in psycholinguistics assert that humans treat polysemy and homonymy as falling onto a continuous gradient (Tuggy, 1993; Crossley et al., 2010). This is corroborated by psycholinguistic experiments which show that both adults and children represent and process polysemous and homonymous senses differently (Frazier and Rayner, 1990; Rodd et al., 2004; Klepousniotou et al., 2008; Rabagliati and Snedeker, 2013; MacGregor et al., 2015). However, these theories of word sense representation lie in stark contrast with many lexicographical approaches, most notably WordNet (Miller et al., 1990). Although WordNet contains a vast store of word senses—and has historically been considered the gold standard ontology of word senses (Jurafsky and Martin, 2014)—it does not encode relations among those senses, and thus does not distinguish between polysemy and homonymy.

Models based on distributional semantics can help bridge the gap between psychological theories of word senses and existing lexicographical resources. Contextualized word embeddings (CWEs), especially BERT (Devlin et al., 2019), which is derived from a Transformer-based architecture (Vaswani et al., 2017), have the potential to capture fine-grained distinctions in relatedness between word senses, because they offer a continuous measure of relatedness between individual uses of words in context (Lake and Murphy, 2020). While fine-tuned BERT models are known to perform exceptionally well in word sense disambiguation (WSD) tasks (Wiedemann et al., 2019; Loureiro and Jorge, 2019; Blevins and Zettlemoyer, 2020), there are still open questions of whether BERT representations capture fine-grained distinctions in sense relatedness.

In the present work, we evaluate whether contextualized embeddings from BERT capture relationships between word senses similar to English speakers. We collect human judgments of the relatedness among different senses of 32 English words through a web-based two-dimensional spatial arrangement task (Goldstone, 1994). We then compare the experimental data to BERT vectors for the same set of words. This is done through extracting and analyzing BERT embeddings for word tokens in the Semcor corpus (Miller et al., 1993), which has been annotated with word sense identifiers from WordNet. Assessing whether relatedness in BERT representations corresponds with human judgments of sense relatedness is an important test of whether CWEs can be used to develop more realistic computational models of word meanings.

2 Background

The distributional hypothesis proposes that a word's meaning can be represented by the lexical context in which it occurs (Harris, 1954). This insight underlies the success of computational models that represent words as continuous-valued vectors representing their surrounding lexical context. Latent semantic analysis (Dumais et al., 1988), and neural models like Word2Vec(Mikolov et al., 2013) encode information about all of a word's senses in a single vector. By contrast, newer models include contextualized embeddings: vector space representations of specific word uses (tokens), reflecting the context of their use. These richer word representations from contextualized embeddings have allowed researchers to ask which aspects of linguistic knowledge are incorporated in their vector spaces (See Rogers et al. (2020) for a review; see also Ethayarajh (2019)). For example, one of the most notable discoveries from this line of work suggests that a sentence's dependency parse tree can be reconstructed from BERT embeddings (Hewitt and Manning, 2019; Reif et al., 2019; Jawahar et al., 2019). However, despite progress investigating how BERT encodes syntactic information, relatively little work has explored how it encodes semantic information such as the relations between word senses.

While older models like Word2Vec may encode some aspects of word sense (Arora et al., 2018), we focus here on Transformer architectures (Vaswani et al., 2017), which may be able to find sense-distinguishing context words at larger distances, and thus perform better for WSD. BERT-based approaches have led to state of the art performance on word sense disambiguation tasks (Wiedemann et al., 2019; Loureiro and Jorge, 2019; Blevins and Zettlemoyer, 2020), but approaches analyzing the model's representation of word senses remain exploratory (Reif et al., 2019; Lake and Murphy, 2020). Evidence from Reif et al. (2019) shows that BERT embeddings for the same word in a large text corpus are largely clustered based on their meanings, but the authors do not investigate the model's ability to encode canonically homonymous or polysemous relationships. Mickus et al. (2020) note that BERT embeddings for the same word type vary as a function of the position in the sentences they occur in. Lake and Murphy (2020) assess BERT's capacity for homonym resolution by comparing relatedness of words that are similar to a homonym in highly constraining contexts. Ettinger (2020) points out the need for more psycholinguistic diagnostics of neural language models like BERT, and compares BERT to human data from tasks such as commonsense inference. Our work falls under this framework, focusing on comparing human judgements of word sense relatedness to BERT representations.

3 Methods

We conducted a metalinguistic experiment (vs. a processing task testing implicit knowledge) where participants used a web interface to assess the relatedness of WordNet senses in a two-dimensional spatial arrangement task. We then obtained BERT embeddings for word types in the Semcor corpus (Miller et al., 1993) and compared them to the experimental data, looking at both cosine distance in the embedding space as well as the accuracy of a sense classifier using BERT's contextualized word embeddings as input. All stimuli, code and visualizations are available at `https://osf.io/fm78w`.

3.1 Data

We select a sample of word types for analysis from Semcor (Miller et al., 1993), which has WordNet sense annotations for 235,000 tokens from the Brown corpus (Francis and Kucera, 1979). We use the corpus reader from the Python Natural Language Toolkit (NLTK) (Bird and Loper, 2004) to access the corpus. The fact that syntax is represented within BERT embeddings (Hewitt and Manning, 2019) implies that BERT embeddings can easily capture distinctions in part of speech, so we focus on lexical ambiguity within part-of speech (specifically nouns and verbs) as a more challenging test case.

For the behavioral experiment, we selected word types across a range of sense entropy values (i.e., uniform to highly peaked sense distributions). We created a multinomial distribution over the senses of each lemma, i.e., (word type, part of speech) pair, and computed its entropy as follows: $-\sum_{s \in L} \frac{c_s}{c_L} \log(\frac{c_s}{c_L})$, where L is a lemma, s is a sense and c corresponds to a frequency, or count in the corpus. We removed stopwords and lemmas with zero entropy (79.3% of all lemmas). This yielded 444 word types.

For experimental stimuli, we chose 32 word types. 20 word types came from Semcor, including 11 low/medium entropy word types and 9 high entropy word types. We defined high entropy to be greater than 1.5 when rounded to the nearest tenth, and medium/low entropy to be less than this value, based on the distribution of sense entropy in the available Semcor data (in Figure 1). To account for variability in participants' placement of tokens in the spatial arrangement task, we needed to normalize measurements in the interface on a per-trial basis, so we selected words with three senses or more. We chose word types with varying entropy values to determine if this quantity had an effect on the correlation between BERT vectors and human judgements; relatedness between embeddings for words with more unpredictable sense distributions may be less consistent with results from the experiment. To avoid overwhelming participants, we selected words with fewer than eight senses. We also chose six additional words of theoretical importance that exemplify patterns of regular polysemy that have been observed across languages from Srinivasan and Rabagliati (2015), and manually chose six words with three senses, one of which was less semantically related to the other two. Because we expected these words to exhibit the greatest differences in pairwise similarity, we elicited judgments from all participants on these items. More details about how these stimuli were presented and exclusion criteria are in Appendix B.

3.1.1 Participants

105 undergraduate students from a major research university participated in the experiment and were compensated with class credit. Upon providing informed consent, participants reported their experience with English and other languages to ensure that data were collected from proficient English speakers (defined as at least 50% of daily language use); one participant was excluded using this criterion.

3.2 Experiment

From the set of 32 word types, each participant received 14 word types as stimuli. We used a two-dimensional spatial-arrangement task (Goldstone, 1994), because it allowed us to efficiently capture psychological judgments, and because tasks of this nature effectively capture relatedness in a high-dimensional semantic space (Richie et al., 2020). Participants were told to place less related sense tokens further apart from one another on the canvas, and more closely related tokens near each other. The experimental interface is shown in Appendix A. To place the sense tokens, participants were given definitions (from WordNet) and example sentences (from Semcor; in some cases shortened for brevity). The task was untimed, and participants were encouraged to introspect for as long as necessary about the meanings of the presented senses before making their placements. Partcipants were encouraged to adjust their placements to reflect all senses.

3.3 Relatedness Matrices

For each word, we collected spatial (x,y) positions of each of the word's senses from each participant. To derive an estimate of the relatedness of senses for each word type, we normalized the distances such that they were rescaled according to the largest reported pairwise distance. This controlled for variation in the absolute amount of space in the canvas that different participants used when making their placements. After excluding participants with unreliable responses (Appendix B), we then averaged relatedness matrices for each word type across the remaining participants. This yielded a single "aggregate relatedness matrix" for each word type which could then be directly compared with model results for a word type. To account for the larger number of participants reporting data for shared stimuli, we selected data from a random set of participants whose size corresponded to the average amount of test items ($n =$ 29). Data from a minimum of 21 participants and a maximum of 37 participants were used to construct the aggregate relatedness matrix for each word type.

3.4 Modeling

We retrieved BERT embeddings for labeled tokens from the Semcor corpus (Miller et al., 1993) and ran classifiers to distinguish between different senses of individual words based on BERT vectors. We compared these data to results from the experiment based on two metrics: distance in the embedding space and classification accuracy, assessing their similarity through correlation (Budanitsky and Hirst, 2006).

Given a word type and a part of speech, we derived word embeddings from BERT as follows. For each sense of the (word type, part of speech) pair, we retrieved sentences from Semcor, and tokenized them using rules specified by the BERT authors (Devlin et al., 2019). We loaded a pre-trained BERT model `BERT-base` from Wolf et al. (2019) and ran the forward pass on each sentence, extracting the activations corresponding to the type, and storing the summed activations of the final four layers, which has produced strong results in word sense disambiguation (Loureiro and Jorge, 2019).

3.5 Word Sense Classifier

As a matter of due diligence, we first evaluated the effectiveness of BERT representations for word sense disambiguation (classification) in the Semcor corpus. While WSD-focused work has used the Semcor dataset for training and tested on other datasets (Raganato et al., 2017), we confirmed that BERT demonstrates similar levels of performance on Semcor. To this end, we assessed performance of multiclass logistic regression models to predict word senses for 401 word types from Semcor. Senses were omitted from this classification whenever there were fewer than 10 tokens. Each logistic regression model was trained to predict WordNet sense labels for each instance of a sense based on its contextual word embedding from BERT. We conducted 5-fold cross validation and applied L1 regularization to prevent overfitting. To confirm consistency with prior work on WSD (Loureiro and Jorge, 2019; Reif et al., 2019; Blevins and Zettlemoyer, 2020), we report the average F1 score (weighted for each sense) across the runs for each word type. Comparable F1 scores relative to this prior work would suggest that it is appropriate to further investigate the geometry implicit in these contextual word embeddings.

Method	All Types in Semcor	Types in Behavioral Expt.
Number of Available Types	401	32
Random Sense	0.480	0.423
Majority Sense	0.441	0.403
Logistic Regression on BERT Embeddings	**0.757**	**0.797**

Table 1: Average F1 scores (across types and train-test splits) for BERT-based word sense disambiguation in the Semcor corpus.

3.5.1 Extracting Cosine Distances Between Word Sense Centroids

After qualitatively reproducing previous word sense disambiguation results using BERT embeddings, we then tested whether the relationship between BERT embeddings of senses parallels human judgments of relatedness between senses. Because BERT generates one vector for each use of a word token, we computed the centroids of the BERT embeddings corresponding to each sense, and then compared different senses by using the cosine distance of these centroids to one another. In a broad range of models, cosine distances between vectors corresponding to word types can encode the degree of semantic relatedness (Dumais et al., 1988; Mikolov et al., 2013; Bojanowski et al., 2017), so we can use this same metric with BERT embeddings to compare word senses to one another. Following the same procedure as the relatedness matrices, we define relatedness as (1 - cosine distance), such that the largest cosine distance (least related pair) takes the value of 0 and the smallest cosine distance (most closely related pair) takes the value of 1 for each word type. We stored these relatedness measures between sense centroids in a matrix analogous to the aggregate relatedness matrices from the behavioral experiment. To evaluate their fit to human data, we computed the Spearman rank correlation coefficient between the upper triangular entries in these two distance matrices. A nonparametric measure of correlation is appropriate given that the relationship is not necessarily linear.

4   Results

First, we verified that BERT can discriminate between senses in Semcor comparably to other test datasets. We then compared relatedness estimates derived from distances in the BERT embedding space to the aggregate relatedness measures from the experiment. We then conduct two exploratory analyses, the first comparing the relatedness of homonymous and polysemous sense pairs, and the second examining the utility of pairwise sense confusion as a measure of relatedness.

4.1   Classification Results for All Semcor Data

We compared the distribution of F1 scores of the classifiers on the 401 words from Semcor (BERT failed to process 43 of the words) with two baselines: random choice and selecting the most frequent sense (Figure 1). Classification performance on all 401 words, including 25 words used in the behavioral experiment, were similar to those reported by Blevins and Zettlemoyer (2020), Loureiro and Jorge (2019), and Reif et al. Reif et al. (2019) (0.739, 0.754, and 0.711, respectively), which used test sets from Raganato et al. (2017). We find that type-wise F1 score is negatively correlated with sense entropy computed from Semcor ($\beta_{sense\_entropy} = -0.074, R^2 = 0.06$; Fig. 1).

4.2   Comparing Human Relatedness with BERT Word Sense Geometry

We computed the Spearman's rank correlation coefficient between human judgments of sense relatedness (from the aggregate relatedness matrices) and measures of word sense relatedness from the centroids of BERT contextualized word embeddings. This yielded a positive correlation (Spearman's $r = 0.565, p < 0.001$), with a 95% confidence interval of (0.459, 0.655). To confirm that this correlation was above that expected by random chance, we compared it to a random baseline established by 1000 draws of randomly generated sense placements for 29 participants (the average number of participants per item). This correlation was much lower (Spearman's $r = 0.062, p < 0.001$, 95% CI: -0.065 - 0.208). We report the correlation between relatedness measures from the embedding space and human judgements by part of speech and high vs. low/medium entropy in Table 2. Correlations between human relatedness

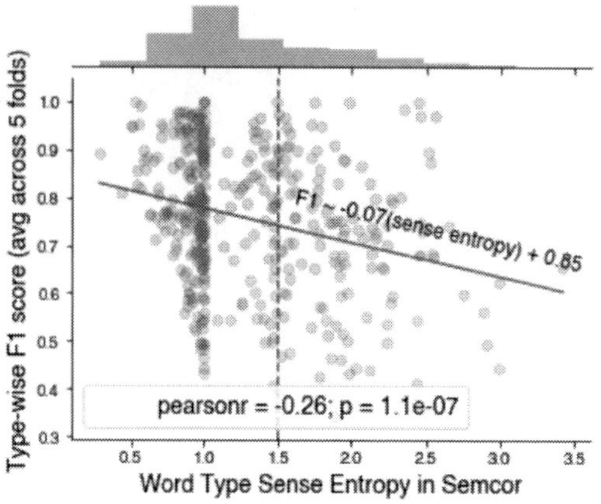

Figure 1: Classifier performance for word types with respect to their sense entropy in Semcor. F1 score for each type is averaged over cross validation folds and weighted by sense frequency. Vertical line represents boundary between low/medium and high entropy word types.

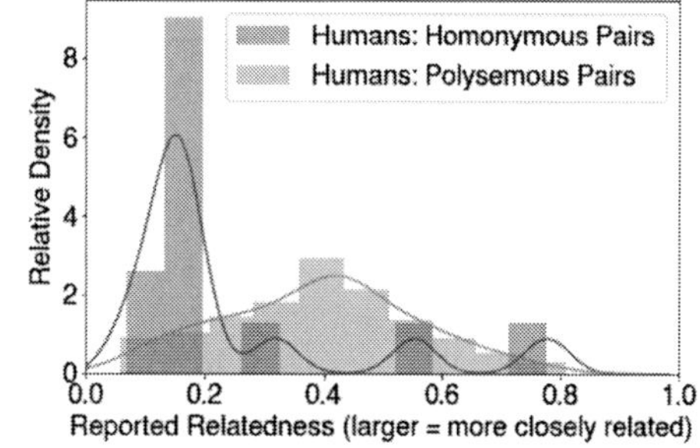

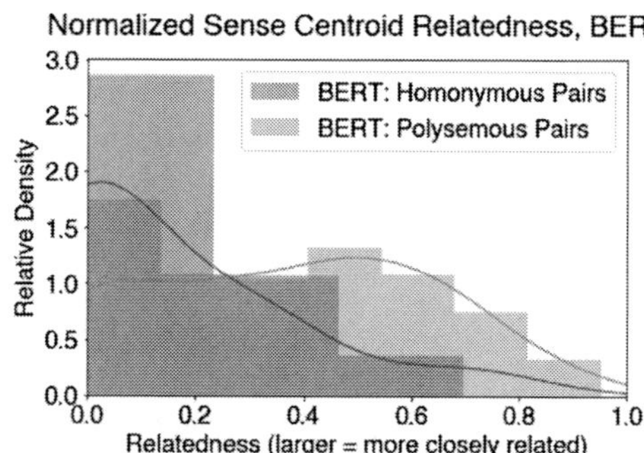

Figure 2: Distribution of distances between pairs of senses from the human data (left) and from BERT (right), across word types.

judgments and BERT relatedness were substantially higher among low to medium than high entropy words(Table 2). We also find that correlations among human and model relatedness are higher among verbs than nouns.

4.2.1 Polysemous vs. Homonymous Sense Pairs

We conducted an exploratory analysis to see if human relatedness judgments differed between homonymous and polysemous relations, and whether the geometry of BERT embeddings captured this distinction between word senses. In the absence of gold-standard datasets labeling polysemous and homonymous word sense relationships,[1] we tagged pairs of senses as polysemous or homonymous ourselves for the set of words in the behavioral experiment. For human judgments, we took the set of average distances between polysemous and homonymous pairs of senses. For BERT embeddings, we took the cosine distances between pairs of polysemous and homonymous sense centroids.

The density plots in Figure 2 show that participants in the behavioral experiment judged the polysemous pairs to be more similar (i.e., less distant) than homonymous pairs (Mann-Whitney $U = 516, p < 0.001$). BERT-based representations reproduced this basic pattern (Mann-Whitney $U = 493, p < 0.001$), though many relatedness estimates were more dispersed for both polysemous and homonymous pairs.

To illustrate the differences between how BERT represents polysemous and homonymous relationships, we show t-SNE and dendrogram visualizations in Figure 3. For `table.n` (Figure 3, top), we

---

[1]We could in principle use natural language dictionaries, some of which list polysemous and homonymous senses under separate entries. However, such definitions would not necessarily map to WordNet labeled data.

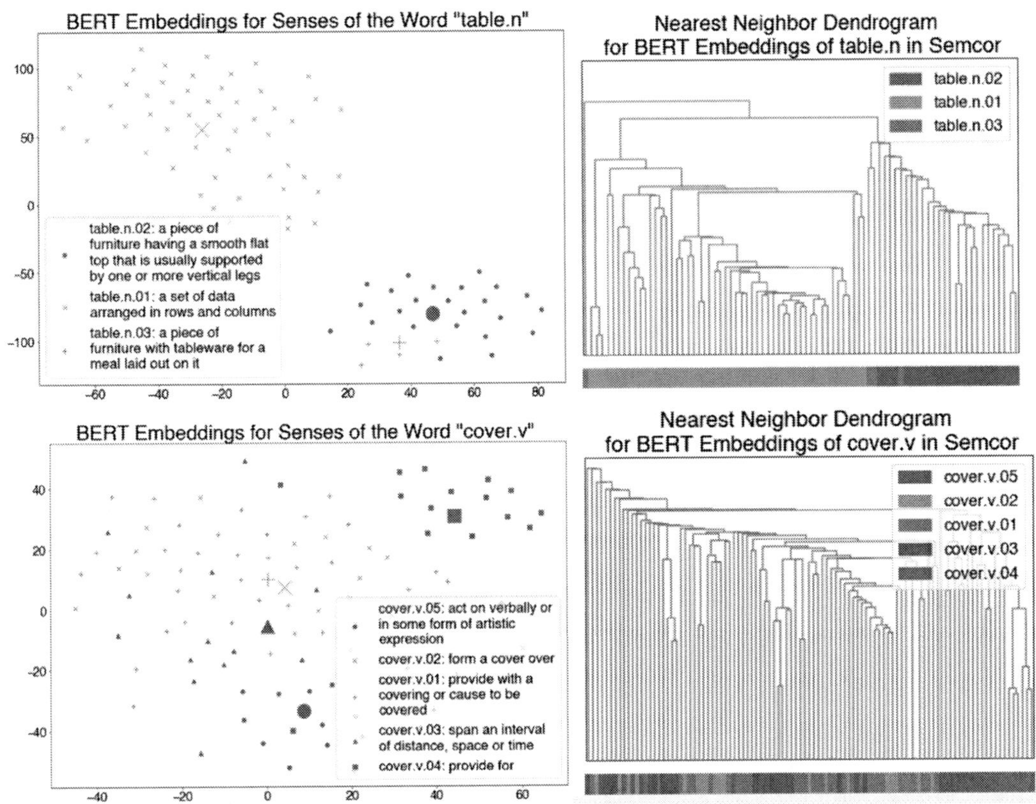

Figure 3: Visualizations of example BERT embeddings for stimuli table.n cover.n. Left column contains results of t-SNE dimensionality reduction with small points indicating word tokens and large points indicating sense centroids. Right column contains results of single linkage agglomerative clustering.

show that two senses related by polysemy (piece of furniture vs. a tablesetting) are judged to be closer together than homonymous pairs (either of the first two senses vs. "a set of data arranged in rows and columns"). For cover.v, all sense pairs were polysemous. Instances of the same sense were still closer to one another in the embedding space, but tokens corresponding to different senses were much less clearly distinguished except for cover.v.04, which may be well-separated from other senses because it refers to a metaphorical meaning of the lemma. We find that the BERT centroids' cosine distances and the aggregated relatedness judgements are strongly correlated (Spearman's $r = 0.851, p < 0.001$), with a 95% confidence interval of $(0.638, 0.943)$.

4.3 Predicting Human Relatedness Judgments with Pairwise Confusion

One possibility is that the cosine distance computed over all dimensions of the BERT embedding space overlooks the possibility that some dimensions may be more or less useful for discriminating word senses depending on the word type. One alternative is to use the pairwise confusion probabilities from multiclass logistic regression (described in Section 3.5) as a measurement of pairwise relatedness in the model. This choice invokes substantive theoretical questions: in principle, sense relatedness and discriminability could be orthogonal. For example, two senses could be judged as closely related by humans, but they could in principle be able to discriminate between instances of those senses without errors. In the absence of human sense discrimination performance data, we leave this question to future work. Nonetheless, we investigated the utility of pairwise sense confusion as an alternative predictor for human judgments of sense relatedness.

Metric	Part of Speech		Word Sense Entropy	
	Nouns	Verbs	High	Low/Medium
Relatedness (1 - Normalized Cosine Distance)	0.487	0.623	0.345	0.570
Pairwise Confusion	0.609	0.627	0.518	0.731

Table 2: Spearman rank correlations between relatedness judgements and confusion matrices in BERT embedding space, split over part of speech and entropy level

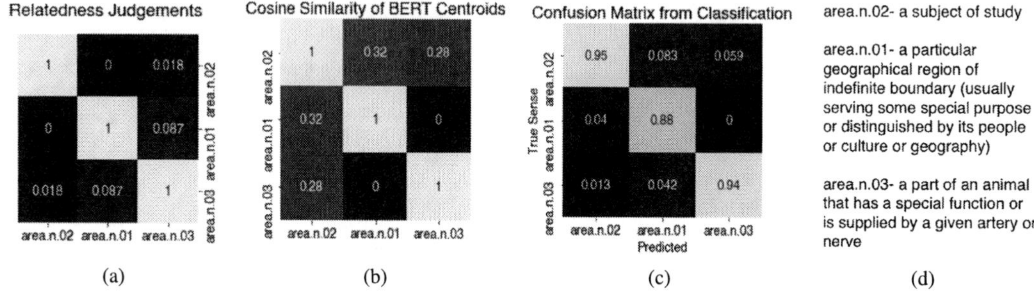

Figure 4: Mean human relatedness judgements, cosine similarity matrix, and confusion matrix for senses of `area.n`.

To this end, we summed the confusion matrices when senses from the stimuli are classified during each iteration of cross-validation from Section 4.1. We normalized each item in the matrix by the number of true labels, such that it represents the probability an item was predicted given its true class. Across all word types with available data (20 out of 32 types, including 150 out of 189 sense pairs), we found a positive Spearman's rank correlation between entries in the confusion matrices and matrices of the corresponding relatedness judgements ($r = 0.649, p < 0.001$), with a 95% confidence interval of (0.592, 0.7). For this measure, we considered all entries in both matrices, as the confusion matrices are not necessarily symmetric. Because this analysis omits word senses with fewer than 10 tokens in Semcor, this evaluation reflects a smaller set of items than the one reported in Section 4.2 for cosine-based relatedness. When we computed the correlation between cosine-based relatedness and human aggregated relatedness matrices on this smaller set, the correlation remains lower (Spearman's $r = 0.518, p < 0.001$), with a 95% confidence interval of (0.391, 0.627). This suggests that pairwise confusion in BERT may be a stronger predictor of human relatedness judgments. We also report correlations stratified by part of speech and type sense entropy in Table 2. To illustrate the approach, we present aggregate relatedness matrices and confusion matrices for the word type `area.n` in Fig. 4. In this case, the experimental data (Fig 4, A) was more closely aligned with the confusion matrix (C) the than the cosine similarity of centroids (B).

We also evaluated sense classification accuracy on the basis of the homonymous and polysemous sense pairs from the preceding exploratory analysis. Among homonymous sense pairs, the classifiers achieved an average F1 score of 0.992. Among the polysemous sense pairs, the classifier achieved an average F1 score of 0.752.

5   Discussion

We investigated the ability of an artificial neural network model that represents word tokens with contextualized word embeddings to capture human-like relations among English word senses. On a subset of word types from the Semcor corpus, we reproduced previous word sense disambiguation results. We then showed that these same BERT embeddings capture a significant amount of information regarding the relationship between word senses, and are able to at least partially reproduce human relatedness judgments. An exploratory analysis revealed that BERT-based measures of the relatedness between pairs of homonymous senses are much lower than for pairs of polysemous senses, matching human intuitions for the same set of senses. Pairwise confusion from the sense classifiers provided a slightly better predictor of human judgments of sense relatedness compared to distance in the embedding space, although this may be unsurprising given that pairwise confusion reflects some additional degree of supervision. Analyzing the error rates of classifiers trained on BERT embeddings of the stimuli, we also provided evidence that their results are more accurate for homonymous sense pairs compared to polysemous sense pairs.

Following in the approach of comparing BERT vectors to experimental data from human participants (Ettinger, 2020), the present research addresses how BERT represents word senses, bridging the gap between human and computational models of lexical ambiguity resolution. Recent progress showing BERT's performance on word sense disambiguation (Wiedemann et al., 2019; Loureiro and Jorge, 2019; Blevins and Zettlemoyer, 2020) indicates that BERT-based models perform better than past approaches, and our work specifies that the representations they use to accomplish this are relatively consistent with human intuitions. Existing exploratory work aims to analyze how BERT represents word senses (Reif et al., 2019; Lake and Murphy, 2020), but we systematically evaluate these claims with both WordNet senses and human data. Our work corroborates claims by Lake and Murphy (2020) that BERT captures relations between homonymous senses. Indeed, poor performance in discriminating polysemous pairs of words senses suggests that more work needs to be done on capturing polysemous relations; one possibility is to explore how BERT could be fine-tuned to capture relations exemplified by regular polysemy. One limitation from these findings is that the dataset only covers 32 word types, which we hope to address in future work.

More generally, our findings suggest that a continuous measure of sense relatedness derived from neural language models could potentially be used to augment existing lexicographic resources like WordNet, in this case providing a measure of relatedness between senses. We encourage other researchers developing sense ontologies, especially those found through word sense induction, to consider representing the relationships among word senses in addition to discovering new sense inventories.

6 Conclusion

Through comparing results from a behavioral experiment with data from contextualized word embeddings, we demonstrate that new Transformer-based neural network architectures may reflect human intuitions about the relationships between word senses, at least in English. Exploratory analyses suggest that these measures of relatedness between sense pairs reflect a distinction between polysemous and homonymous relationships between word senses, but that these models are much more effective in discriminating homonymous sense pairs than polysemous ones. By demonstrating basic levels of consistency with human judgements, we hope to stimulate further research that combines contextualized word embedding techniques with discrete, symbolic ontologies to develop a more cognitively informed model of the lexicon.

Acknowledgements

We would like to thank Steven Piantadosi, Ruthe Foushee, Sammy Floyd, and Jessica Mankewitz for thoughtful discussion of this work, and Jon Wehry for ensuring the experiment ran smoothly. We also thank the reviewers for helpful feedback, and the workshop organizers for giving us the opportunity to share this work.

References

Ju D Apresjan. 1974. Regular polysemy. *Linguistics*, 12(142):5–32.

Sanjeev Arora, Yuanzhi Li, Yingyu Liang, Tengyu Ma, and Andrej Risteski. 2018. Linear algebraic structure of word senses, with applications to polysemy. *Transactions of the Association for Computational Linguistics*, 6:483–495.

Steven Bird and Edward Loper. 2004. NLTK: The natural language toolkit. In *Proceedings of the ACL Interactive Poster and Demonstration Sessions*, pages 214–217, Barcelona, Spain, July. Association for Computational Linguistics.

Terra Blevins and Luke Zettlemoyer. 2020. Moving down the long tail of word sense disambiguation with gloss informed bi-encoders. In *Proceedings of the 58th Association for Computational Linguistics*.

Piotr Bojanowski, Edouard Grave, Armand Joulin, and Tomas Mikolov. 2017. Enriching word vectors with subword information. *Transactions of the Association for Computational Linguistics*, 5:135–146.

Alexander Budanitsky and Graeme Hirst. 2006. Evaluating wordnet-based measures of lexical semantic relatedness. *COMPUTATIONAL LINGUISTICS*, 32(1):13–47.

Scott Crossley, Tom Salsbury, and Danielle McNamara. 2010. The development of polysemy and frequency use in english second language speakers. *Language Learning*, 60(3):573–605.

Jacob Devlin, Ming-Wei Chang, Kenton Lee, and Kristina Toutanova. 2019. BERT: Pre-training of deep bidirectional transformers for language understanding. In *Proceedings of the 2019 Conference of the North American Chapter of the Association for Computational Linguistics: Human Language Technologies, Volume 1 (Long and Short Papers)*, pages 4171–4186, Minneapolis, Minnesota, June. Association for Computational Linguistics.

Susan T Dumais, George W Furnas, Thomas K Landauer, Scott Deerwester, and Richard Harshman. 1988. Using latent semantic analysis to improve access to textual information. In *Proceedings of the SIGCHI conference on Human factors in computing systems*, pages 281–285.

Kawin Ethayarajh. 2019. How contextual are contextualized word representations? comparing the geometry of BERT, ELMo, and GPT-2 embeddings. In *Proceedings of the 2019 Conference on Empirical Methods in Natural Language Processing and the 9th International Joint Conference on Natural Language Processing (EMNLP-IJCNLP)*, pages 55–65, Hong Kong, China, November. Association for Computational Linguistics.

Allyson Ettinger. 2020. What bert is not: Lessons from a new suite of psycholinguistic diagnostics for language models. *Transactions of the Association for Computational Linguistics*, 8:34–48.

W Nelson Francis and Henry Kucera. 1979. Brown corpus manual. *Letters to the Editor*, 5(2):7.

Lyn Frazier and Keith Rayner. 1990. Taking on semantic commitments: Processing multiple meanings vs. multiple senses. *Journal of memory and language*, 29(2):181–200.

Robert L Goldstone. 1994. Influences of categorization on perceptual discrimination. *Journal of Experimental Psychology: General*, 123(2):178.

Zellig S Harris. 1954. Distributional structure. *Word*, 10(2-3):146–162.

John Hewitt and Christopher D Manning. 2019. A structural probe for finding syntax in word representations. In *Proceedings of the 2019 Conference of the North American Chapter of the Association for Computational Linguistics: Human Language Technologies, Volume 1 (Long and Short Papers)*, pages 4129–4138.

Ganesh Jawahar, Benoît Sagot, and Djamé Seddah. 2019. What does BERT learn about the structure of language? In *Proceedings of the 57th Annual Meeting of the Association for Computational Linguistics*, pages 3651–3657, Florence, Italy, July. Association for Computational Linguistics.

Dan Jurafsky and James H Martin. 2014. Speech and language processing. vol. 3.

Ekaterini Klepousniotou, Debra Titone, and Carolina Romero. 2008. Making sense of word senses: The comprehension of polysemy depends on sense overlap. *Journal of Experimental Psychology: Learning, Memory, and Cognition*, 34(6):1534.

Ekaterini Klepousniotou. 2002. The processing of lexical ambiguity: Homonymy and polysemy in the mental lexicon. *Brain and language*, 81(1-3):205–223.

Brenden M. Lake and Gregory L. Murphy. 2020. Word meaning in minds and machines. *arXiv preprint, arXiv:2008.01766*.

Daniel Loureiro and Alípio Jorge. 2019. Language modelling makes sense: Propagating representations through WordNet for full-coverage word sense disambiguation. In *Proceedings of the 57th Annual Meeting of the Association for Computational Linguistics*, pages 5682–5691, Florence, Italy, July. Association for Computational Linguistics.

John Lyons. 1995. *Linguistic semantics: An introduction*. Cambridge University Press.

Lucy J MacGregor, Jennifer Bouwsema, and Ekaterini Klepousniotou. 2015. Sustained meaning activation for polysemous but not homonymous words: Evidence from eeg. *Neuropsychologia*, 68:126–138.

Timothee Mickus, Denis Paperno, Mathieu Constant, and Kees van Deemter. 2020. What do you mean, bert? assessing BERT as a distributional semantics model. *Proceedings of the Society for Computation in Linguistics*, Vol. 3, Article 34.

Tomas Mikolov, Ilya Sutskever, Kai Chen, Greg S Corrado, and Jeff Dean. 2013. Distributed representations of words and phrases and their compositionality. In C. J. C. Burges, L. Bottou, M. Welling, Z. Ghahramani, and K. Q. Weinberger, editors, *Advances in Neural Information Processing Systems 26*, pages 3111–3119. Curran Associates, Inc.

George A Miller, Richard Beckwith, Christiane Fellbaum, Derek Gross, and Katherine J Miller. 1990. Introduction to wordnet: An on-line lexical database. *International journal of lexicography*, 3(4):235–244.

George A Miller, Claudia Leacock, Randee Tengi, and Ross T Bunker. 1993. A semantic concordance. In *Proceedings of the workshop on Human Language Technology*, pages 303–308. Association for Computational Linguistics.

Steven T Piantadosi, Harry Tily, and Edward Gibson. 2012. The communicative function of ambiguity in language. *Cognition*, 122(3):280–291.

James Pustejovsky. 1998. *The generative lexicon*. MIT press.

Hugh Rabagliati and Jesse Snedeker. 2013. The truth about chickens and bats: Ambiguity avoidance distinguishes types of polysemy. *Psychological science*, 24(7):1354–1360.

Alessandro Raganato, Jose Camacho-Collados, and Roberto Navigli. 2017. Word sense disambiguation: A unified evaluation framework and empirical comparison. In *Proceedings of the 15th Conference of the European Chapter of the Association for Computational Linguistics: Volume 1, Long Papers*, pages 99–110.

Christian Ramiro, Mahesh Srinivasan, Barbara C Malt, and Yang Xu. 2018. Algorithms in the historical emergence of word senses. *Proceedings of the National Academy of Sciences*, 115(10):2323–2328.

Emily Reif, Ann Yuan, Martin Wattenberg, Fernanda B Viegas, Andy Coenen, Adam Pearce, and Been Kim. 2019. Visualizing and measuring the geometry of bert. In *Advances in Neural Information Processing Systems*, pages 8594–8603.

Russell Richie, Bryan White, Sudeep Bhatia, and Michael C Hout. 2020. The spatial arrangement method of measuring similarity can capture high-dimensional semantic structures. *Behavior Research Methods*, pages 1–23.

Jennifer M Rodd, M Gareth Gaskell, and William D Marslen-Wilson. 2004. Modelling the effects of semantic ambiguity in word recognition. *Cognitive science*, 28(1):89–104.

Anna Rogers, Olga Kovaleva, and Anna Rumshisky. 2020. A primer in bertology: What we know about how bert works. *arXiv preprint, arXiv:2002.12327*.

Mahesh Srinivasan and Hugh Rabagliati. 2015. How concepts and conventions structure the lexicon: Cross-linguistic evidence from polysemy. *Lingua*, 157, 01.

Mahesh Srinivasan, Catherine Berner, and Hugh Rabagliati. 2019. Children use polysemy to structure new word meanings. *Journal of Experimental Psychology: General*, 148(5):926.

David Tuggy. 1993. Ambiguity, polysemy, and vagueness. *Cognitive linguistics*, 4(3):273–290.

Ashish Vaswani, Noam Shazeer, Niki Parmar, Jakob Uszkoreit, Llion Jones, Aidan N Gomez, Łukasz Kaiser, and Illia Polosukhin. 2017. Attention is all you need. In *Advances in neural information processing systems*, pages 5998–6008.

Gregor Wiedemann, Steffen Remus, Avi Chawla, and Chris Biemann. 2019. Does bert make any sense? interpretable word sense disambiguation with contextualized embeddings. *arXiv preprint, arXiv:1909.10430*.

Thomas Wolf, Lysandre Debut, Victor Sanh, Julien Chaumond, Clement Delangue, Anthony Moi, Pierric Cistac, Tim Rault, Rémi Louf, Morgan Funtowicz, Joe Davison, Sam Shleifer, Patrick von Platen, Clara Ma, Yacine Jernite, Julien Plu, Canwen Xu, Teven Le Scao, Sylvain Gugger, Mariama Drame, Quentin Lhoest, and Alexander M. Rush. 2019. Huggingface's transformers: State-of-the-art natural language processing. *arXiv preprint, arXiv:1910.03771*.

Yang Xu, Khang Duong, Barbara C Malt, Serena Jiang, and Mahesh Srinivasan. 2020. Conceptual relations predict colexification across languages. *Cognition*, 201:104280.

Appendices

A Experiment Details

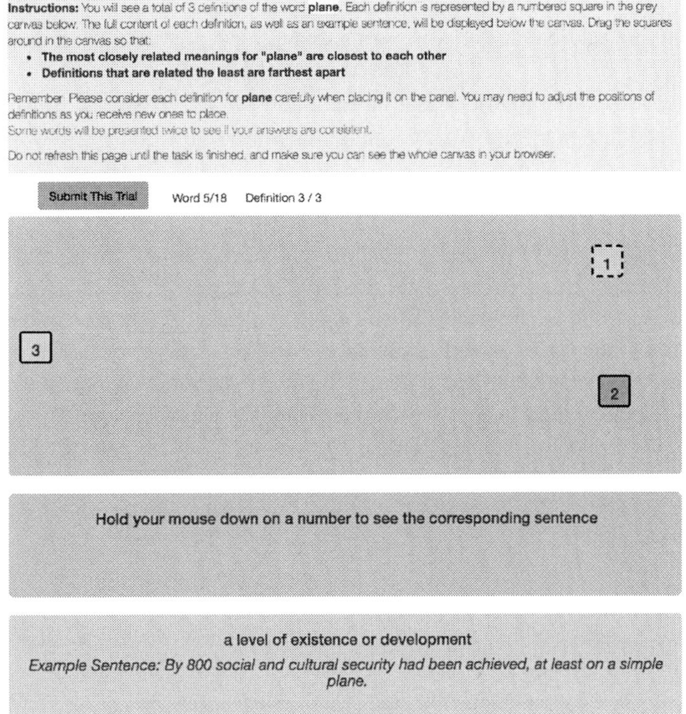

Figure 5: A sample trial in the experiment

B Trial Types and Exclusion Criteria

The first two of the eighteen trials participants received were presented as *training* trials to ensure that participants were familiar with the interface; data from these trials were discarded. Participants received a mixture of *shared* trials completed by all participants, and *test* trials where only a subset of participants provided judgments. The inclusion of both trial types gave us a consistent set of word types for which all participants contributed data (allowing us to evaluate which participants gave unreliable responses compared to all other participants), while at the same time characterizing a broad set of word types with more sparse responses. Test trials were drawn from the set of 26 lemmas consisting of words from Srinivasan and Rabagliati (2015). To identify participants who provided low-quality data, we computed hold-one-out correlations for each participant using their relatedness matrices for the shared trials, and excluded participants whose data had a rank correlation with the hold-one-out averages that was lower than 0.4. This threshold corresponds roughly to the 92nd percentile of scores if sense tokens are placed randomly in the interface.

In addition to the shared and test trials, participants also saw two *repeat* trials, drawn from the same set as the test trials, to evaluate the reliability of their responses within the same testing session. Participants with rank correlations in reported distances between their original and repeat trials lower than 0.2 were excluded from analysis, corresponding to the 70th percentile of correlations if sense tokens are placed randomly (this threshold was lower because of variation in both the number of senses and the recency of the test trial). Ten participants who failed to meet both criteria were excluded from further analysis.

Automatic Word Association Norms (AWAN)

Jorge Reyes-Magaña[1,2]   **Gerardo Sierra**[1]   **Gemma Bel-Enguix**[1]

jorge.reyes@correo.uady.mx   gsierram@iingen.unam.mx   gbele@iingen.unam.mx

Helena Gómez-Adorno[3]

helena.gomez@iimas.unam.mx

[1]Universidad Nacional Autónoma de México, Instituto de Ingeniería,
Ciudad de México, México

[2] Universidad Autónoma de Yucatán, Facultad de Matemáticas, Mérida, México

[3] Universidad Nacional Autónoma de México, Instituto de Investigaciones
en Matemáticas Aplicadas y en Sistemas, Ciudad de México, México

Abstract

Word Association Norms (WAN) are collections that present *stimuli* words and the set of their associated responses. The corpus is widely used in diverse areas of expertise. In order to reduce the effort to have a good quality resource that can be reproduced in many languages with minimum sources, a methodology to build Automatic Word Association Norms is proposed (AWAN). The methodology has an input of two simple elements: a) dictionary, and b) pre-processed Word Embeddings. This new kind of WAN is evaluated in two ways: i) learning word embeddings based on the *node2vec* algorithm and comparing them with human annotated benchmarks, and ii) performing a lexical search for a reverse dictionary. Both evaluations are done in a weighted graph with the AWAN lexical elements. The results showed that the methodology produces good quality AWANs.

1 Introduction

Word associations is a technique that helps researchers to learn how words are connected by their meanings and the relationships among them in the human mind. Although vocabulary diversity and lexicon size depend on a variety of social elements among individuals, the final result is a kind of word distribution in the population. The method is used in psychology and linguistics to discover how the human mind structures knowledge (De Deyne et al., 2013). This type of resources reflect both semantic and episodic contents (Borge-Holthoefer and Arenas, 2009). In free association tests, a person is asked to say the first word that comes to mind in response to a given *stimulus* word. The set of lexical relations obtained with these experiments is called Word Association Norms (WAN).

The development of technological tools that will help gather these kinds of resources is starting to draw attention, mostly taking advantage of distributed technologies like the Internet. Small World of Words[1] is a clear example of that. We believe that this way of collaborative construction could bring a variety of problems, biasing the final results. On the other hand, the classic methodologies of WAN's construction are very time-consuming. Just to mention some disadvantages, many people are needed to compile the data. Furthermore, good control of the environment conditions of the experiments is important, as well as carefully selecting a set of metadata that must be annotated: age, education years, gender, etc.

In the end, the complete WAN could take years to be polished and shared with the scientific community. Nevertheless, this effort is worthwhile, as WAN could help diverse areas of study: psychologists, linguists, neuroscientists and others, to test new theories about how we represent and process language.

In this paper, a methodology to build automatic WAN is presented. We called the resource generated Automatic Word Associaton Norms (AWAN). The language used to prove our methodology is Spanish, more specifically Mexican Spanish.

The only WAN corpus for Mexican Spanish is the *Normas de Asociacion de Palabras para el Español de México* (Arias-Trejo et al., 2015) (from here, this corpus will be referred to as Mexican Spanish WAN; i.e., MSWAN), which was built using a classic methodology.

---

[1]https://smallworldofwords.org/en/project

Proceedings of the Workshop on Cognitive Aspects of the Lexicon, pages 142–153
Barcelona, Spain (Online), December 12, 2020

The AWAN methodology presented here pretends to infer semantic relatedness between stimuli and their responses. The main reason is that word association has been of great interest as a tool to research mechanisms related to semantic memory (Barrón-Martínez and Arias-Trejo, 2014). The main relations shown in MSWAN are: metonymy, meronymy, functionality, cohyponymy, qualification, hyponymy, 'made of' and synonymy (Mijangos et al., 2017). Our objective is to capture the semantic relatedness but not the types of relation.

Gómez-Adorno et al. (2019) presented Word Embeddings based on *node2vec* (Grover and Leskovec, 2016) and a graph constructed with the MSWAN corpus. Besides, the work presented by Reyes-Magaña et al. (2019a) used the MSWAN to develop a lexical search model for the implementation of a reverse dictionary. With these two works, we can obtain a gold standard to be compared with our AWAN running on the same tasks.

The elements we used to build the AWAN are a general dictionary and a set of pretrainned word vectors. Specifically, we used the Mexican Spanish Dictionary, *Diccionario del Espanol de México* (DEM, 2010), as the main input for our methodology and the pretrained embeddings available for Spanish [2]. The algorithms that were used to train these embeddings are: FastText(Bojanowski et al., 2017), Word2Vec (Mikolov et al., 2013), and Glove (Pennington et al., 2014).

The rest of the paper is organized as follows. In Section 2, the related work is discussed. In Section 3, a description of the methodological framework for the construction of the Automatic Word Association Norms is presented. Section 4 shows the evaluation of the generated norms, using a word similarity dataset in Spanish and the lexical search model. Finally, in Section 5, we establish some conclusions and discuss possible directions of future work.

2   Related Work

In linguistics and psycholinguistics, semantic networks (Sowa, 1992) are defined as graphs relating words (Aitchison, 2012). Their use is not exclusive to learn the organization of the vocabulary, but also to draw the structure of knowledge.

WAN are a special kind of semantic networks, and they are available in many languages. The creation of WAN is not new. The first example is Roget (1911), and two very well-known resources are the *Edinburgh Associative Thesaurus*[3] (EAT) (Kiss et al., 1973) and the collection of the University of South Florida (USF) (Nelson et al., 1998)[4]. Thanks to the Internet and new technologies, WAN lists have been more efficiently compiled in the last years, with the help of a large number of volunteers. Some examples are: *Jeux de Mots*[5], in French (Lafourcade, 2007) and the multilingual dataset *Small World of Words* [6].

For Spanish, there exists several corpora of word associations. Algarabel et al. (1998) integrate 16,000 words, including statistical analyses of the results. Macizo et al. (2000) build norms for 58 words in children, and Fernández et al. (2004) work with 247 lexical items that correspond to Spanish (Sanfeliu and Fernández, 1996).

As stated above, the only resource designed and compiled for Mexican Spanish is the MSWAN. Reyes-Magaña et al. (2019a) introduced a method for lexical search based on that compilation that worked from clue words or definitions to the concept, i.e., from the responses to the *stimuli*.

In some cases, authors create this type of corpus from scratch and in other cases, they extend the available WAN to learn more responses to the *stimuli*. In recent years, Bel-Enguix et al. (2014) used techniques of graph analysis to calculate associations from large collections of texts. Additionally, Garimella et al. (2017) published a model of word associations that was sensitive to the demographic context. This was based on a neural network architecture with n-skip-grams and improved the performance of the generic techniques, which do not take into account the demography of the participant.

Sinopalnikova and Smrz (2004) showed that Word Association Thesaurus (WAT) is comparable to balanced text corpora and can replace them in case of absence of a corpus. The authors presented a

---

[2]https://github.com/dccuchile/spanish-word-embeddings

[3]http://www.eat.rl.ac.uk/

[4]http://web.usf.edu/FreeAssociation

[5]http://www.jeuxdemots.org/

[6]https://smallworldofwords.org/

methodological framework for building and extending semantic networks with WAT, including a comparison of quality and information provided by WAT vs. other language resources.

Borge-Holthoefer and Arenas (2009) used free association information for extracting semantic similarity relations with a Random Inheritance Model (RIM). The obtained vectors were compared with LSA-based vector representations and the WAS (word association space) model. Their results indicate that RIM can successfully extract word feature vectors from a free association network.

In the work by De Deyne et al. (2016), the authors introduced a method for learning word vectors from WANs using a spreading activation approach in order to encode a semantic structure from WAN. The authors used part of the *Small World of Words* network. The word-association-based model was compared with a word embeddings model (Word2Vec) using relatedness and similarity judgments from humans, obtaining an average of 13% of improvement over the Word2Vec model.

In the recent work by Bel-Enguix et al. (2019), the authors used two WAN in English, EAT and USF to produce word embeddings that were tested against human-annotated benchmarks and some external tasks, Showing that this kind of learning method produces good quality vectors without a training corpus based on billions of words.

WANs are proved to be good in a reverse dictionary task since they suitably represent the connections between words and the way concepts are linked in the human mind. The whole scenario of onomasiological searches changed with the universalization of the Internet and language technologies that allowed to build online resources powered by the huge corpus the World Wide Web provides. In the last two decades, several online dictionaries have been designed that allow natural language searches. Users enter their own definition in natural language and the engine looks for the words that match such definition.

One of the first online dictionaries allowing this type of search was the one created for French by Dutoit and Nugues (2002). Bilac et al. (2004) designed a dictionary for Japanese where the users can freely enter their definitions. It has an algorithm that calculates the similarity between concepts comparing the words.

El-Kahlou & Oflazer (El-Kahlout and Oflazer, 2004) built a similar resource for Turkish. They took into account some synonymy relations between words, as well as the similarity of definitions by means of a counter of similar words in the same order and in subsets of such words. For English, there exists an online onomasiological dictionary, OneLook Reverse Dictionary,[7] that retrieves acceptable results.

One of the main works in Spanish is the one by Sierra and McNaught (2000). DEBO is an onomasiological dictionary that works with user queries given in natural language and a search engine, which was later improved; the database structure was also optimized (Sierra and Hernández, 2011).

Finally, the use of WANs to build a reverse dictionary in Spanish is presented by Reyes-Magaña et al. (2019a). The authors used the corpus MSWAN and graph-based techniques, specifically a measure of betweenness centrality, to perform searches in the knowledge graph. The results of the search model overcome the information retrieval systems it was compared to. The same methodology is successfully applied to English in Reyes-Magaña et al. (2019b). In the latter work, another graph algorithm was presented additionally to perform the search, the PageRank. Nevertheless, the results show that betweenneess centrality is more suitable for the reverse dictionary task.

3   Methodology of Automatic Word Association Norms

The aim of this work is to present a general methodology that could serve as a model to build WAN for any language. The main process consists in parsing the entire dictionary, working with the entries and their definitions. We consider that all the entries become the stimuli words, and each one of the words that define the entries become the associate responses to them. The process also involves the inference of a numeric value that measures the relationship between words, allowing us to obtain the weight the classic WANs have.

Algorithm 1 presents the overall schema of our model. The dictionary, *Diccionario del Español de México* (DEM, 2010), is the result of a set of investigations of the vocabulary used in Mexico since 1921. The investigations have been carried out since 1973 at the Center for Linguistic and Literary Studies of *El Colegio de México*. The Mexican Dictionary of Spanish is a comprehensive dictionary of Spanish in

---

[7]https://www.onelook.com/reverse-dictionary.shtml

Algorithm 1: Automatic Word Association Norms

Data: Dictionary, Word embeddings
Result: AWAN
pre-process(Dictionary)
for *each entry* **do**
   for *each word in definition* **do**
      similarity = cosine_similarity(entry,word);
      weight = similarity * tf_idf(words);
   ordering(words)

---

its Mexican variety, prepared on the basis of an extensive study of the Corpus of contemporary Mexican Spanish (1921-1974) and a set of data after that last date to the present.

Sometimes, the definitions of each one of the entries bring examples of use. All of this additional information was removed because we consider that this kind of data could contaminate the final WANs. Then, in order the prepare the definitions, we performed some preprocessing steps, as described.

- All the words are lemmatized using Freeling (Padró and Stanilovsky, 2012) for the Spanish language.

- All the functional words were removed using the Spanish *stop words* list available in the *NLTK* package (Bird and Loper, 2004).

- Some specific words were added to the *stop list* in order to be removed as well. These words are very common in dictionaries but do not provide meaningful data for our purpose of building AWAN. Some of them are: 'etc.', 'approximately', 'generally', 'specifically', 'type', among others.

Later, with the remaining words, we calculate the cosine similarity between the entry and each word corresponding to its definition. For this purpose, we use pretrainned word embeddings[8] for Spanish language. Table 1 presents the main characteristics of each embeddings model. The corpora used to train these embeddings are the following: FastText, Glove and Word2Vec with a Spanish Billion Word Corpus, and FastWiki with Wikipedia Spanish Dump.

Short name	Model file	Dimensions	# vectors	Algorithm
FastText	FastText from SBWC	300	855,380	FastText with Skipgram
Glove	GloVe from SBWC	300	855,380	GloVe
Word2Vec	Word2Vec from SBWC	300	1,000,653	Word2Vec with Skipgram
FastWiki	FastText from Spanish Wikipedia	300	985,667	FastText with Skipgram

Table 1: Description of the pretrained vectors in Spanish used to measure similarities.

With the remaining lexical elements, the *tf-idf* of each word is calculated; every definition is considered as a different document. The value will be used as adjustment factor of the cosine similarity between words. The weight is calculated as follows:

$$W_{as}(stimulus, response) = tf\_idf(response) * cosine\_similarity(stimulus, response) \quad (1)$$

We called this weight Approximation Strength (W_{as}). The final step is to order from high to low the weights of all the associated responses (words in a definition) to the entries (*stimuli*).

---

[8]https://github.com/dccuchile/spanish-word-embeddings

The corpus of the AWANs is available in github[9]. We generate four different collections, one for each embedding used to calculate the cosine similarity.

3.1 AWAN Corpus and Graph

The corpus AWAN has a total of 17,330 *stimuli*. The vocabulary size of each AWAN is : a) FastText with 22,699 b) Glove with 21,867 c) Word2Vec with 22,045 and d) FastWiki with 22,517. The discrepancy in the vocabulary sizes is due to the embeddings corpus, not all the words that appear in the definitions are in the vector resources. The richest AWAN, in terms of amount of lexical items, is the FastText version.

The graph representing the AWAN is elaborated with all the lexical items. It is formally defined as: $G = \{V, E, \phi\}$ where:

- $V = \{v_i | i = 1, ..., n\}$ is a finite set of nodes of length n, $V \neq \emptyset$, that corresponds to the *stimuli* and their *associates*.

- $E = \{(v_i, v_j) | v_i, v_j \in V, 1 \leq i, j \leq n\}$, is the set of edges.

- $\phi : E \rightarrow R$, is a function over the weight of the edges.

The graph is undirected so that every stimulus is connected to their associated words without any precedence order. For the weight of the edges we use the Approximation Strength measure. Table 2 presents a brief snapshot of the AWAN corpus, in specific for the stimulus *stimulus* Bee *(Abeja)* and its responses, using the FastText and Glove embeddings. It can be observed that they share the same responses, but they are located in different positions. The cosine similarity obtained on each embedding corpus produces the arrangement adjustment.

4 AWAN evaluation

To measure the quality of the AWANs, two types of experiments were performed. The first one allows us to know the representativeness of the embeddings that were trained using AWAN and node2vec, trying to describe similarity against human-annotated benchmarks. The second experiment is about the lexical search model used in the reverse dictionary. This evaluation is done because the WANs prove to be well-performing lexical searches using this kind of corpus as input (Reyes-Magaña et al., 2019a). Each one of the experiments will be compared with the results of these tasks using MSWAN. We select these outcomes as the gold standard because the WAN corpus used to perform the experiments corresponds to Mexican Spanish, same as our AWANs.

4.1 Node2vec

Node2vec (Grover and Leskovec, 2016) finds a mapping $f : V \rightarrow R^d$ that transforms the nodes of a graph into vectors of d-dimensions. It defines a neighborhood in a network $N_s(u) \subset V$ for each node $u \in V$ through a S sampling strategy. The goal of the algorithm is to maximize the probability of observing subsequent nodes on a random path of a fixed length.

The sampling strategy designed in *node2vec* allows it to explore neighborhoods with skewed random paths. In this work, we used the implementation of the project *node2vec*, which is available on the web[10] considering a dimension of 300.

With the embeddings trained on AWAN, we evaluated the ability of word vectors to capture semantic relationships through a word similarity task. Specifically, we used two widely-known corpora: a) the corpus *WordSim-353* (Finkelstein et al., 2001) composed of pairs of terms semantically related to similarity scores given by humans and b) the MC-30 (Miller and Charlees, 1991) benchmark containing 30 word pairs. Both datasets in their Spanish version (Hassan and Mihalcea, 2009).

We calculated the cosine similarity between the vectors of word pairs contained in the above mentioned datasets and compared it with the similarity given by humans using the Spearman correlation. To deal with the non-inclusion of every word of the testing datasets in our AWAN, we introduced the concept

---

[9]https://github.com/jocarema/AWAN
[10]http://snap.stanford.edu/node2vec/

Table 2: Responses for stimulus Bee, using FastText and Glove.

Abeja (Bee)			
FastText		**Glove**	
Response	**Approximation Strength**	**Response**	**Approximation Strength**
mellifera	0.599	*apis*	0.521
miel	0.580	*miel*	0.442
zángano	0.552	*mellifera*	0.441
apis	0.550	*hembra*	0.393
himenóptero	0.546	*zángano*	0.353
aguijón	0.532	*reina*	0.343
insecto	0.520	*nido*	0.336
néctar	0.511	*insecto*	0.321
cera	0.506	*macho*	0.320
hembra	0.485	*cera*	0.310
polen	0.482	*aguijón*	0.304
macho	0.464	*panal*	0.303
polinizador	0.461	*néctar*	0.290
apidae	0.431	*polen*	0.286
nido	0.412	*estéril*	0.259
reina	0.403	*apidae*	0.195
panal	0.367	*himenóptero*	0.181
domesticar	0.339	*fértil*	0.179
estéril	0.318	*colonia*	0.164
amarillo	0.315	*amarillo*	0.160
rojizo	0.311	*alimentar*	0.131
colonia	0.300	*solo*	0.126
obrero	0.284	*vivir*	0.117
fértil	0.273	*domesticar*	0.107
solo	0.257	*obrero*	0.106
vello	0.240	*rojizo*	0.099
producto	0.230	*misión*	0.081
galería	0.220	*vello*	0.076
alimentar	0.214	*existir*	0.073
medir	0.195	*producto*	0.064
vivir	0.185	*construir*	0.062
existir	0.176	*galería*	0.061
constituir	0.171	*frecuencia*	0.058
frecuencia	0.169	*polinizador*	0.056
numeroso	0.163	*cubrir*	0.055
cubrir	0.162	*medir*	0.047
misión	0.155	*constituir*	0.043
aprovechar	0.146	*aprovechar*	0.035
subterráneo	0.146	*subterráneo*	0.025
proveer	0.138	*numeroso*	0.007
construir	0.107	*proveer*	0.003

of overlap in the experiments, and calculated the total number of common words between the lists that are being compared. The others are excluded from the evaluation. In principle, having large overlaps is a positive feature of this approach. Tables 3 and 4 present the Spearman correlation of the similarity given by human taggers with the similarity obtained with word vectors (learned from MSWAN and AWAN separately). We also report the overlap, which is the number of words that can be found in both, the given WAN corpus (MSWAN or AWAN) and the evaluation dataset (ES-WS-353 or MC-30).

Table 3: Spearman rank order correlations between Mexican Spanish WAN embeddings (300 dimension) and the ES-WS-353 dataset.

WAN	Weighting function	Overlap	Correlation
	Inv. Frequency		0.489
MSWAN (Gómez-Adorno et al., 2019)	Inv. Association	140	0.463
	Time		0.461
AWAN FastText			**0.595**
AWAN Glove	Inv. Approximation	291	0.555
AWAN Word2Vec			0.550
AWAN FastWiki			0.572

Table 4: Spearman rank order correlations between Spanish WAN embeddings (300 dimension) and the MC-30 dataset

WAN	Weighting function	Overlap	Correlation
	Inv. Frequency		0.305
MSWAN (Gómez-Adorno et al., 2019)	Inv. Association	11	0.563
	Time		0.545
AWAN FastText			0.747
AWAN Glove	Inv. Approximation	22	0.698
AWAN Word2Vec			0.706
AWAN FastWiki			**0.771**

It can be observed that the word embeddings obtained from the AWAN corpus achieved better correlation with the human similarities than the embeddings obtained from the MSWAN corpus in both datasets, ES-WS-53 and MC-30.

4.2 Lexical Search Model

Given a definition, the search in the graph is done considering the word that better matches with it. For this purpose, centrality measures identify the most important nodes in a graph; the variation of the *betweenness centrality* (BT) algorithm (Freeman, 1977) which instead of computing BT of all pairs of nodes in a graph, calculates the centrality based on a sample (subset) of nodes (Brandes, 2008). This approximation is formally described as follows:

$$C_{btw\_aprox}(v) = \sum_{i \in I, f \in F} \frac{\sigma_{i,f}(v)}{\sigma_{i,f}} \tag{2}$$

where: I is the set of initial nodes, F is the set of final nodes, $\sigma_{i,f}$ is the number of shortest paths between i and f, and $\sigma_{i,f}(v)$ is the number of those paths that passes through some node v that is not i or f.

In a non-weighted-graph, the algorithm looks for the shortest path. In a weighted graph, such algorithm finds the path that minimizes the sum of the weight of the edges. When using WAN as the input corpus, we obtain the weighted one.

We employ the approximation of the BT algorithm in order to search for the concept related to a given definition because it only uses a subset of nodes to find the most central nodes in the graph. Therefore, we define a subgraph composed by the words (nodes) of the definition. This subgraph is used as both initial and final nodes to calculate the shortest paths from each of the nodes of the initial nodes set to each one of the nodes of the final nodes set. Finally, the nodes are ranked taking the measure of BT as a parameter for the comparison of the most important nodes found by the algorithm.

We constructed the AWAN graph considering only the 234 *stimuli* of MSWAN but having the response associated and the weights, using the algorithm 1 previously described.

For the experiments, we use the small corpus available in github[11]. It is reported that this corpus contains 5 definitions for 56 concepts corresponding to *stimuli* of the MSWAN, with a total number of 280 definitions. The corpus was gathered with the collaboration of students who gave their own description of the word. For the evaluation of the inference process, we used the technique of precision at k ($p@k$) (Manning et al., 2009), for example, $p@1$ shows that the concept associated to a given definition was ranked correctly in the first place; in $p@3$ the concept was in the first three results, and the same applies to $p@5$.

The results are shown in Table 5. It is clear that when the model searches over MSWAN graphs weighted with any function, the results are higher than when searching on the AWAN graph. We consider that the precision obtained with the AWAN corpus is still competitive. We can affirm this because in the work of Reyes-Magaña et al. (2019a), the authors describe and implement other retrieval information systems applied to the reverse dictionary, being all outperformed by our AWAN graphs. These methods were: Boolean IR, *Onelook reverse dictionary* [12], BM-25 (Robertson and Zaragoza, 2009) and CAS (Ghosh et al., 2014).

Table 5: Lexical Search Results in terms of precision.

WAN	Weighting function	p@1	p@3	p@5
	Inv. Frequency	0.616	0.741	0.774
MSWAN (Reyes-Magaña et al., 2019a)	Inv. Association	**0.655**	**0.804**	**0.829**
	Time	0.362	0.550	0.652
AWAN FastText		0.329	0.526	0.584
AWAN Glove	Inv. Approximation	0.333	0.544	0.587
AWAN Word2Vec		0.340	0.537	0.584
AWAN FastWiki		0.326	0.526	0.580

We did some additional experiments to prune the graph. For this purpose, on each AWAN we vary the weight with incremental intervals of .05. Figure 1 shows the precision of the lexical search; this value is seen on the vertical axis. The horizontal axis represents from left to right the reductions of responses that satisfy the filter, meaning that, if we have the value of .1, the responses to be considered will be those whose weights vary from 1 to .1. In the case of .55, we only select responses with weight from 1 to .55, and so on. With this technique, we could see if there is an improvement of precision as we vary the values in weights. The reason to perform this experiment is that in some cases, a more compact graph yields more efficient searches. When the reduction reaches a value of .60, the filtered responses are bigger, having fewer words to work with and making the precision of lexical search, turns almost to 0. We can see that in the first intervals, reducing the graph does not make a significant difference in the precision outcomes. A slight peak can be reached before the precision starts to decrease. For this reason, we provide full AWANs without any reduction.

5   Conclusions and Future Work

We introduced a method for learning Word Association Norms in Mexican Spanish from a dictionary. Although we could use a general Spanish dictionary like the *Real Academia de la Lengua (RAE)*, the experiments did not yield good results, mainly because the test corpus is based on definitions made by people that use Mexican Spanish as their mother tongue. Nevertheless, the methodology we provide in this paper can be applied to any kind of dictionary. To evaluate the AWANs, we used two types of test. The first one is the intrinsic test which uses the *node2vec* algorithm to learn word vectors on the graph built with the AWAN corpus. The results determine that these vectors overcome the Spearman correlation presented with the MSWAN corpus. The second one is the extrinsic test which presents a more realistic

---

[11] https://github.com/jocarema/Natural-Language-definitions
[12] https://www.onelook.com/reverse-dictionary.shtml

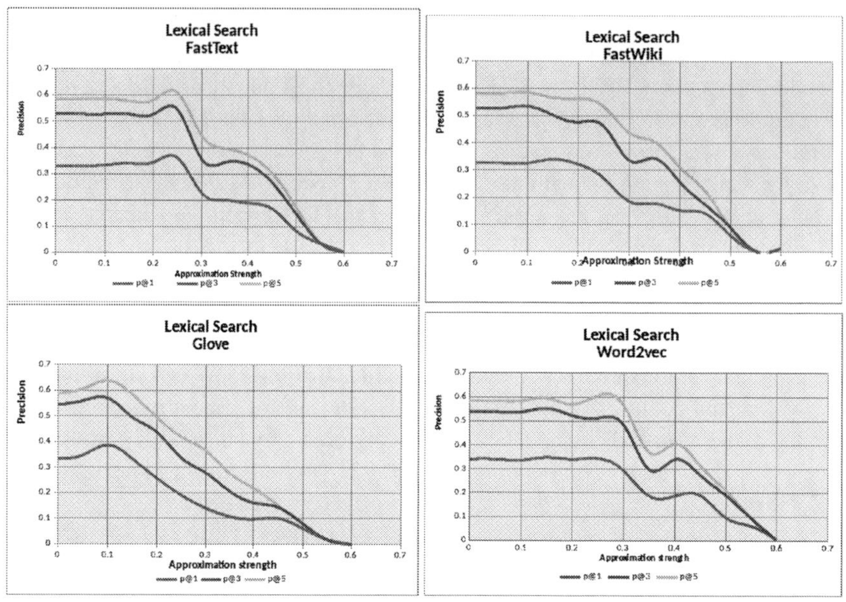

Figure 1: Lexical Search precision based on AWAN

use of this type of corpus; the lexical search model shows that even if we did not outperformed the results of the MSWAN, it is competitive enough to outperform classic information retrieval systems. We employ a weighting function on the graph edges considering the inverse approximation strength because all the tests use the shortest paths.

We consider that the methodology proposed is a helpful tool for the construction of Word Association Norms. The input elements to produce AWANs are somehow easy to get, and consist mainly of a dictionary, and the pretrained word embeddings. We also believe that the MSWAN collected and processed by humans, will bring more accurate results depending on the task that will be used. Nevertheless, in some cases where time and availability of WAN is urgent or simply impossible to collect in the classic way, the creation of AWAN is a reliable and fast solution. In a more advanced stage, the success of the technique can make unnecessary the effort and resources that are currently dedicated to collect WANs.

Besides, as a parallel result, we provide the Word Embeddings [13] that we trained using the *node2vec* algorithm, having as the most important feature that these vectors are based on Mexican Spanish. We claim that this methodology can be used to produce embeddings for specific variants of a language without a huge amount of data.

As future work, we plan to do some additional experiments to increase the precision in lexical search in order to apply some additional filters in the response words, like having only nouns, verbs, and/or adjectives, with all the possible combinations a POS tagging can produce. Roth and im Walde (2008) showed that the WANs can be enriched using diverse types of corpora in addition to a dictionary. Hence, as future work, we plan to add some encyclopedic and co-ocurrence corpora resources in order to improve the tasks performance on WANs. Also, it is possible to have the incorporation of multi-terms is possible to have, adding the vector representation of each word in the multi-term. This could be done by applying the same methodology.

Acknowledgments

This work was supported by UNAM-PAPIIT AG400119, IA401219, TA100520 and CONACyT A1-S-27780. We thank *El Colegio de México* for the availability of the *Diccionario del Español de México*.

---

[13] https://drive.google.com/drive/folders/1nmApEvi4ywQl1CDjK5umiSQE79MuGP9C

References

Jean Aitchison. 2012. *Words in the mind: An introduction to the mental lexicon.* John Wiley & Sons.

Salvador Algarabel, Juan Carlos Ruíz, and Jaime Sanmartín. 1998. *The University of Valencia's computerized Word pool.* Behavior Research Methods, Instruments & Computers.

Natalia Arias-Trejo, Julia B. Barrón-Martínez, Ruth H. López Alderete, and Francisco A. Robles Aguirre. 2015. *Corpus de normas de asociación de palabras para el español de México [NAP].* Universidad Nacional Autónoma de México.

Julia B Barrón-Martínez and Natalia Arias-Trejo. 2014. Word association norms in mexican spanish. *The Spanish journal of psychology*, 17.

Gemma Bel-Enguix, Reinahrd Rapp, and Michael Zock. 2014. A graph-based approach for computing free word associations. In *Proceedings of the 9th edition of the Language Resources and Evaluation Conference*, pages 221–230.

Gemma Bel-Enguix, Helena Gómez-Adorno, Jorge Reyes-Magaña, and Gerardo Sierra. 2019. Wan2vec: Embeddings learned on word association norms. *Semantic Web.*

S Bilac, W Watanabe, T Hashimoto, T Tokunaga, and H Tanaka. 2004. Dictionary search based on the target word description. In *Proceedings of the Tenth Anual Meeting of the Assocviation for Natural Language Processing*, pages 556–559.

Steven Bird and Edward Loper. 2004. Nltk: the natural language toolkit. In *Proceedings of the ACL 2004 on Interactive poster and demonstration sessions*, page 31. Association for Computational Linguistics.

Piotr Bojanowski, Edouard Grave, Armand Joulin, and Tomas Mikolov. 2017. Enriching word vectors with subword information. *Transactions of the Association for Computational Linguistics*, 5:135–146.

Javier Borge-Holthoefer and Alex Arenas. 2009. Navigating word association norms to extract semantic information. In *Proceedings of the 31st Annual Conference of the Cognitive Science Society.*

Ulrik Brandes. 2008. On variants of shortest-path betweenness centrality and their generic computation. *Social Networks*, 30(2):136–145.

Simon De Deyne, Daniel J. Navarro, and Gert Storms. 2013. Associative strength and semantic activation in the mental lexicon: Evidence from continued word associations. In *Proceedings of the 35th Annual Conference of the Cognitive Science Society.* Cognitive Science Society.

Simon De Deyne, Amy Perfors, and Daniel J Navarro. 2016. Predicting human similarity judgments with distributional models: The value of word associations. In *Proceedings of COLING 2016, the 26th International Conference on Computational Linguistics: Technical Papers*, pages 1861–1870.

2010. *Diccionario del Español de México (DEM).* El Colegio de México, A.C.

M Dutoit and P Nugues. 2002. A lexical database and an algorithm to find words from definitions. In *Proceedings of the 15th European Conference on Artificial Intelligence*, pages 450–454.

I.D El-Kahlout and K Oflazer. 2004. Use of wordnet for retrieving words from their meanings. In *2nd Global WordNet Conference.*

Ángel Fernández, Emilio Díez, M. Ángeles Alonso, and M. Soledad Beato. 2004. Free-association norms form the spanish names of the snodgrass and vanderwart pictures. *Behavior Research Methods, Instruments & Computers*, 36:577–583.

Lev Finkelstein, Evgeniy Gabrilovich, Yossi Matias, Ehud Rivlin, Zach Solan, Gadi Wolfman, and Eytan Ruppin. 2001. Placing search in context: The concept revisited. In *Proceedings of the 10$_{th}$ International Conference on World Wide Web*, pages 406–414. ACM.

Linton C Freeman. 1977. A set of measures of centrality based on betweenness. *Sociometry*, pages 35–41.

Aparna Garimella, Carmen Banea, and Rada Mihalcea. 2017. Demographic-aware word associations. In *Proceedings of the 2017 Conference on Empirical Methods in Natural Language Processing*, pages 2285–2295.

Urmi Ghosh, Sambhav Jain, and Paul Soma. 2014. A two-stage approach for computing associative responses to a set of stimulus words. In *Proceedings of the 4th Workshop on Cognitive Aspects of the Lexicon (CogALex-IV). COLING 2014 25th International Conference on Computational Linguistics*, pages 15–21.

Helena Gómez-Adorno, Jorge Reyes-Magaña, Gemma Bel-Enguix, and Gerardo E Sierra. 2019. Spanish word embeddings learned on word association norms. In *13th Alberto Mendelzon International Worshop on Fundations of Data Managment*.

Aditya Grover and Jure Leskovec. 2016. node2vec: Scalable feature learning for networks. In *Proceedings of the 22nd ACM International Conference on Knowledge Discovery and Data Mining*, pages 855–864. ACM.

Samer Hassan and Rada Mihalcea. 2009. Cross-lingual semantic relatedness using encyclopedic knowledge. In *Proceedings of the 2009 Conference on Empirical Methods in Natural Language Processing: Volume 3-Volume 3*, pages 1192–1201. Association for Computational Linguistics.

G.R. Kiss, Ch. Armstrong, R. Milroy, and J. Piper. 1973. *An associative thesaurus of English and its computer analysis*. Edinburgh University Press, Edinburgh.

Mathieu Lafourcade. 2007. Making people play for lexical acquisition. *In Proceedings of the 7th SNLP 2007, Pattaya, Thaïland*, 7:13–15, December.

Pedro Macizo, Carlos J. Gómez-Ariza, and M. Teresa Bajo. 2000. Associative norms of 58 spanish for children from 8 to 13 years old. *Psicológica*, 21:287–300.

C.D. Manning, P. Raghavan, and H. Schutze. 2009. *Introduction to Information Retrieval*. Cambridge University Press.

Victor Mijangos, Julia B Barrón-Martınez, Natalia Arias-Trejo, and Gemma Bel-Enguix. 2017. A graph-based analysis of the corpus of word association norms for mexican spanish.

Tomas Mikolov, Kai Chen, Greg Corrado, and Jeffrey Dean. 2013. Efficient estimation of word representations in vector space. *Computing Research Repository*, arXiv:1301.3781.

G.A. Miller and W.G. Charlees. 1991. Contextual correlates of semantic similarity. *Language and cognitive processes*, 6(1):1–28.

Douglas L. Nelson, Cathy L. McEvoy, and Thomas A. Schreiber. 1998. *Word association rhyme and word fragment norms*. The University of South Florida.

Lluís Padró and Evgeny Stanilovsky. 2012. Freeling 3.0: Towards wider multilinguality. In *Proceedings of the Language Resources and Evaluation Conference (LREC 2012)*, Istanbul, Turkey, May. ELRA.

Jeffrey Pennington, Richard Socher, and Christopher D Manning. 2014. Glove: Global vectors for word representation. In *Proceedings of the 2014 conference on empirical methods in natural language processing (EMNLP)*, pages 1532–1543.

Jorge Reyes-Magaña, Gemma Bel-Enguix, Helena Gómez-Adorno, and Gerardo Sierra. 2019a. A lexical search model based on word association norms. *Journal of Intelligent & Fuzzy Systems*, 36(5):4587–4597.

Jorge Reyes-Magaña, Gemma Bel-Enguix, Gerardo Sierra, and Helena Gómez-Adorno. 2019b. Designing an electronic reverse dictionary based on two word association norms of english language. *Electronic lexicography in the 21st century (eLex 2019): Smart lexicography*, page 142.

S. Robertson and H. Zaragoza. 2009. The probabilistic relevance framework: Bm25 and beyond. *Foundations and Trends in Information Retrieval*, 3(4):333–389.

R. Roget. 1911. *Roget's Thesaurus of English Words and Phrases (TY Crowell co.*

Michael Roth and Sabine Schulte im Walde. 2008. Corpus co-occurrence, dictionary and wikipedia entries as resources for semantic relatedness information. In *Proceedings of the Sixth International Conference on Language Resources and Evaluation (LREC'08)*.

Carmen Sanfeliu and Ángel Fernández. 1996. A set of 254 snodgrass' vanderwart pictures standardized for spanish: Norms for name agreement, image agreement, familiarity, and visual complexity. *Behavior Research Methods, Instruments, & Computers*, 28:537–555.

Gerardo Sierra and Laura Hernández. 2011. A proposal for building the knowledge base of onomasiological dictionaries. *Journal of Cognitive Science*, 12(3):215–232.

Gerardo Sierra and John McNaught. 2000. Design of an onomasiological search sistem: A concept-oriented tool for terminology. *Terminology*, 6(1):1–34.

Anna Sinopalnikova and Pavel Smrz. 2004. Word association thesaurus as a resource for extending semantic networks. pages 267–273.

John F Sowa. 1992. Conceptual graphs as a universal knowledge representation. *Computers & Mathematics with Applications*, 23(2):75–93.

Association for Computational Linguistics
209 N. Eighth Street
Stroudsburg, Pennsylvania 18360

ISBN 978-1-7138-2823-5